WINDS OF REVOLUTION

TimeFrame AD 1700-1800

RUSSIA

NORTH AMERICA

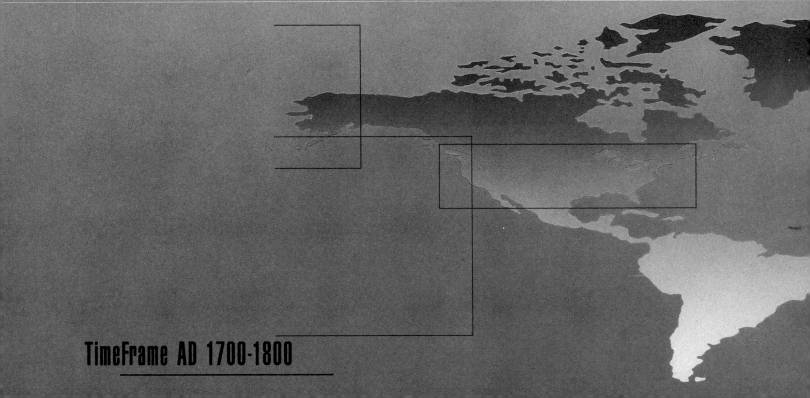

TimeFrame AD 1700-1800

FRANCE

THE PACIFIC

PRUSSIA

Other Publications:
AMERICAN COUNTRY
VOYAGE THROUGH THE UNIVERSE
THE THIRD REICH
THE TIME-LIFE GARDENER'S GUIDE
MYSTERIES OF THE UNKNOWN
FIX IT YOURSELF
FITNESS, HEALTH & NUTRITION
SUCCESSFUL PARENTING
HEALTHY HOME COOKING
UNDERSTANDING COMPUTERS
LIBRARY OF NATIONS
THE ENCHANTED WORLD
THE KODAK LIBRARY OF CREATIVE PHOTOGRAPHY
GREAT MEALS IN MINUTES
THE CIVIL WAR
PLANET EARTH
COLLECTOR'S LIBRARY OF THE CIVIL WAR
THE EPIC OF FLIGHT
THE GOOD COOK
WORLD WAR II
HOME REPAIR AND IMPROVEMENT
THE OLD WEST

For information on and a full description of
any of the Time-Life Books series listed above,
please call 1-800-621-7026 or write:
Reader Information
Time-Life Customer Service
P.O. Box C-32068
Richmond, Virginia 23261-2068

WINDS OF REVOLUTION

TimeFrame AD 1700-1800

BY THE EDITORS OF TIME-LIFE BOOKS

TIME-LIFE BOOKS, ALEXANDRIA, VIRGINIA

Time-Life Books Inc.
is a wholly owned subsidiary of
THE TIME INC. BOOK COMPANY

President and Chief Executive Officer:
Kelso F. Sutton
President, Time Inc. Books Direct:
Christopher T. Linen

TIME-LIFE BOOKS INC.

EDITOR: George Constable
Executive Editor: Ellen Phillips
Director of Design: Louis Klein
Director of Editorial Resources:
Phyllis K. Wise
Director of Photography and Research:
John Conrad Weiser

EUROPEAN EDITOR: Sue Joiner
Executive Editor: Gillian Moore
Design Director: Ed Skyner
Assistant Design Director: Mary Staples
Chief of Research: Vanessa Kramer
Chief Sub-Editor: Ilse Gray

PRESIDENT: John M. Fahey, Jr.
Senior Vice Presidents: Robert M.
DeSena, Paul R. Stewart, Curtis G.
Viebranz, Joseph J. Ward
Vice Presidents: Stephen L. Bair,
Bonita T. Boezeman, Mary P. Donohoe,
Stephen L. Goldstein, Juanita T. James,
Andrew P. Kaplan, Trevor Lunn, Susan J.
Maruyama, Robert H. Smith
New Product Development: Yuri Okuda,
Donia Ann Steele
Supervisor of Quality Control: James King

PUBLISHER: Joseph J. Ward

Correspondents: Elisabeth Kraemer-Singh
(Bonn); Christina Lieberman (New York);
Maria Vincenza Aloisi (Paris); Ann
Natanson (Rome). Valuable assistance
was also provided by: Angie Lemmer
(Bonn); Ann Wise (Rome).

TIME FRAME
(published in Britain as
TIME-LIFE HISTORY OF THE WORLD)

SERIES EDITOR: Tony Allan

Editorial Staff for *Winds of Revolution:*
Editor: Chris Middleton
Designer: Lynne Brown
Researchers: Caroline Smith,
Louise Tucker
Sub-Editor: Frances Willard
Design Assistant: Rachel Gibson
Editorial Assistant: Molly Sutherland
Picture Department: Amanda Hindley
(administrator), Zoë Spencer (picture
coordinator)

Editorial Production
Chief: Samantha Hill
Traffic Coordinator: Emma Veys
Editorial Department: Theresa John,
Debra Lelliott

U.S. EDITION

Assistant Editor: Barbara Fairchild
Quarmby
Copy Coordinator: Elizabeth Graham
Picture Coordinator: Jennifer Iker

Editorial Operations
Copy Chief: Diane Ullius
Production: Celia Beattie
Library: Louise D. Forstall

Computer Composition: Gordon E. Buck
(Manager), Deborah G. Tait, Monika D.
Thayer, Janet Barnes Syring, Lillian
Daniels

Special Contributors: James Chambers,
John Cottrell, Ellen Galford, Alan Lothian
(text); Barbara Moir Hicks (research);
Ann L. Bruen (copy); David E. Manley
(index)

CONSULTANTS

General:
GEOFFREY PARKER, Professor of History,
University of Illinois, Urbana-Champaign,
Illinois

CHRISTOPHER BAYLY, Reader in Modern Indian History, Saint Catharine's College, Cambridge University, Cambridge,
England

Russia:
ANTHONY G. CROSS, Professor, Department of Slavonic Studies, Cambridge
University, England

Prussia:
H. M. SCOTT, Lecturer in Modern History,
University of Saint Andrews, Scotland

The Pacific:
GLYN WILLIAMS, Professor of Modern
History, University of London, England

North America:
HUGH BROGAN, Reader in History, University of Essex, England

France:
COLIN LUCAS, Fellow of Balliol College,
Oxford University, England

**Library of Congress Cataloging in
Publication Data**

Winds of revolution, AD 1700-1800 / by the
editors of Time-Life Books.
   p.   cm. — (Time frame)
  Includes bibliographical references.
  ISBN 0-8094-6458-6
  ISBN 0-8094-6459-4 (lib. bdg.)
  1. History, Modern—18th century.
  2. Revolutions—History—18th century.
I. Time-Life Books. II. Series.
D286.W52 1990   909.7—dc20   90-10720
                                      CIP

Time-Life Books Inc. offers a wide range of fine
recordings, including a *Rock 'n' Roll Era* series.
For subscription information, call 1-800-621-
7026 or write Time-Life Music, P.O. Box C-
32068, Richmond, Virginia 23261-2068.

CONTENTS

THE AGE OF REASON

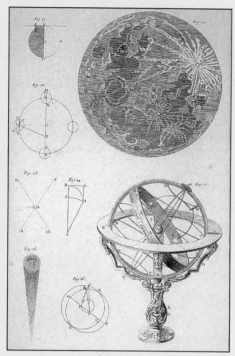

Astronomy

From one end of Europe to the other, the anthem of the eighteenth century was the simple but dangerous word "Why?" Time-honored certainties crumbled: Old assumptions about the authority of kings, the structure of the universe, even the very existence of God, were called into question. The thinkers of the age would take nothing on trust; old habits of unquestioning obedience to religious, political, and social authority were replaced by the scrutiny of all ideas under the penetrating light of human reason. Philosophers were exhilarated by the notion that theirs was a time of profound and accelerated change. Few would argue with their German contemporaries, who named the era Die Aufklärung —the Enlightenment.

"Dare to know!" commanded the German philosopher Immanuel Kant, expressing the spirit of the century. "Have the courage to use your intelligence."

In Britain, France, Italy, Switzerland, the

Netherlands, and the German states, in Poland, Russia, and even in the far-off American colonies, writers and scholars rose to the challenge. But this intellectual ferment was not restricted to men of letters, scribbling away in their ivory towers. New ways of looking at the world would lead inexorably to bold attempts to change it: By the end of the century, an American republic would be born out of the throes of revolution; and in France, crowned heads would roll, and a monarchy would topple.

The thinkers who planted the seeds of these transformations came from a wide variety of backgrounds and traditions. Philosopher David Hume, for instance, had his roots in the spartan rigors of Scottish Presbyterianism; Charles-Louis de Secondat, Baron de Montesquieu, student of history and statecraft, was the scion of an increasingly decadent French aristocracy; his countryman Voltaire—poet, polymath, and leading publicist of the age—emerged from the ranks of the bourgeoisie; Jean-Jacques Rousseau—perhaps the most profoundly influential of all the era's social visionaries—was the son of a lowly watchmaker; the Marchese di Beccaria was an Italian jurist, schooled in legal traditions harking back to the medieval universities.

They were never parochial in their interests. None perceived a division between arts and sciences: The classification of plant and animal species, the movements of the heavenly bodies, the definition of beauty, the technicalities of playwriting, the workings of the human mind, the meaning of history, the creation of wealth, the obligations of monarchs, and the rights of commoners were all deemed equally worthy of consideration.

In France, where the era of Enlightenment reached its apogee, its apostles were known as philosophes, derived from the Greek for "friends of wisdom." But wherever they worked, whatever their chosen fields of study, or however fiercely they disputed one another's conclusions, the scholars of the Enlightenment were united in a search for truth and understanding.

Rational inquiry was their method, empirical data their basis for investigation, and a growing faith in humankind's capacity for self-improvement their impetus.

They were the heirs to a 300-year endeavor to widen the horizons of human knowledge. In the fifteenth and sixteenth centuries, the men of the Renaissance had become reacquainted with the brilliant classical civilizations of the ancient Greeks and Romans: They had absorbed Aristotle's discourses on rhetoric, poetics, and philosophy, and apprehended the system of logic propounded by Plato—a step-by-step guide for the testing of ideas using the simple exercise of reason.

As this spirit of inquiry spread, it led to critical reappraisals of the Christian religion. In the sixteenth century, Protestant reformers turned away from the Catholic church and established new versions of the faith based on a strict interpretation of the biblical texts; while thinkers such as Copernicus challenged old notions of the relationship between heaven and earth, shocking Christians with the heretical suggestion that the earth was not itself the center of God's universe, but revolved around the sun instead.

Seventeenth-century thinkers built on these foundations. Philosophers such as Francis Bacon in England and René Descartes in France sought to devise new patterns of thinking that owed nothing to theological dogma or received philosophical theory, but were shaped purely by the evidence of the senses and logic. The Italian scientist Galileo expanded the work of Copernicus, challenging the traditional laws of astronomy that had been laid down by Ptolemy of Alexandria 1,500 years before and suggesting that the rules of mathematics might play a significant part in the workings of the universe. Alarmed by the implications of these theories, the Pope ordered Galileo to be put on trial for heresy: The astronomer spent the last eight years of his life under house arrest.

But it was to England that the eyes of the learned world turned when, in 1665, the young inventor of calculus, Isaac Newton, proved through painstaking observation and scholarship that the solar system was governed by the laws of gravitation. His discovery opened a door to the mysteries of the universe, offering a simple—but rigorously tested—mechanical principle that could be applied to the movements of celestial and earthly bodies alike. If one significant law could be uncovered, so New-

Physiognomy

Chemistry

ton's contemporaries reasoned, others would surely follow. In an epigram written a few decades later, Newton's compatriot, the poet Alexander Pope, expressed the optimism of the age:

Nature and Nature's laws lay hid in night:
God said, "Let Newton be!" and all was light.

Newton and his contemporaries had not perceived their studies as a challenge to established religion; whatever mechanical laws they might discover, they still believed in a divine presence that governed these operations. Even the alleged heretic Galileo had attempted to reconcile scientific theories with religious truth in a work entitled *The Authority of Scripture,* while Newton himself directed his energies to biblical studies as well as to the exploration of science and mathematics. But if he and other thinkers of the late seventeenth century were disinclined to carry their ideas to more dangerous, heretical conclusions, the philosophers of the generations that followed became less inhibited.

The propositions of Galileo and Newton had undermined the old architecture of a Christian cosmos with God at the top and man in the center. At the beginning of the eighteenth century, fresh cracks appeared in these foundations, caused by the application of inventions such as the microscope and the telescope, which displayed unex-

pected complexities not only in the heavens but in the tiniest fragments of the terrestrial world. Complacency was not encouraged by the disturbing news that a flea boasted a structure as intricate as that of a human being, or that investigators, peering through a glass at an egg and spermatozoa, claimed to have uncovered the very sources of life.

As the new century progressed, scientists had other revelations in store. In France, Antoine-Laurent Lavoisier conducted experiments to discover the composition of water and elucidated the age-old mystery of fire by demonstrating the role that oxygen played in the process of combustion. Across the Atlantic in the American colonies, the versatile statesman-scientist Benjamin Franklin probed the terrifying force of electricity that shot through the skies in bolts of lightning.

Meanwhile, the travelers and explorers of the age brought home disquieting ac-

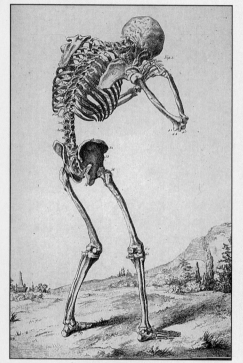

Skeletal anatomy

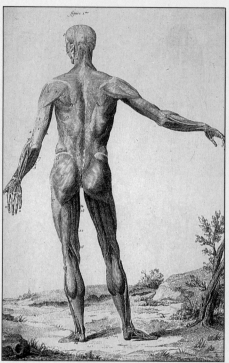

Muscular anatomy

counts of hitherto unknown lands, where men and women worshiped deities entirely unconnected to Christianity, and whose lives—unblessed by baptism—nonetheless gave every evidence of virtue and morality. The highly developed society of China, with its rigid codes of conduct, was an object of particular fascination. The German philosopher Baron Gottfried Wilhelm Leibniz, for instance, suggested that the Chinese should send missionaries to civilize the Christian West.

The majority of Europeans, preoccupied with their daily struggle for survival, took little notice of these intellectual upheavals and remained steadfast, or at least unquestioning, in their faith. But inhabitants of the world of ideas, such as Voltaire, felt that their altered perceptions demanded a new approach to religion. Voltaire did not altogether abandon the concept of a supreme being. "If God did not exist," he observed, "it would be necessary to invent him." But

clergymen, sacraments, liturgies, and the biblical version of human history were not deemed equally indispensable.

To reflect their changing view, Voltaire and many of his like-minded contemporaries embraced a faith they called deism. They accepted the fact that a supremely intelligent and benevolent creator had designed the world according to universal laws, and had bestowed upon mortal men and women both natural virtue—instead of Original Sin—and the gift of reason, to forge a destiny of their own choosing. The wonders of the universe, which fresh scientific discoveries daily confirmed and amplified, demonstrated beyond dispute the celestial dimensions of the scheme. Deism won many adherents in the intellectual circles of France and England, and even far beyond: Thomas Jefferson, American statesman and a future president of the new republic, declared himself to be a believer in the creed.

A religion based on rationality carried the danger that the very tool that had created it might be wielded in its destruction. Some thinkers took empiricist logic to its ultimate conclusions. The Scottish skeptic and essayist David Hume argued that fallible human senses could not guarantee certain knowledge of the divine, while the German radical Baron Paul-Henri-Dietrich d'Holbach dispensed with God altogether, proclaiming that the universe was mere matter in motion, indifferent to the fate of its inhabitants.

Yet if the human race was, as the baron suggested, unimportant to the forces that had forged it, it was an object of ever-increasing fascination to the philosophes. They explored such questions as the mechanics for acquiring knowledge, the role of memory and the senses, and the dynamics of human behavior. In *An Essay Concerning Human Understanding*, published in 1690, the Englishman John Locke set the agenda for much of the eighteenth-century debate. He postulated the theory that human beliefs and behavior were not innate or inborn—as implied by the old Christian concept of Original Sin—but were created by external stimuli: An individual was the product of his or her environment.

As the century reached the halfway mark, an English doctor named David Hartley sought to uncover the precise connection between external stimuli and the mind. In a tome ponderously entitled *Observations on Man, his Frame, his Duty, and his Expectations*, he laid the foundations of modern psychology. Hartley's theory was that upon reaching the senses, outside stimuli set off vibrations, which then traveled by way of the nervous system to the brain, where they were translated into ideas. Through repetition, the brain learned to associate stimuli with ideas, to the extent that small stimuli could trigger ranges of mental reactions normally linked to more complex sensory input.

Such ideas were, as yet, unproved, but their immediate implications were not lost on the philosophes. If human behavior was indeed molded by sensory impressions, then the human character could be forged or transformed by the application of the proper stimuli. They turned their attention to the matter of education.

Although he himself had abandoned his five children to the care of the state, the French essayist and novelist Jean-Jacques Rousseau became a zealous advocate for a new and more enlightened approach to the teaching of children. In his didactic novel *Émile,* he emphasized the importance of natural development. Rejecting the old approach to education—which tended in general to treat children like miniature adults, forced them to obey a series of rigid rules, and used the rod as the primary means of instilling information—he proposed a kindlier method, better attuned to the needs of a growing child.

Rousseau urged parents to appoint sensitive tutors to guide their offspring into adulthood. Ideally these mentors should be paragons of gentleness, who would retire

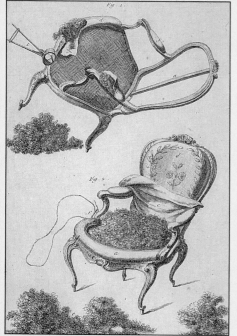

Upholstery

with their young charges to some wholesome, rustic retreat, where they would teach them to look closely at the natural world around them, before moving on to literacy and other practical skills.

Children were not the only objects of concern to the social visionaries of the age. In Italy, the Marchese di Beccaria published an influential work advancing the revolutionary argument that criminals

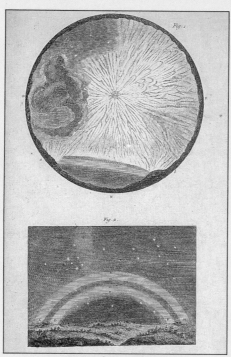

Meteorology: rainbows

should be educated out of their ways rather than subjected to the barbarous retribution usually dispensed by the courts. Where punishment was unavoidable, he recommended the passing of sentences commensurate with the offense—a novel idea at a time when in England, for example, a man could be hanged for stealing goods worth little more than a few cents.

This interest in the principles of justice extended beyond the purely theoretical. Voltaire, tireless scourge of injustice and fanaticism alike, took up the cudgels when

his twin foes reared their heads in the case of Jean Calas, a victim of religious bigotry. Calas—a Protestant—was falsely accused of murdering his son to prevent the young man's conversion to Catholicism. In 1762, Calas was convicted, sentenced to death, and broken on the wheel. Tirelessly proclaiming Calas's innocence, Voltaire used his influence to help the dead man's family, and fired off campaigning pamphlets

Meteorology: snowstorms

and essays. Finally, after three years of struggle, Voltaire succeeded in having the conviction quashed and Calas's name posthumously cleared.

While Voltaire and his fellows expounded their visions of a more just and rational society, other thinkers were mapping out the route to human happiness along a road of economic reforms. In France, François Quesnay and a group calling themselves the Physiocrats claimed that the process of the creation of wealth was controlled by natural forces; they recommended that for this reason, agricultural produce and manufactured goods should be allowed to circulate freely, unhindered by any intervention by the state.

Across the English Channel, the Scottish economist Adam Smith expanded upon this theory in his *Inquiry into the Nature and Causes of the Wealth of Nations,* published in 1776. Providence, he explained, had provided humankind with the wherewithal to create unlimited wealth, but it had also arranged matters in such a way that self-interest would not conflict with the common good:

> *Every individual exerts himself to find out the most advantageous employment for whatever his capital can command. The study of his own advantage necessarily leads him to prefer what is most advantageous to the society.*

The entrepreneurs building the mills and factories that were the engines of Britain's incipient Industrial Revolution could take heart from Smith's message: Their quest for maximum profit would not exclude them from entrance into the kingdom of heaven, and—better still—they could contribute most substantially to the common good if allowed to operate without the interference of the state.

Nor was government itself exempt from the searching gaze of Enlightenment philosophers. French thinkers in particular, uneasy in a realm whose king held absolute, unchecked power, offered their own political prescriptions. Montesquieu, as a member of the nobility, advocated a strong aristocracy to provide a balancing mechanism that would curb any ruler's autocratic tendencies. Bourgeois Voltaire was as mistrustful of the aristocracy's reformist potential as he was contemptuous of the populace at large. A firm supporter of the monarchic system, he recommended that royal power be tempered by the civilizing influence of enlightened advisers. Rousseau, whose plebeian origins gave him no

stake in the status quo, argued for an entirely different form of government; in his *Social Contract,* published in 1762, he favored a republican state where citizens freely surrendered their individual will to the general will of society but retained the right to a voice in shaping the laws that ruled their lives.

Although they were hardly likely to endorse such dangerous republican sentiments, some of Europe's rulers were inspired by Enlightenment ideas and began, for the first time, to demonstrate a consciousness that their peoples were entitled to something in return for paying their taxes and sending their sons to war. In Prussia, Frederick the Great—an admirer of Voltaire and enthusiastic patron of an academy of arts and sciences—abolished torture and censorship, overhauled his country's legal system, and carried out agrarian and industrial reforms. In neighboring Austria, Emperor Joseph II advocated religious tolerance and attempted, though without suc-

cess, to abolish serfdom. The Russian sovereign Peter the Great struggled to drag his vast and backward dominion out of the Dark Ages; he developed a powerful modern army and navy, and he set up an improved bureaucracy to administer his state. His successor, Catherine the Great, brought equal enthusiasm to the task of modernization. Influenced by Enlightenment ideals, she introduced a program of educational and humanitarian reforms in an effort to transform Russia into a forward-looking European state.

Yet no monarch went so far as to endanger the principle of autocratic rule. Frederick and his peers were, at best, benevolent despots. They might be prepared to consent to—or even initiate—piecemeal reforms, and they were delighted to be acclaimed by their contemporaries as philosopher-kings; but they maintained an iron grip on the caste-ridden societies of their realms and ensured that power stayed firmly at the center.

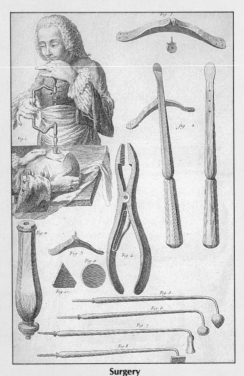

Surgery

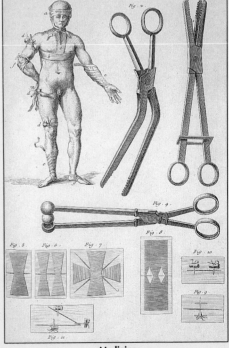

Medicine

It was inevitable that the moving spirits of the Enlightenment should come from a privileged elite. Only members of the aristocracy or the affluent middle classes had the leisure to cultivate their minds, and they alone had the resources to purchase the books and undertake the foreign travel that would expand their own horizons. But the ideas discussed by the intelligentsia soon spread far beyond their gilded salons and supper rooms.

The extension of various forms of public education ensured that increasingly large proportions of the populace were learning to read. In France and Britain particularly, the printed word thrived as never before. The majority of French adults enjoyed a basic degree of literacy, while across the English Channel, lending libraries proliferated, feeding an insatiable demand for reading matter.

From London and Amsterdam to Vienna and Milan, printing presses produced an ever-growing flood of books and periodicals. Although many writers catered to the tastes of the barely literate, others made it their mission to educate and inform. In England, Joseph Addison edited the *Spectator* magazine, which boasted sales of 30,000 copies per issue; his declared intention was to bring philosophy "out of closets and libraries, schools and colleges, to dwell in clubs and assemblies, at tea tables and coffee houses."

Some luminaries employed popular literary forms to explicate their ideas. In 1733, England's Alexander Pope published his poetical *Essay on Man* in four books of approximately 200 to 300 lines each—an exploration in rhyme of man's place in nature, the power of reason, the role of Providence, the definition of human happiness, and other themes of the age. Voltaire and Rousseau used the medium of the novel to give their ideas wider currency: In 1759, Voltaire's moral tale, *Candide,* required eight large printings to satisfy demand in France alone, while Rousseau's *La Nouvelle Héloïse* went through seventy French editions between 1761 and 1789.

Translations of these and other texts spread their authors' fame to the reading public throughout western Europe.

But it fell to another work to encapsulate the intellectual scope of the age: Denis Diderot's epic *Encyclopédie.* This vast compendium of contemporary knowledge covered every subject within the sphere of the Enlightenment. All aspects of human inquiry, from philosophy to farming, from

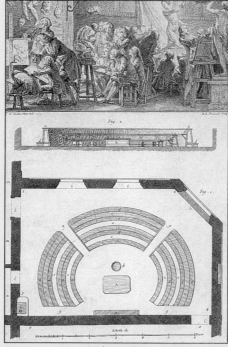

Art instruction

carpentry to surgery, were lucidly recorded in seventeen volumes of text, illustrated by eleven books of plates.

Between 1751 and 1772, in a publication schedule that spanned two decades, Diderot engaged artisans and intellectual luminaries alike; while Rousseau, Holbach, and Voltaire penned articles for the massive work, other contributors interviewed the best craftsmen of the realm and even built tools and machines before describing them. Implicit in the *Encyclopédie's* equal emphasis on practical skills and theoretical

doctrines was a great faith in innovation and a belief that all members of the human race had a right to share its fruit.

Such principles as these, embodying new visions of human rights and opportunities, would be translated into action before the century was out. In North America, England's thirteen colonies severed themselves from the mother country to forge a republic. In 1776, the revolutionaries issued the Declaration of Independence, with a text that rang out with enlightened precepts, ranging from the practical notion of government accountability to the credo that every individual had a natural right to life, liberty, and the pursuit of happiness.

It would take eight years of bitter war before the declaration could be put into practice, and when it was, the power relationships within the new state revealed that Enlightenment had its limits: North America's original inhabitants were remorselessly driven into the wilderness, slavery was legal, and only a small percentage of the male population—and none of the female—enjoyed the right to vote. Nevertheless, the principles of tolerance, self-determination, and equal citizenship in a democratic republic had become a reality, and the force of these ideas would prove to be unstoppable.

Soon thereafter, the Old World experienced its own revolutionary upheaval. In 1789, France's disaffected bourgeoisie and downtrodden poor rose up together against their weak but autocratic king. The men who came to power when the monarchy fell were the children of the Enlightenment. They had imbibed the unsentimental rationalism of Voltaire, the broad historical perspectives of Montesquieu, and the passionate social idealism of Jean-Jacques Rousseau. The bloody course of the French Revolution, with its years of terror and turmoil, might have horrified these mentors, but the Revolution's rallying cry of *"Liberté! égalité! fraternité!"* was a triumphant answer to a century of searching and fundamental questions.

RUSSIA LOOKS WEST

In a detail from an equestrian portrait, Catherine the Great, empress of all the Russias, adopts a triumphal pose at the start of a reign that, like Peter the Great's before her, was both to aggrandize and liberalize her country. Peter had secured Russian access to the Baltic Sea and, with the help of ideas and expertise drawn from western Europe, built up an efficient army, navy, and bureaucracy. Catherine showed similar dedication to modernization and development. She built schools and towns, and she tirelessly promoted culture and science. But, like Peter, she found her long-term achievements limited by the difficulties of imposing centralized government on a nation that was already vast, and was made still larger by her acquisitions of territory.

Ostensibly, January 1, 1700, was a typical New Year's Day in Moscow—a day when the thousand golden-domed churches of the sprawling Russian capital became the scene of mass religious observances, and every home the setting for festivities. As in other years, all the people held family feasts and decorated their wooden houses with evergreen pine and juniper branches. As usual, Red Square, at the heart of the city, was the center of the nation's celebrations. Its shops and stalls were closed for the day; instead, beneath the towering white walls of the Kremlin and the fantastic steeples and onion-shaped domes of Saint Basil's Cathedral, Russian troops massed at noon to deliver celebratory salvos of artillery and musket fire. In the evening, as was customary, the rejoicing climaxed with a spectacular fireworks display.

However, these New Year's rituals were unlike any the Russians had known before. The populace was not rejoicing spontaneously, but by command of a czar who had decreed that everyone should attend church services on this day; that all his subjects should "display their happiness by loudly congratulating one another"; and that all houses were to be illuminated and open for seven days of feasting. The people passively obeyed the will of the czar, but their hearts were not in it. For their religion taught them that New Year's Day was not January 1, but September 1, and that this was the year 7208, not 1700.

For centuries past, Russians had numbered their years from the date of the Creation: September 1, 5508 BC, according to the calculations of the Orthodox church. Now, all at once, their calendar was being made to conform with the Julian system of western Europe. The diehard traditionalists of the Russian church, known as the Old Believers, were especially horrified. The earth, they argued, could not possibly have been created in January, for how could the serpent have tempted Eve with a ripe apple plucked in icy midwinter? But they protested in vain. Peter I, twenty-seven-year-old czar of all the Russias, was unshakable in his conviction that it was time for his people to be propelled into the modern world.

"Modern," as Czar Peter defined the word, meant "European." Having made an eighteen-month tour of western Europe—the first time a Russian ruler had ever ventured abroad in peacetime—he was now embarking on a long succession of ruthless and radical reforms, designed to shake off the chains of tradition and to put a stop to the kind of narrow-minded thinking that assumed that winter in Russia was winter for all the world.

Thus, while the winds of revolution were sweeping across the Western world, Russia as well was undergoing an extraordinary metamorphosis of its own. For the unconventional and unstoppable Czar Peter was only the first of two great eighteenth-century rulers who forced their country to move forward from the Middle Ages. Later, Peter's progressive ideas were given fresh impetus by an equally remarkable ruler:

the German-born Catherine II, who was empress of Russia from 1762 to 1796. Together, they transformed their nation from a semibarbaric country into a European state of the first magnitude.

In 1700, Russia was territorially the largest nation on earth—a land of vast forests, plains, and deserts, stretching from the Arctic Ocean in the north to the landlocked Caspian Sea in the south; and from the Polish border in the west to the Pacific Ocean in the east. Russia's estimated population was eight million, which, though smaller than France's sixteen million, was far greater than that of more advanced countries such as England (five million), and Sweden and Holland (two million each). In terms of political influence, economic prosperity, and technological progress, however,

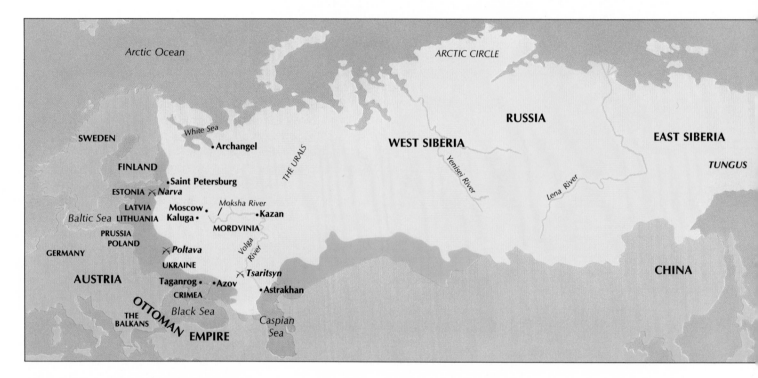

By the end of the eighteenth century, Peter and Catherine the Great had brought Russia closer to the West not only culturally but also geographically, acquiring territories here colored orange. In the first quarter of the century, Peter won access to the Baltic Sea and the Sea of Azov. In the last third, Catherine gained a large portion of Poland, seized parts of south and central Asia from Turkey's Ottoman Empire, and expanded into Alaska, not to be sold to America until 1867. The nation now stretched more than 6,000 miles from east to west, and centralized government became increasingly difficult, because of the vast distances involved and the ever-growing diversity of peoples within the empire, as shown in the colored engravings on the following pages by the German artist C. M. Roth.

Russia remained among the most feeble and backward of European states.

Russia was also the most isolated of all the large nations, both geographically and politically. Denied access to the Baltic Sea (by Sweden) and to the Black Sea (by the Ottoman Empire), Russia had only one harbor—Archangel, on the White Sea—and that port was frozen solid for the better part of six months out of every year. However, at least some of this isolation was self-inflicted. For centuries, all Russians had been forbidden to travel abroad lest they become contaminated by free-thinking ideas; similarly, the 3,000 foreigners living in Russia had been restricted since the middle of the seventeenth century to a separate enclave, which was known as the German Suburb, three miles northeast of Moscow.

Militarily, Russia was a bear without claws. Until the reign of Peter, its navy had been virtually nonexistent, and its army both poorly disciplined and ill equipped. Regular soldiers were known as *streltsy*, or "sharpshooters," and were divided into twenty-two Moscow-based regiments, each 1,000 men strong. The streltsy had been established in the sixteenth century both as a personal guard for the czar and his family and as an elite assault force in time of war. Over the years, however, they had developed into a hereditary, archconservative class, fiercely protective of their special privileges, such as the right to engage in tax-free trading. Their growing commercial interests, combined with their Moscow police role in peacetime, invited corruption; furthermore, they were prone to political intrigue and even rebellion when their favored status seemed to be threatened. Together with the Church, they provided the most stubborn resistance to social reform and foreign influence.

In the same way, Russia's self-interested and ignorant aristocracy presented another barrier to change. The ranks of the nobility were headed by the boyars, who held hereditary landed estates; beneath them were the lesser nobles, who had been granted estates for life in return for services to the royal family. But, whether high- or lowborn, almost all these nobles were illiterate and devoid of progressive ideas, their wealth derived exclusively from land maintained by serfs: peasants who were bound by law to till the same patch of ground in perpetuity. From these unfortunates, a landowner demanded regular payment both in cash and produce; attempts at escape were met with fearsome beatings.

Meanwhile, the day-to-day administration of the czar's central government was in the hands of approximately forty *prikazy*, or "departments of state"—all appallingly inefficient, with duties that often overlapped and a long tradition of corruption.

But the biggest deterrent to social and economic development was the sheer size of Russia and the dispersion of its ethnically divided peoples. This was a land of myriad villages, where peasants dwelled in smoky, one-room houses made of logs or clay, and survived by farming, forestry, and hunting. Russian industry, meanwhile, was limited to small factories and workshops, which were located in towns and

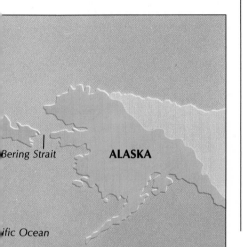

Bering Strait   **ALASKA**

ific Ocean

Woman of Kaluga

Tatar from Kazan

Mordvinian woman

produced handicrafts and household implements for the idle aristocracy and for a small, up-and-coming class of merchants and artisans.

Given all these impediments to progress, there remained only one means whereby Russia might be profitably subjected to the influence of the outside world. This was by the will of the czar, who alone had the power to override the archconservatism of the Church and the tradition-bound self-interest of the nobles and the streltsy. The czar was omnipotent—an unchallenged autocrat, who could introduce laws, impose taxes, and change centuries-old custom as he pleased.

It had been that way ever since the fifteenth century, when Ivan III, a powerful Moscow prince, established the independent Russian state and took the title of "czar," the Russian equivalent of "caesar." From that time on, the fate of the nation had depended to a dangerous degree on the quality of its hereditary ruler. Some, like Ivan the Terrible, grandson of the first czar, were excessively tyrannical. Some were too young or too handicapped, physically or mentally, to govern on their own.

Peter the Great, though, was unlike any czar that his people had known before. Physically, he was extraordinary: a veritable giant, more than six and one-half feet tall. Loose-limbed and angular, he possessed immense strength and exceptional energy. He was as intellectually alert as he was physically active, with an insatiable curiosity and a thirst for knowledge, which he could quench only by exploring the more advanced nations of the West.

His unorthodox outlook stemmed from his upbringing. The son of Czar Alexis I, young Peter was kept out of court circles by his calculating half sister, Sophia, who ruled in his stead as regent. Thus he did not receive the usual cloistered education of a future czar, but was taught by a relatively liberal-minded tutor, Nikita Zotov, an amiable fellow who had been elevated from his position as a clerk in the Church's tax-collecting department.

Tungus Hunter

Old woman from Moksha Valley

Woman from northern Siberia

Peter's education, largely by his own demand, was practical rather than theoretical. He made himself proficient as a carpenter, blacksmith, and printer. And, from the age of thirteen, he commanded a self-created regiment of boy-soldiers, armed with real pistols, muskets, and cannon, whom he deployed in a series of elaborate war games. Over the next four years, he turned this force of 600 boys into a well-disciplined and well-equipped little army, under the command of highly professional foreign officers. Thus, in 1689, when the regent Sophia lost the support of her Kremlin guards, Peter had enough military backing to seize control of the state. At the age of seventeen, he rode in triumph into Moscow and promptly secured his position by banishing the deposed Sophia to a convent.

Nominally, he was sharing the czardom with his half brother, Ivan, but the latter was a sickly individual and died seven years later, having taken little part in government. In the beginning, Peter seemed equally uninterested in state matters; he loathed paperwork and court ceremony and used his newly won power only to indulge in frivolity.

His despairing mother arranged for him to marry Eudoxia Lopukhina, the shy young daughter of a Moscow nobleman. Peter duly complied, and one year later became the father of a boy, the Czarevich Alexis. However, marriage failed to produce the intended stabilizing effect. Peter's life now became geared to an interminable round of orgiastic banquets, interrupted only by sailing trips and ever more elaborate war games. In 1694, he staged a mock battle involving 30,000 men, which was so realistic that more than twenty soldiers were killed and some eighty wounded. And, in his most notorious action, he and his drinking companions formed a riotous, pleasure-seeking group called the Jolly Company, which they later renamed the All-Joking, All-Drunken Synod of Fools and Jesters.

Dedicated to the worship of Bacchus, the Greek god of wine, the synod was

Peasant woman from Saint Petersburg area

Finnish woman in festive costume

Merchant of Kaluga

In a contemporary oil painting, Peter the Great wears the costume of a Dutch shipbuilder, as he did in the course of his quest to obtain the secrets of European technology. During an eighteen-month tour of the West, at the age of twenty-five, he worked incognito as a carpenter at the port of Zaandam, but was forced to abandon this arrangement after only a week when his imperial disguise was penetrated. Later, he worked for four months at a closed dockyard in Amsterdam and was certified as a qualified shipwright. Peter's pragmatic nature impelled him to seek his country's advancement through technological progress, and during his reign, he persuaded many hundreds of European experts to come to Russia, among them craftsmen, canal builders, naval officers, and doctors.

presided over by a "prince pope," Peter's now-alcoholic ex-tutor, Zotov. Traditionalists of the Russian Orthodox church regarded the synod as blasphemous, and the public revelries of its members reinforced the belief in some quarters that Czar Peter I was the Antichrist.

Peter never outgrew the synod. However, from the age of twenty-two, he began to balance his merrymaking with some serious endeavors. For a long time, it had been his ambition to secure a strategic naval base, and to this end, in 1695, he set out to capture Azov, a Turkish-held fortress-city controlling access to the sea of the same name. However, the venture ended in disaster, not least because the Russians lacked a navy with which to complete the city's encirclement. Peter's response was to mobilize tens of thousands of carpenters who, following his personal example, labored all that winter to construct a squadron of galleys and hundreds of barges. When the siege was resumed the following spring, the blockade was total; within a month, the Turks surrendered.

All at once, Peter was a national hero. In Moscow, the entire city turned out to welcome his return. But the watching Muscovites were baffled when the victorious army finally appeared. Contrary to tradition, there was no religious pageantry; stranger still, there was no conquering hero riding on a white charger at the head of his troops. Instead, the triumphal procession—several miles long—was led by a doddering civilian seated in a six-horse carriage.

The civilian was the Drunken Synod's prince: the aging tutor, Zotov, grandly attired in full armor. As for the czar of Russia, he was to be found marching some distance behind, instantly recognizable because of his height, but dressed as an ordinary naval captain. In this, his supreme moment of glory, Peter could not suppress his penchant for farce.

The celebrations had scarcely ended when Peter began issuing edicts that sent shock waves through Russia's privileged classes. First, some 3,000 streltsy, together with as many peasant families, were directed to move at once to Azov, to colonize the area. Next, the Church and all wealthy boyars and merchants were ordered to contribute to the cost of building a navy. Every large monastery and every great landowner was required to build one ship. These were to be completed within eighteeen months and then assembled at Taganrog, a new naval harbor to be constructed on the north shore of the Sea of Azov by a drafted labor force of 20,000 Ukrainians. Finally, in November 1696, Peter announced that fifty highborn Russians were to be sent abroad to study shipbuilding, seamanship, and navigation. Each was to go at his own expense, and no one was to return until he had acquired a certificate of proficiency, signed by a foreign employer.

The aristocracy reacted with horror at the prospect of conscripted nobles—many of them married with young families—being torn from their wives and children and exposed indefinitely to the temptations of western Europe. But their shock was far greater at the news that followed: The czar himself was to make an unprecedented fact-finding tour of the West. Moreover, he was going to travel incognito, under the name of Petr Mikhaylov, as one of thirty-five apprentice "volunteers" whose purpose was to learn technical skills from foreigners.

Peter's companions were commanded, on pain of death, always to address him as Mikhaylov. Foreign courts, too, respected his desire for anonymity, although he was frequently recognized, both because of his height and the fact that he traveled with an embassy of 250 people.

Everywhere he went, Peter amazed foreigners with his phenomenal energy and his insatiable appetite for knowledge. He studied newfangled printing methods, took part in surgical operations, and developed such enthusiasm for dentistry that forever after he would practice his rudimentary skills on unfortunate servants and courtiers, proudly collecting their extracted teeth in a bag. Microscopes, barometers, wind gauges—anything of practical value fascinated him.

Above all, he pursued his passion for ships. In Sweden, he went out drinking with ordinary Baltic seamen. In Holland, where he shared a small, wooden house with a blacksmith, he signed on as a carpenter in the shipyards and stayed there until he had qualified as a shipwright. And in England, he worked at the royal dockyards at Deptford, on the Thames, roaming the streets of London as he pleased.

One of the main purposes of the tour was to recruit foreign experts, and more than 800 Europeans, most of them Dutch, were enlisted. They included naval officers, navigators, shipwrights, hydraulic engineers, carpenters, mathematicians—and barbers, whom he set to work on the Russian nobles' beards as soon as he got home.

The tour was cut short, however, when news reached Peter of a rebellion by four regiments of the streltsy, who were protesting against their postings away from Moscow and against the increasing influence of foreign officers. Peter hurried home to find that the rebellion had been put down by loyal troops. The ringleaders had been executed, and more than 1,800 of their followers imprisoned. But Peter was not satisfied. He felt sure the revolt was part of a high-level plot, instigated by unknown boyars, to restore Sophia's regency.

A political conspiracy could never be proved, even though the prisoners were tortured in traditional style—beaten, whipped, and roasted over an open fire like animals on a spit. Lack of evidence did not deter the czar, however. He wanted to be rid of the streltsy forever, and to this end, he not only had 1,200 rebels executed but also disbanded the remaining streltsy regiments. The soldiers were stripped of their property, exiled from Moscow, and forbidden ever again to engage in military service. In their place, Peter was to raise a new standing army, trained and equipped along Western lines, and composed of conscripted townspeople and peasants, with officers drawn from the nobility.

At this point, however, Peter made a gross miscalculation. In August 1700, before his army had been expanded and modernized, he declared war on Sweden in a bid to seize two key provinces on the Baltic Sea. The result was disaster. In November, at the Estonian town of Narva, the Swedish cavalry inflicted a humiliating defeat on a Russian army that outnumbered them four to one.

This setback gave dramatic impetus to the forming of a new Russian army. Mass conscription was introduced, army training radically overhauled, great fortifications built, and the production of flintlocks and cannon greatly increased. Such was the sense of urgency that, within six months, the czar had had one-quarter of all the church bells in Russia melted down and recast as cannon.

Nine years later, at Poltava in the central Ukraine, the bloody fruit of these labors was reaped. The Swedish army, now only 19,000 strong, was overwhelmed by a force of 42,000 Russians. All the same, the czar was lucky to survive; one Swedish bullet passed through his hat, another buried itself in his saddle, and a third was miraculously deflected by a metallic ornament around his neck.

Peter's early successes in this Great Northern War gave him access to the Baltic coast, and it was there that he set about building his new capital city, Saint Petersburg. However, the war itself dragged on for another twelve years after Poltava, prolonged, in large part, because Peter was diverted by a disastrous conflict with the Turks. Finally, in 1721, the Treaty of Nystad was signed, under which Russia gained the eastern shore of the Baltic (modern-day Estonia, Latvia, and Lithuania) and most of southeast Finland, thus replacing Sweden as the greatest power in the region. Amid the lavish celebrations that followed, the Senate in Saint Petersburg awarded the czar the title of Peter the Great, Father of his Country, Emperor of all the Russias.

As he himself acknowledged, Peter was not a brilliant general. He was, nevertheless, the architect of Russia's military success. In the quarter of a century between the

Battle of Narva and the end of his reign, Peter built up Russia's regular army from 25,000 to 200,000 men, plus 100,000 irregulars. The infantry was fully armed with flintlock muskets and bayonets, the artillery with cannon and mortars of the most up-to-date design. In addition, Peter endowed Russia with a formidable navy of 48 battleships and nearly 600 galleys.

Furthermore, through his relentless demands for more ships, guns, and efficiency, the czar stirred Russia into sudden and spectacular industrial growth. All at once, a country with minimal industry was compelled to develop cannon foundries, powder mills, and musket-making factories; great textile mills for the manufacture of woolen uniforms and sailcloth; and leather works for the production of saddles, harnesses, and boots. At the same time, priority was given to the finding and mining of iron, copper, and coal. Prospectors scoured the land, and a decree was passed making concealment of mineral deposits by a landowner a capital offense.

It was not enough, however, to gear the nation to a war economy. Peter needed to boost state revenue by developing trade and industry in general. He therefore reduced imports by imposing high customs tariffs, and he provided domestic entrepreneurs with incentives such as interest-free loans and subsidies, as well as exemption from state service and taxation.

Exemption from state service was an especially powerful incentive. Under Peter's rule, all physically able men among the landowning classes were required, from the age of fifteen, to serve in the armed forces or the bureaucracy as a condition of retaining their social position and lands. Russian society had always been based on

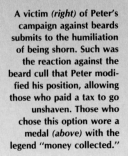

A victim *(right)* of Peter's campaign against beards submits to the humiliation of being shorn. Such was the reaction against the beard cull that Peter modified his position, allowing those who paid a tax to go unshaven. Those who chose this option wore a medal *(above)* with the legend "money collected."

AN ATTACK ON TRADITION

On the day after he returned from his tour of western Europe in 1698, Peter the Great suddenly produced a pair of scissors and cut off the luxuriant beard of one of his courtiers. This typically idiosyncratic act marked the beginning of one of Peter's most visible attempts to move Russia away from its archaic past.

The czar forbade all men except members of the clergy to wear beards, a proclamation that caused widespread outrage, since traditional teachings held that beards were gifts from God, and their removal a sin against the Almighty.

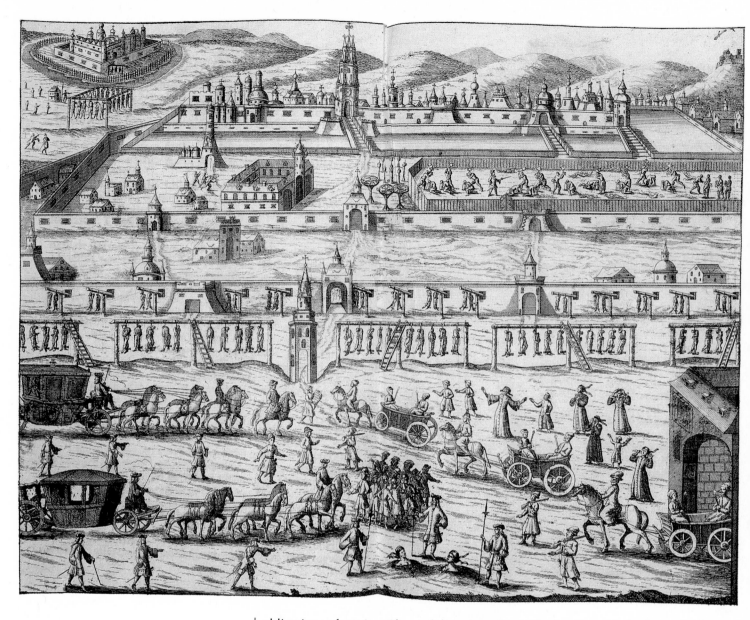

obligations of service: The serfs owed service to the landowner; the landowner owed service to the czar. But Peter changed this concept; now everyone's overriding obligation was to the state.

Just as a conscripted peasant might be torn from his village to endure a lifetime of military service or industrial labor, so now were the members of the ruling class removed from their homes and families, for years or even decades. This was often at considerable cost to themselves, in terms of lost income, to their estates, which were allowed to run down, and to their serfs, whose welfare was inevitably neglected during the landlord's absence. There remained, of course, the possibility of promotion and higher pay, but there was no longer the prospect of being rewarded by the czar with estates and money. Instead, Peter artfully adopted the altogether less expensive practice of conferring ceremonial honors.

This was one of a number of economic measures that arose directly from lessons he had learned abroad. One area in which he was unable to match the West, however, was in developing a Russian merchant navy. This was firmly blocked by the two maritime powers, England and Holland, who insisted on retaining responsibility for shipping goods to and from Russian ports. Nevertheless, as a result of increased productivity, along with the improvement in foreign relations following his grand tour, Peter's reign saw foreign trade increase sevenfold.

For all his successes, though, he had no great overall plan for economic reform. Almost all the changes he instituted—social, political, and economic—were in imitation of Western practices that impressed him; or else they evolved haphazardly, arising as and when he encountered obstacles.

More and more, he promoted the principle of meritocracy. In 1722, this culminated in the establishment of a table of ranks, a completely new class structure that defined a person's place in society by individual achievement rather than by birth. The table created three parallel categories of state servant—civil, military, and judicial—and each category was divided into fourteen classes. Entry to any level was open to persons of the humblest origins, and promotion was strictly decided on merit and length of service. A commoner who reached fourteenth place on the military ladder, or eighth place on the civil or court ladder, was automatically accorded the status of hereditary noble. Thus, in theory, the predominance of the boyars was broken, although in practice, many of the old families continued to enjoy positions of power and influence.

In the interest of greater efficiency, Peter also changed the traditional law of inheritance, whereby a landowner's estate was divided equally among his sons. Instead, only one son—not the eldest, but the ablest—was to be made the sole heir. From the state's point of view, this was beneficial, since estates were no longer broken up into progressively smaller holdings that became less productive and hence less lucrative sources of tax revenue. But the new law led to family upheavals and violent feuds, and it was so unpopular with the landowners that it was repealed five years after Peter's death.

Peter introduced some compassionate reforms, which did endure. He banned the old custom of smothering deformed babies at birth. He delighted young Russians by decreeing that marriages should no longer be arranged, but undertaken voluntarily. And he freed noblewomen from their confinement to the *terem,* the females-only quarter of the house.

This did not mean, however, that these changes were adopted across the length and breadth of the empire. The reforms were mainly aimed at—and most strictly imposed upon—the urban gentry. In the more remote quarters of Russia, the new decrees were often not accepted by the people or else not implemented because of the lack of a police force. Sometimes, too, there was violent opposition, such as occurred in 1705 in the city of Astrakhan, on the edge of the Caspian Sea. Here, antipathy toward Peter's Western-style reforms fueled existing economic grievances and sparked a revolt, which the czar put down with bloody severity.

One major obstacle that Peter encountered in his attempts to raise standards in the public services was the general lack of education in Russia. Peter responded by becoming the first czar to sponsor education along secular lines. To facilitate basic learning, he had the Russian alphabet simplified and promoted the publication of textbooks. At a higher level, he set up colleges specializing in languages, mining,

State executioners inflict a multitude of hideous punishments on members of the *streltsy,* Russia's elite military force, who had attempted to overthrow Peter while he was away in Europe. In the foreground of this engraving, two women, probably wives of the insurrectionists, have been buried up to their necks in an attempt to extract information about the plot. In the middle distance, scores of men are being executed, many with their hands and feet cut off; most had already undergone torture by rack, burning, and flaying. Peter's savage response was conditioned by childhood memories of a rebellion in 1682, when the streltsy had killed his relatives and installed his half sister, Sophia, as regent. Peter strongly suspected her of involvement in this revolt, but could prove nothing.

A NEW CAPITAL ON THE BALTIC

When Peter began building Saint Petersburg in 1703, it was a fetid bog surrounded by forests in which wild bears and wolves prowled. He was determined, however, that this should be the location both for Russia's first Baltic naval base and a new, Western-style capital. To make the vision a reality, he drafted forced-labor gangs; many thousands of these men died during the construction work. The result, as seen in a painting from the middle of the eighteenth century, was a showpiece city in which waterborne traffic of all kinds proceeded past majestic buildings such as the Winter Palace, dominating the left bank of the Neva River, and the Academy of Sciences, on the right. Peter even provided some of the population, ordering the bodily transportation of unwilling noblemen and their families to live in Saint Petersburg.

engineering, and military techniques. In addition, several hundred young men were sent abroad to study at the state's expense.

Education, however, was still limited almost entirely to sons of nobles and state officials, and even on this narrow scale, progress fell far short of Peter's aims. In 1714, he made it compulsory for all sons of nobles, from the age of ten, to have five years of schooling in reading, writing, elementary arithmetic, and geography. But two years later, he reversed this decree in the face of overwhelming opposition from landowners who resented the disruption of their traditions.

Peter had greater success with his administrative reforms. In 1711, he replaced the old, outdated council of boyars with the Senate, a nine-member body, which he appointed and made responsible for the coordination of central and local government and for the collection and expenditure of revenue. Then, in 1718, he scrapped the notoriously inefficient and corrupt prikazy. In their place, he adopted the Swedish system of nine "colleges," or government ministries. All the college presidents were appointed to the Senate, which, in effect, became a council of ministers. He even set up a bureau of official informers—the hated *fiskal*—in an attempt (unsuccessful, as it turned out) to eliminate corruption among state officials.

By now, Peter's autocracy was unchallenged. He had created a centralized bureaucracy entirely subservient to his authority. He had rid himself of the scheming, threatening streltsy. And he had reduced the influence of the boyars to an insignificant level. Only the traditionalists of the Russian Orthodox Church remained a force to be reckoned with.

He brought them to heel in 1721, when he formally abolished the Patriarchate of Moscow as the head office of the Church, and replaced it with the Holy Governing Synod, a spiritual college organized on the same lines as his civil ministries. The synod was composed of nine members, all of them obedient to the czar's will; like the Senate, it had a secular official to oversee its activities. At a stroke, the Church was reduced to the status of a government department of spiritual affairs and prevented from becoming a rallying point for popular protest.

In taming the Church, Peter effectively completed his dominance over the peasant masses. By now, they were virtual slaves of the state. They had been crippled by excessive taxes, and drafted by the hundreds of thousands to serve in the army, to labor in factories and shipyards, and to toil on gigantic construction projects. Tens of thousands had perished in the erection of Saint Petersburg, commonly known as "a city built on bones." Everywhere, forced-labor gangs worked in appalling conditions and lived in fear of the Secret Office, a newly created police department with a brief to sniff out treason.

Many times, in the early years of Peter's reign, the peasants had risen in revolt; always they had been defeated by the overwhelming power of the czar and the nobility. Thousands had fled from oppression, to find refuge in the lonely frontier lands of southern Russia and Siberia. For the majority, however, there was no escape.

In 1718, Peter proclaimed that every male in Russia, except the clergy and the nobility, was to pay a minimum levy of seventy-four kopecks a year, which in many cases was the equivalent of an entire household's annual rent. Following a census, which listed about 5.79 million taxable individuals, this so-called soul tax was first collected in 1724. It was a spectacular success for the state, producing almost half its entire revenue for the year. But in the long term, it had disastrous consequences. Russia's peasants were already forbidden to leave a landowner's estate without

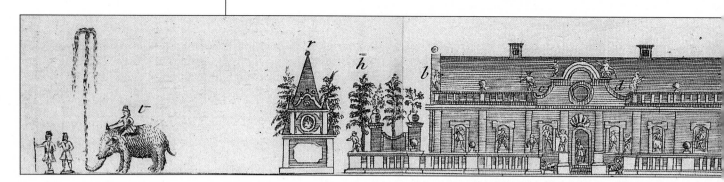

written permission. Now they were tied even more tightly to the estate, since their landlord was made responsible for collecting their taxes and was required to pay out of his own pocket the tax of any listed "soul" that was missing. Peasants thus came to represent calculable sums of money; not only could they be "requisitioned" by the state but they could be bought and sold by their masters like cattle. The division between the ruling class and the workers thus became more sharply and dangerously defined than ever before.

In November 1724, while sailing in the Gulf of Finland, Peter spotted some soldiers in danger of drowning. Characteristically, he plunged into the icy waters to lead a successful rescue operation. At fifty-two, however, his giant body was prematurely aged—weakened by decades of excessive drinking, by venereal disease, and lately by a bladder infection. He developed a severe chill, which he ignored, and later a raging fever, before finally falling into a coma. On January 28, 1725, all the church bells of Saint Petersburg tolled their grim message: Czar Peter, first emperor of all the Russias, was dead.

In death, as in life, Peter the Great inhabited legend. He became celebrated as the czar who had worked miracles, and in truth his achievements had been extraordinary. His reign had been one of continuous territorial and industrial expansion. Moreover, as his admirers noted, he had waged war for twenty-one years; created a navy and a mighty, modern army; and built a new capital, harbors, fortresses, and a gigantic network of canals—all without borrowing a single gold piece in foreign loans. Instead, his triumphs had been purchased with the sweat and blood of the commonfolk of Russia, for whom his reign had been in many ways a disaster.

He himself had served Russia unstintingly, except in one important area: He had left Russia without a male heir to the throne. Early in his reign, he had forced his devoted but dull first wife, Eudoxia, to enter a convent and become a nun. Later, when their only surviving son, Alexis, supported opposition to the czar's reforms, Peter had him arrested and charged with treason. The young czarevich was mercilessly tortured and subsequently died in prison.

For fifteen years after Czar Peter's death, the Russian throne was the most insecure in Europe, beset by factional struggles and occupied by a confused succession of rulers. Peter's second wife, Catherine, reigned for only two years before dying of a fever; his eleven-year-old grandson ruled only a few months longer, before succumbing to smallpox. And although his niece, Anna, was empress for a full decade (1730 to 1740), she was dominated throughout by her German lover and former

Built as an elaborate practical joke by command of the Empress Anna, a palace made of ice *(above, left)* stands in a garden made of ice trees, guarded by three ice soldiers in Persian costume and an ice elephant blowing a jet of water. Inside the palace *(above)*, a frozen bedchamber awaits its unfortunate occupants. They were two of Anna's court jesters, a disgraced prince and an ugly peasant woman, who were forced not only to marry each other but also to spend their wedding night on the icy bed, providing great amusement for the peeping empress and her court. Such crude escapades were typical of Russian court life during Anna's reign, belying the outwardly urbane and westernized appearance of the people who indulged in them.

secretary, Ernst Biron, a man both cruel and inflexible in his implementation of imperial authority.

For a time, in the mid-eighteenth century, the monarchy was stabilized by Peter's daughter, Empress Elizabeth, who, with the support of the Imperial Guard, seized power in 1741. Two years later, she scored a notable military and diplomatic victory over the Swedes, who, in 1741, had renewed hostilities in a bid to win back territory ceded at the Treaty of Nystad. She also was chiefly responsible for maintaining the alliance of Austria, France, and Russia against Prussia and Great Britain in the conflict that lasted from 1756 to 1763 and later became known as the Seven Years' War. And it was she who established Moscow University in 1755 and the Academy of Fine Arts in Saint Petersburg three years later. But then, on Christmas Day, 1761, her death brought to power a man totally unfit to be czar: her German-born nephew Karl Peter Ulrich.

Peter III, as he became known, was neurotic, immature, near-alcoholic, and probably impotent. He made no attempt to learn Russian and, to make matters worse, was known as a fanatical admirer of Prussia, with whom Russia was at war. In the eyes of his subjects, he had only one asset to commend him: a wife possessed of charm, spontaneous wit, and intelligence, who endeared herself to the Russian people by wholeheartedly absorbing their language, customs, and traditions. Like Peter, she was German-born: Princess Sophia Augusta Fredericka, from the small, obscure state of Anhalt-Zerbst. At the age of fourteen, she had been brought to Russia specifically to marry Peter, who was her cousin. She had been restyled the Grand Duchess Catherine Alekseyevna, and the wedding had taken place in 1744, when she was sixteen and he an adolescent seventeen.

It may be—despite Peter's predilection for playing with his toy soldiers in the conjugal bed—that their arranged marriage was consummated. But it is doubtful. In 1754, when Catherine was at last delivered of a child—a son and recognized heir, Pavel Petrovich—the father was almost certainly Sergey Saltykov, a married nobleman and court chamberlain to her husband. Two years later, when she had a daughter, Anna Petrova, the father was probably her new favorite, Stanislaw Augustus Poniatowski, a young Polish count.

Catherine II was by no means a beauty; her brow was too high, her nose and chin rather too long and pointed. But she had large, expressive blue eyes and such elegance and personality that it was not surprising, given a loveless marriage, that she should eventually be drawn into the amorous intrigues that so pervaded the Russian court. Peter, meanwhile, openly paraded his paramours and took pleasure in humiliating his wife in public. In so doing, he merely enhanced her popularity. By the time her husband became czar, Catherine had won not only admiration for her stylish bearing and devotion to Russia but also sympathy as the partner of a ruler repellent both in character and in his small, pox-scarred features.

Most important, Catherine was adored by the Imperial Guard at Saint Petersburg, and by one officer in particular. In January 1762, when her husband became the czar,

Catherine was six months pregnant by Grigory Orlov, a dashing and heroic captain of the artillery. By necessity, she remained discreetly in the background, until, in April, she was secretly delivered of her illegitimate child: a little boy who was promptly spirited away to foster parents.

In the meantime, Peter had been remarkably swift in implementing new policies. One of his first—and most significant—acts was to free the gentry from compulsory state service. This meant that for the first time ever in Russia, some citizens were at liberty to conduct their lives independently of both czar and state.

But any esteem he won was quickly canceled out. He proceeded to outrage the Church, by initiating the nationalization of all monastery lands, and the army, by suing for peace with Prussia, even though Russian forces were in the ascendant. He further alienated his army by ordering them to wear German-style uniforms, and by appointing his German uncle as colonel-in-chief of the Horse Guards.

Opposition to his rule was now so overwhelming that on June 28, Catherine, with the support of the Guards regiments and the acquiescence of the Church, was able to lead a bloodless coup d'état. The czar was imprisoned. Eight days later, the newly proclaimed empress of all the Russias was told that her husband had been killed in a drunken brawl with the Guards. The official public pronouncement, however, was that he had succumbed to a hemorrhoidal colic, which had affected his brain and brought on apoplexy.

Thus, at the age of thirty-three, Catherine gained control of the empire, beginning a reign that was to span almost three and a half decades. Like Peter the Great, she was dedicated to the creation of a prosperous and powerful state. Like him, too, she plundered the technology of western Europe. She provided incentives for skilled foreign workers to settle in Russia, sent geologists exploring far and wide for mineral deposits, and made grants to landowners who experimented with new farming techniques from England.

But unlike Peter, Catherine was also interested in abstract ideas. During her early years at the Russian court, she had read an enormous range of books, particularly those of Voltaire—"his works formed my mind and spirit," she claimed—and in the process had become fascinated with the liberal philosophies of the Enlightenment.

Yet her immediate priorities, on coming to the throne, were economic, not intellectual. She had to reduce the huge foreign debt that had built up as a result of Empress Elizabeth's costly involvement in the Seven Years' War. In this, she was wholly successful. Previously, almost all branches of trade had been run by state or private monopolies. Catherine now decreed that anyone living outside Moscow or Saint Petersburg was free to start up a factory. As a result, there sprang up a whole range of cottage industries, producing linen, pottery, leather goods, and furniture.

At the same time, she boosted foreign trade by abolishing export duties. In addition to maintaining a thriving trade with England, she signed a series of commercial treaties with Spain, Portugal, Denmark, and, later in her reign, France. With measures like these, she transformed, in three years, a budget deficit of 7 million rubles into a surplus of 5.5 million.

Now she was free to pursue her dreams of a more humane society. She had no ready-formulated plans, so she summoned to Moscow a legislative commission, composed of more than 500 of her subjects, drawn from all social classes except the serfs. It was, despite its name, a purely consultative body, the aim being merely to find out the wishes of the people and to gather suggestions for ways to achieve them.

A serene Catherine sits with son Pavel and husband Peter, the heir apparent to the Russian throne, for a family portrait by A. R. Lisiewska. The united image was misleading: The marriage had been strained from the start, and Pavel's father was probably one of Catherine's lovers. Both Peter and Catherine were German-born, but whereas Peter made it clear he preferred his native country to the one he was about to rule, Catherine enthusiastically embraced her adopted culture, achieving fluency in the Russian language and entering the Orthodox faith. Her motive was power. In 1757, she had admitted: "My ambition is as great as is humanly possible." In 1762, she overthrew her husband just six months after he had become Czar Peter III.

In two sketches of Russian rural life by western European travelers, a peasant woman draws water from the village well *(above)* and bearded serfs huddle around a table in their cheerless cabin *(right)*. Most Russian peasants lived in similar one-room dwellings, made either of clay or of logs insulated with moss. Usually, they shared their homes with whatever livestock they possessed. Forbidden to leave the land on which they toiled, they appeared on official records merely as the property of the landowner. Catherine the Great espoused liberal treatment of the serfs, but she frequently made grants of land—and the laborers who lived on it—as rewards to her favorites. This practice served to expand the bonded labor system, which at the beginning of her reign she had aspired to dismantle.

Nevertheless, it was an extraordinary innovation. For the first time, the Russian peasants were able to voice their many grievances without fear of retribution.

At the first meeting of the commission, Grigory Orlov opened the proceedings by reading key passages from a sixty-page document written by Catherine, entitled *Nakaz (Instruction)*. This work began, significantly, with the words "Russia is a European country." It went on to outline the need for a more civilized society, for religious toleration, and, above all, for just and humane laws. The document was regarded as being so dangerously radical that its publication was subsequently banned in absolutist France.

Between 1767 and 1769, the legislative commission met no fewer than 203 times, but free though the debate was, there emerged no immediate reforms. Furthermore, Catherine's energies were now being directed elsewhere, for in 1768, she launched a war against the Turks, with the aim of expanding Russia's frontiers toward both the Balkans and the Black Sea.

Five years later, with the war still in progress, any possibility that Catherine might significantly ease the plight of the serfs was foreclosed by a peasant rebellion in southeast Russia, led by Emelyan Pugachev, an army deserter. By June 1774, the peasant forces were threatening to march on Moscow. But a timely end to the Russo-Turkish War meant that the full imperial army was now free to fight and, after initial setbacks, defeat the rebels at Tsaritsyn, on the Volga River. Pugachev was brought to Moscow and executed.

Catherine wrote to Voltaire: "If it were only me he had harmed, his hopes could

Chained but seemingly uncowed, Emelyan Pugachev awaits judgment for leading a rebellion in the southern Urals. Claiming to be the deposed Czar Peter III, the charismatic Pugachev had recruited peasants and nomads to his cause, promising land, money, arms, and freedom. His forces had rampaged throughout the southeastern provinces, slaughtering nobles and looting their estates. It had taken Catherine's forces nearly a year to put down the revolt, by which time Pugachev's army numbered 20,000. The rebels were finally defeated in August 1774, and Pugachev was brought in an iron cage to Moscow, where he was tried and beheaded.

be justified, and I should pardon him, but this trial involved the empire and its laws." She still wanted to be seen as an enlightened despot and to have Russia recognized as a civilized European state. But thenceforth her attitude toward the peasantry would be increasingly governed by fear rather than by compassion. More and more, she became aware that to liberate the serfs would be to undermine the authority of the landowning classes, upon whom her power ultimately depended.

At the same time, Catherine introduced a number of measures to restrict enserfment in Russia. She ended the practice of bonding prisoners of war; and she rescinded laws specifying that a man automatically forfeited his freedom on marrying a serf, and that orphans and illegitimate children became the serfs of their foster parents.

But while condemning cruelty in general, she made no attempt to introduce legislation protecting serfs from their owners, perhaps recognizing that such a law would have been almost impossible to enforce. She could do nothing but hope that the maltreatment of serfs would be checked both by her public education policy (her *Instruction* on social justice was read three times a year in every law court), and by a gradual refinement of behavior among the nobles.

In other areas, Catherine made a more positive contribution to the advancement of Russian civilization. Torture by the judiciary was almost completely eliminated, and corporal and capital punishment were greatly reduced. The administration of justice was brought nearer to the population by the creation of a vast network of courts at both provincial and district levels. And with an initial endowment from the empress, every province set up a board of public welfare to establish and supervise schools, hospitals, poorhouses, and correctional institutions.

In 1775, the newly created Commission of National Schools became responsible for overseeing schools, training teachers, and providing textbooks; and in 1786, Catherine's Statute for National Education set up a two-tier network of high schools and primary schools in provincial capitals, along with primary schools in district towns. Attendance was not compulsory, but the schools were to be free and open to children of both sexes and all social classes.

At the time of Catherine's accession, Russia had only a handful of state schools. By the end of her reign, some 62,000 children were being educated in 548 institutions sponsored by the government—only a minute fraction of the national child population, but the empress had nevertheless established the principle that education was the responsibility of the state.

She also decreed that each provincial capital must have a hospital and that each district should have a doctor, a surgeon, an assistant surgeon and a student doctor. She countered the shortage of medical practitioners by attracting large numbers of German physicians with the offer of an 800-ruble retirement pension.

Catherine founded a number of hospitals, including one in Saint Petersburg that treated (anonymously) patients suffering from venereal disease; and she introduced smallpox inoculation, which she herself received in order to allay people's fears.

At the same time, the empress remained an absolute autocrat and maintained all the trappings of majesty. She spent millions of rubles on palaces and country estates. She transformed Saint Petersburg from a city of wooden structures into an imposing metropolis of granite. She sought to rival the French court at Versailles for splendor and style, and for the extent of her library and her art collection. She was a tireless promoter of Russian culture, and she greatly encouraged intellectual and artistic activity through her patronage of composers, painters, poets, novelists, and playwrights. She herself wrote a number of satirical plays and operatic librettos. Literature and journalism also flourished, stimulated by her so-called free-press edict of 1783, which for the first time allowed private citizens to set up their own publishing houses.

During the course of Catherine's reign, the members of her court came to enjoy greater luxury than ever before. Yet despite the lavishness of her surroundings, the empress herself surrendered to only one personal extravagance: the unrelenting pursuit of romance.

"The trouble," she once wrote, "is that my heart is loath to remain even one hour without love." An irrepressible romantic, she took a succession of lovers, at least twenty-one all together, most of them progressively younger than herself. As though installed by royal appointment, each paramour in turn was given a princely salary and his own private apartments; and, when he was replaced, he was usually rewarded with a title and a landed estate.

In 1764, Catherine even contrived to have one devoted ex-lover, the amiable Stanislaw Poniatowski, elected king of Poland. Once on the throne, the poor man was hopelessly torn between his loyalty to Catherine, who gave him indispensable financial support, and his need to appease Polish nationalists resentful of her interference. The breaking point came when Catherine tried to make the Polish Diet, or Parliament, give the same voting rights to the country's Orthodox and Lutheran minorities as were enjoyed by the Catholic majority. Civil war broke out, as Catholic leaders banded together to fight for Catholicism and Polish independence.

The Polish rebels were crushed by Russian troops in 1772. Over the next quarter of a century, their country was divided up among Russia, Prussia, and Austria. By

In a 1791 caricature by the English cartoonist Richard Newton, the devil tempts Catherine with the evidently appealing prospect of acquiring Warsaw and Constantinople. Entitled *Queen Catherine's Dream,* the illustration demonstrates the English suspicion that Catherine's war against the Turks, begun in 1787, was motivated by greed for new territory and not, as she claimed, by a Christian desire to regain the Ottoman Empire—and its capital Constantinople—from the Muslims. Although she did win large amounts of territory from the Turks, she never took Constantinople. Her troops captured Warsaw, but the city was allotted to the Prussians when Russia, Austria, and Prussia divided Poland in 1795.

1795, Poland, as a sovereign state, had ceased to exist; poor Poniatowski retired to take up the study of botany.

As a result of the partitions of Poland, Russia acquired the Polish Ukraine and Lithuania. Catherine's reign also saw Russian expansion into the steppes beyond the Urals; across the Bering Strait from Siberia into Alaska, which a century later would be sold to the United States; and, most spectacularly, into the Crimea, which was wrested from the Turks.

For these territorial gains, Catherine was greatly in debt to another of her lovers, Grigory Potemkin, a dynamic and ambitious army officer. Potemkin was the most adored of all her suitors, and the only man with whom she was ever willing to share power. Their tempestuous love affair began in 1774 and lasted for only two years; but long afterward he remained her chief minister, virtually a prince consort, profoundly influencing her policies at home and abroad, and even taking responsibility for the selection of her new lovers.

It was Potemkin who, in 1787, organized what was undoubtedly the high point in Catherine's reign: a grand and glittering tour of her newly acquired territories in southern Russia, on which she took with her 14 carriages, 124 sleighs, and 3,000 troops. After this, however, her fortunes, and those of Russia, began to wane. In 1788, Sweden invaded Russian-occupied Finland and won a major naval victory in the course of the ensuing, inconclusive two-year war. Then, as the excesses of the French Revolution began to cast their shadows over Europe's monarchies, news reached Catherine that Potemkin had died of malaria.

By now, the empress was sixty-two years old, white-haired, and round of figure.

In this commemorative engraving, Catherine the Great watches from the balcony of the Saint Petersburg Senate House, on the left, as the great bronze statue of Peter the Great is unveiled. The date was August 7, 1782, the centenary of Peter's enthronement. Catherine had commissioned the statue from the French sculptor Étienne Maurice Falconet, but the two of them fell out, and Falconet left Saint Petersburg before the unveiling. The inscription on the statue read, "To Peter the First from Catherine the Second," confirming that the project was an attempt by the empress to foster a link in people's minds between her own reign and that of her legendary predecessor.

Fearful of the antiroyalist forces unleashed in France, she began to retreat from her previously tolerant attitudes toward the intelligentsia. The publisher Nikolay Novikov was arrested, and his books were confiscated and burned; the distinguished author Alexander Radischev was exiled to Siberia for expressing views on the treatment of serfs, which Catherine herself would have welcomed in earlier years. She revoked her free-press edict and banned the writings of her former friend and mentor, Voltaire.

In November 1796, the great empress died at the age of sixty-seven, following a stroke. Decades before, she had written her own epitaph:

> Here lies Catherine II, born at Stettin May 2, 1729. . . . Enthroned in Russia, she desired nothing but the best for her country, and tried to procure for her subjects happiness, liberty, and wealth. She forgave easily and hated no one. Tolerant, undemanding, of a gay disposition, she had a republican spirit and a kind heart.

Ultimately, however, her desire to create a just, orderly, and humane society had proved to be an impossible dream. The Russian Empire was growing too quickly, and its economy was still too dependent on serfdom to permit any major social reorganization, at least during her lifetime. In a sense, Catherine had even extended the feudal system, by her generous awards of land—and the work force that went with it—to loyal ministers, to court favorites, and, not least, to her ex-lovers.

Nevertheless, Russia in the eighteenth century had undergone a remarkable transformation. Peter and Catherine's reforms had affected every aspect of national life, from government and warfare to culture and religion. The two great innovators left Russia far stronger, militarily and economically, than it had been in 1700, and far larger, with new territories the size of France and a population that had risen from 8 million to 35 million.

Yet in expanding its frontiers, the nation was storing up problems for the future; Russian administration was imposed on resentful Polish Catholics, Baltic Germans, and Lithuanian Jews, with blatant disregard for their cultural and religious traditions. At home, the continued dependence on serfdom would cause a buildup of popular resistance that future rulers would find increasingly difficult to contain.

THE GRAND TOUR

In an age when the yearning for enlightenment was matched by a reverence for the classical past, a grand tour of Europe—culminating in a thorough exploration of Italy's cities—came to be perceived as a desirable conclusion to every wealthy young man's education. The fashion reached its peak during the years of peace between the end of the Seven Years' War in 1763 and the beginning of the French Revolution in 1789. For the first time, travelers could move freely throughout Europe, shown here on a map of the time, visiting

North America, but the nation that dispatched its manhood in the greatest numbers was England. Contemporary writers estimated that as many as 40,000 Englishmen were touring Europe at any one time. Their trips usually lasted three years, much longer than those of their counterparts from other countries. One reason for this was that after a turbulent Channel crossing of up to twelve hours, the average Englishman was in no hurry to repeat the experience. He therefore tended to treat his grand tour as a once-in-a-lifetime voyage of discovery.

Young men on the tour generally traveled with a tutor, whose job it was to steer his charges through dangers and distractions, both physical and moral, and to instruct them about the places they visited. Families and newlyweds also went on the tour, along with others who sought to improve either their minds or their health.

France was the favored route to Italy, and the cold and difficult struggle across the Alps was generally pre-

all the major places of interest without fear of being persecuted on grounds of religion or nationality. Most found the experience both thrilling and invigorating, as shown by the quotations on the following pages.

The travelers came from all over western Europe and in some cases from as far as

ferred to either the pirate-plagued sea crossing from Marseilles to Genoa or the longer overland journey through Germany and Austria. The traveling could be bone-jolting and the bedbugs bothersome, but for many, the splendors of Italy made up for all the discomforts. As the German literary giant Johann Goethe wrote: "I count it as a second birthday, a true rebirth, from the day I entered Rome."

PARIS: THE SHOWPLACE OF FASHION

"When an Englishman comes to Paris, he cannot appear until he has undergone a total metamorphosis. At his first arrival, he finds it necessary to send for the tailor, perruquier, hatter, shoemaker, and every other tradesman concerned in the equipment of the human body."

Tobias Smollett. Paris, October 19, 1763. *Travels in France and Italy.*

In a contemporary engraving *(right)* from the *Encyclopédie* of Denis Diderot, an eager French tailor measures a young customer. Only when clad in a suitably fashionable outfit, perhaps trimmed with lace or made of multicolored velvet, could a young traveler have the confidence to be seen among the dazzling notables of Parisian society, some of whom take a leisurely promenade through the gallery of the Palais Royal in Philibert-Louis Debucourt's 1787 painting *(below).*

Seated apprehensively in his sledge, an Alpine tourist comes down a slope the quick way in an anonymous eighteenth-century sketch *(inset, right)*. Any such opportunity of speeding up the journey was readily seized upon. It could take six days to cross the mountains from France to Italy, traveling on muleback or else being carried by porters in a roughly carved sedan chair. Despite the difficulties, however, the numbers of visitors to the Alps began to increase during the middle of the century, as writers and poets emphasized the majesty rather than the monstrousness of the peaks. In a painting by Caspar Wolf dated 1776 *(far right)*, a group of visitors to Lake of Thun in Switzerland, dwarfed by the walls of a giant cave, gaze out in wonderment at the surrounding scenery.

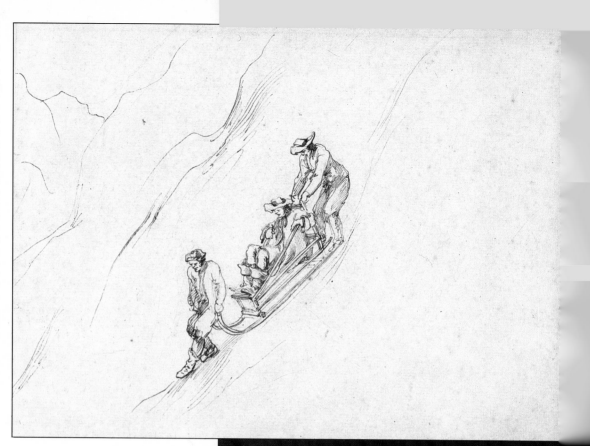

THE ALPS: A PERILOUS BEAUTY

"The farther we penetrate, the more the sight is animated with the beauties of this romantic region. The views become still more and more engaging as we advance; every valley appears like a new country from its different form; overhanging rocks of a prodigious height, and torrents pouring down in sheets from their very summits, are such wonders of nature as it is impossible to look upon without a mixture of astonishment and awe."

T. Bourrit. *Relation of a Journey to the Glaciers in the Dutchy of Savoy,* translated from the French by C. and F. Davy, 1775.

VENICE: A CENTER OF PLEASURE

"Their gaming houses are called ridotti, apartments in noblemen's houses where none but noblemen keep the bank, and fools lose their money. They dismiss the gamesters when they please, and always come off winners. There are usually ten or twelve chambers on a floor with gaming tables in them, and vast crowds of people; a profound silence is observed, and none are admitted without masks. Here you meet ladies of pleasure, and married women who under the protection of a mask enjoy all the diversions of the carnival, but are usually attended by the husband or his spies."

Sir Thomas Nugent. *The Grand Tour containing an exact description of Most of the Cities, Towns & Remarkable Places of Europe,* 1749.

Masked revelers mingle anonymously in one of Venice's notorious gaming houses, in a mid-eighteenth-century painting by Gianantonio Guardi. Tourists were welcome, provided they wore masks and were prepared to lose money.

In a late-1730s painting *(below)* by the prolific Canaletto, a golden barge waits amid a flotilla of gondolas to carry the doge of Venice to the Ascension Day ceremony at which he will throw a ring into the Adriatic, to symbolize a marriage between the city and the sea. The spectacle attracted many out-of-season tourists.

FLORENCE: THE HOME OF ART

"The most precious productions are kept in a place called the Tribuna, which is the holy of holies of this temple of the arts. This Tribuna forms a very elegant closet, of a round or rather octagonal form, with a roof in the shape of a dome, which receives the light: Here are the select pieces of the gallery—the Venus of the Medicis with five other ancient statues, several pictures by Raphael, an excellent Madonna by Correggio, a Venus by Titian, and several more."

J. W. von Archenholz. *A Picture of Italy*, translated from the German by Joseph Trapp, 1791.

Visiting art enthusiasts from England cluster reverently around the exhibits in the viewing room of Florence's Uffizi gallery, in a painting *(far left)* by Johann Zoffany, dated between 1772 and 1778. Zoffany had been commissioned by the British royal family to produce a record of the gallery's greatest masterpieces. In the foreground, a museum official holds Titian's reclining *Venus of Urbino*, and amid a cluster of visitors at the left of the picture, Zoffany himself holds up Raphael's *Cowper Madonna*. But in an English cartoon of 1801 *(inset, left)*, a less-discerning connoisseur inspects a bust that has been crudely disfigured to give it the look of an antique. This was just one of the ways in which unscrupulous dealers took advantage of the travelers' desire to return home with art treasures of their own.

In the foreground of Giambattista Piranesi's sweeping sketch *(far left)*, dated 1745, a young gentleman listens to his guide's lecture amid the decaying splendor of the Colosseum, the amphitheater of ancient Rome. Much of eighteenth-century education concentrated on the classical past; arriving in Rome therefore represented the ultimate goal of a young gentleman's grand tour, and, as well as spending much of his time exploring the ruins, he would also want to record his impressions of this majestic city. The young traveler *(inset, left)*, captured in a lightning sketch by the portraitist Sir Joshua Reynolds in 1752, seems utterly absorbed in his drawing of a Roman landscape.

ROME: THE ETERNAL CITY

"We entered the famous Colosseum, which certainly presents a vast and sublime idea of the grandeur of the ancient Romans. It is hard to tell whether the astonishing massiveness or the exquisite taste of this superb building should be more admired. A hermit has a little apartment inside. We passed through his hermitage to climb where the seats and the corridors of the theater once were ... it was shocking to discover several portions of this theater full of dung. It is rented to people who use it in this fashion."

James Boswell. Tuesday, March 26, 1765. *Course in Antiquities and Arts in Rome.*

THE RISE OF PRUSSIA

It should have been the eighteenth century's most brilliant encounter. The French writer Voltaire, bright star of Europe's Enlightenment, arrived in the Prussian capital of Berlin, in response to the insistent invitations of his exalted admirer, Frederick the Great, king of Prussia. Both host and guest were aware of their positions as two of the marvels of the age. The monarch, with his zeal for political reform and his literary aspirations, saw himself as the modern embodiment of that ancient ideal, the philosopher-king. Voltaire, unhindered by false modesty, knew that his visit could only enhance the reputation of the Prussian court, and was not averse to praise.

"I find beauties beyond number in your works," Frederick had written at the beginning of their correspondence. "If my destiny should not favor me enough to be able to possess you, at least let me hope that I shall one day see the man whom I have admired from afar for a long time."

The response was gratifying. "Believe me," Voltaire had declared, "the only truly good kings have been those who began, like you, by educating themselves, by knowing mankind, by loving truth, by detesting persecution and superstition."

In the summer of 1750, ten years after Frederick ascended the throne, the glorious moment arrived: Voltaire took up residence in Prussia. The early days were idyllic—long nights of witty conversation at the palace of Sans Souci, or "Carefree," concerts, dinner parties with the intellectual elite, hours of fruitful collaboration. Frederick hoped that Voltaire would help him improve his French prose style, as well as editing the literary, historical, and political texts that flowed from the prolific royal pen.

But the honeymoon did not last. "My dear child," wrote Voltaire to his niece in France, "the weather is beginning to get cold." He had financial difficulties, was entangled in a lawsuit with a local banker, and—far worse—had grown disillusioned with his patron. "There are absolutely no resources here," he complained in another letter home. "There are a prodigious number of bayonets, and very few books."

When a row split the Berlin Academy, scholars whom Frederick had reconvened for the greater glory of his reign, Voltaire wrote a scathing satire against the man the king had chosen to head the institution. Frederick did not take kindly to Voltaire's attack on his protégé: He called Voltaire a "vile scribbler" and had the pamphlet burned in public. Voltaire was scandalized. By this act, Frederick gave the lie to his image as an enlightened monarch, who had banned censorship within days of mounting the throne. The poet packed up and returned to Paris. But before Voltaire could reach home, he was intercepted and placed under house arrest at Frankfurt. He was charged with stealing a book of the king's own poems. When—five weeks later—he was released, his captors handed him a bill for his board and lodging.

"The most dishonest man alive" was the writer's verdict at the end of his two-and-a-half-year stay with Frederick. "His greatest talent is to lie like a lackey."

Voltaire may have spoken out of injured pride, but he had perceived, correctly, that the king of Prussia was a bundle of contradictions. Frederick may have talked of turning his realm into a modern state, but he also wielded power as absolute as that of any Roman emperor and took pains to control every aspect of government.

Frederick had ascended the throne at a time when his formerly impoverished and insignificant kingdom stood poised for momentous changes, and he would himself be the architect of developments that turned Prussia into a leading player on the European stage. But Prussia's transformation from a minor German principality to Europe's most formidable military power had started long before his birth.

The realm that Frederick inherited had been ranked as a kingdom for only two generations. In the mid-seventeenth century, Germany had been a patchwork of several hundred nominally independent principalities. These fragmented states had formally achieved their autonomy as a result of the hideously destructive Thirty Years' War, in which they had successfully challenged the overlordship of the Holy Roman Empire—the unwieldy dynastic institution presided over by the Austrian Hapsburg family, whose nominal writ ran from the border of France to the margins of Poland.

Frederick the Great's paternal great-grandfather, Frederick William, prince of the

Prussia in the early eighteenth century comprised a scattered collection of territories *(shaded yellow)* that had been conquered or annexed by its Hohenzollern rulers. Within a year of his accession in 1740, King Frederick II, later to be known as Frederick the Great, seized and held Austria's rich and populous territory of Silesia. But his conquests were not secured until the end of the Seven Years' War (1756-1763), an exhausting conflict that involved all the major European powers. In 1772 Frederick acquired West Prussia as his share from the partition of Poland, and with this and his other acquisitions *(green)* finally linked East Prussia with the Brandenburg heartlands to form a cohesive state.

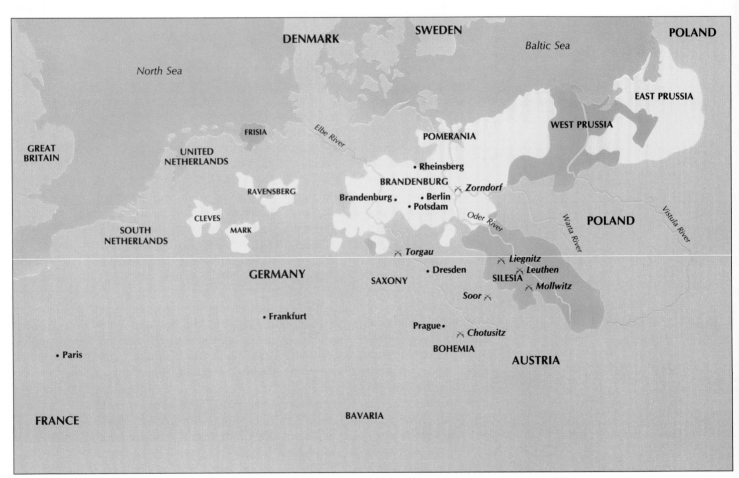

house of Hohenzollern and elector of Brandenburg, had ruled over a number of widely scattered territories in the north of this empire. Warfare, diplomacy, and—more commonly—astute marriages had brought together possessions that were distant and disparate: The old heartland of the electorate, the sandy plains surrounding the city of Berlin, was more than 400 miles away from its easternmost Baltic province of East Prussia and was separated from it by a sizable slab of the kingdom of Poland. Far to the west lay the smaller counties of Cleves, Mark, and Ravensberg; the first of these, straddling the Rhine, stood much nearer to Amsterdam than it did to Berlin.

The Great Elector began to weld these scattered entities into a state ruled by a centralized government and connected by a network of improved communications. In 1701, the elector's son was granted a crown from the Holy Roman emperor and styled himself Frederick I, king in Prussia. The wording was judicious: Frederick could not be a king of Prussia, since eastern Prussia was ruled by Poland. And a king of Brandenburg would have had the right to grant titles of nobility within the Holy Roman Empire—a profitable enterprise the Hapsburgs wanted for themselves.

The new monarch reveled in the full pomp and panoply of kingship and indulged his taste for expensive luxuries, despite having little in his coffers to pay the bills. Nine years after his coronation, his realm was struck by a sequence of disasters: a savage winter followed by bad harvests and famine. His sparsely settled, wind-swept domains—particularly those in the east—were further depopulated by plague, which killed thousands and sent still more fleeing to uncontaminated lands.

Frederick William I, who succeeded his father in 1713, demonstrated a different style of kingship. He abandoned the French manners and ostentation of his predecessor's court, lived frugally, and continued his grandfather's work of strengthening the state. His first priority was to continue the expansion and improvement of the army. Instead of relying heavily, as so many European monarchs had done, on foreign mercenaries, he built up a force that eventually numbered mostly native soldiers. The rank-and-file troops were provided primarily by his "cantonal" system of conscription, whereby almost all peasants in a canton, or district, were made liable for two years' military service, followed by additional terms as and when the state required. The officer class was supplied by the Prussian aristocracy, or Junkers—from the German for "young noble"—among whom military service was a traditional career. By the time he died in 1740, Frederick William had mustered 80,000 troops, an army equal to that of Austria, a country ten times the size of his own.

Nevertheless, the king did not rely on numerical strength alone. He sought to forge a fighting force more tightly disciplined, and more efficient, than Europe had hitherto seen. Strict rules governed every aspect of military conduct, dress, and training. Foreigners were amazed by the extraordinary and unprecedented spectacle of an army that marched in measured, synchronized step—a refinement invented by a Prussian field marshal who appreciated the psychological impact of a force that comported itself like a single, superhuman killing machine. Not only did this many-headed creature walk in time; it knelt, aimed muskets, fired, and reloaded in time as well. Thanks to another Prussian invention, the iron ramrod, it was capable of firing twice the number of salvos its rivals could produce in the same time.

Prussian soldiers were drilled to maintain a uniform posture, move at a uniform pace, and look as identical as possible: Pigtails had to be trimmed to a precise length, beards shaped to a prescribed pattern. Soldiers unable to produce the necessary configuration of whiskers were ordered to fill in the correct outlines with paint.

Officers were expected to rule the men under their command with a rod of iron. Discipline was so severe that even the most hard-bitten soldiers could be driven beyond the breaking point. There were times when the suicide rate at the Berlin barracks rose to one fatality per fortnight. Frederick William had little sympathy for those who chose to defect in this manner. To set an example, he ordered that the corpses of soldier-suicides be tied by the feet and dragged away by an army horse.

The king's passion for regulations extended into civil life. He set up a central body, the General Directory, whose responsibility it was to translate royal decisions into written instructions, and then supervise their implementation in detail. He even drew up a thirty-five-chapter, 297-page manual for all public employees, dictating every aspect of their professional lives, from office hours to menus, crockery, and serving staff appropriate for working lunches. To emphasize the importance of these strictures, he decorated the text at appropriate points with sketches of gallows. No bureaucrat convicted of embezzlement could hope to escape the scaffold.

When Frederick William's queen, Sophia Dorothea—a princess of the German house of Hanover and sister to England's future George II—bore an heir in 1712, the king tried to regulate his son's life with the same precision. The future Frederick the Great was to be prepared for kingship with a regimen of early rising, scripted prayers, military dress, a detailed timetable of academic studies and physical training, and an early bedtime. The only breaks in this routine were to be allowed when the boy reached a suitable age to accompany his father on troop inspections and sit in on late-night pipe-smoking sessions with the king and his military cronies.

"It is the intention of the king," remarked one visitor to court, "that the boy should prefer the military to all other sciences, learn thrift and frugality early, and not fall in love with comfort and pleasure!" But such an approach to child-rearing extracted its toll. The same witness went on to note of the boy that "he looks and walks as stiff as if he had already taken part in many campaigns."

The prince had, indeed, seen combat, but it had largely taken place around the family dinner table. The puritanical attitudes of his father sat uneasily with his mother's artistic enthusiasms and fondness for music, card games, and other sociable diversions. The king thundered that his wife was turning their son into a milksop; he deplored the boy's unmanly enthusiasm for flute-playing and novel-reading, his aversion to gunfire, and his apparent inability to sit a horse.

To teach his son to mend his ways, the king subjected him to a series of public humiliations. He forced him to sit below the salt, at the farthest end of the family table, kicked and beat him in front of visitors, and on one occasion mortified onlookers when he grabbed the prince by his hair and dragged him along the ground.

At the age of eighteen, Frederick tried to escape from his father's clutches. He confided in a close friend, Hans Hermann von Katte, and solicited his aid. Katte, scion of an old Prussian military family, shared Frederick's love of music, art, and witty conversation; he sympathized with his friend's need to free himself from parental tyranny. The pair planned to flee the realm together. The prince entrusted Katte with some of his jewels, to be sold secretly for the purpose of raising funds, and sent a clandestine appeal to his uncle, the king of England, begging for asylum.

The eagle-eyed Frederick William got wind of the plot. He placed Frederick and Katte under arrest and charged his own son on several counts, including military desertion and attempted conspiracy with a foreign monarch. At the king's command, the prince was placed in solitary confinement at the fortress of Küstrin, while his

A court portrait of Frederick II at the age of about eleven *(below)* shows him as a little soldier, a role forced on him from infancy by his tyrannical father, Frederick William I. In his youth Frederick loathed his father's militaristic values and longed for the cultured world of his frivolous mother. In fact, although the old king ranted against his son's love of music and literature, he enjoyed the arts, and was himself a painter. In a picture painted in 1738 *(right)*, he depicts himself *(third from right)* accompanied by servants and some of his renowned Potsdam Grenadiers—a cherished regiment of unusually tall soldiers.

partner in crime was tried by a court-martial and sentenced to death. On the morning of November 6, 1730, Katte was beheaded in the Küstrin courtyard: Frederick, by his father's command, was pushed to the window of the cell by his jailers and forced to watch his friend die. He was also found guilty, but in his case the judges were not prepared to pass the death sentence on a member of the royal family.

A shaken Frederick formally submitted to his father. He would swallow his pride, do the parental bidding, and follow whatever course the king dictated. Mollified, Frederick William sent his son to learn the workings of Prussian government from the bottom up, beginning in a junior bureaucratic post in the War and Domains Chamber. Without audible protest, the crown prince applied himself to his political education and did not demur at the strict regimen his father set for him. It was a return to the proscriptions of his childhood: He was forbidden to dance, play music, read anything but religious or educational texts, or order such delicacies as oysters for his table.

When Frederick William pronounced himself satisfied by the prince's diligence, he gave him command of a military regiment so he might enhance his preparation for the throne by a careful study of the arts of war. He also arranged a suitable marriage for his heir, with a German princess, Elisabeth Christine, from the small principality of Brunswick-Wolfenbüttel. The charms of his eighteen-year-old bride were lost on Frederick, who evinced little lust—or indeed liking—for women. When the king allowed Frederick to establish his own princely court in an old manor house at Rheinsberg, Elisabeth Christine remained there only on sufferance. Soon, Frederick had her installed in her own residence just outside Berlin, and although she had grown to love and admire him, he rarely consented to see her or speak to her for the rest of his life. It was clear from an early stage, therefore, that this unhappy union would not produce an heir.

Enjoying the unaccustomed freedom of his own establishment, Frederick decorated his new home with murals, painted garlands, and statuary; he stocked his library with classics and important contemporary works and applied himself to the study of philosophy, literature, and the sciences. Guests were invited for lively supper parties, masked balls, theatricals, and musical evenings, and the young prince launched into his celebrated correspondence with Voltaire. But such indulgences no longer provoked the wrath of the king: The crown prince, through belated obedience and diligent efforts, had by now convinced his ailing father that he was capable of fulfilling the full range of roles—military, administrative, and diplomatic—that were incumbent upon a Prussian monarch: "I die content," declared Frederick William in his last days, "with so worthy a son to succeed me."

On May 31, 1740, the twenty-eight-year-old Frederick acceded to the throne of Prussia. He set to work immediately, with a set of military and civil reforms. Government officials were ordered to put the interests of "the people" above all, even above the interests of the king. Generals were instructed to keep a tight rein on their troops, so as to protect the king's subjects from oppression by his soldiery. Instructions—not always obeyed—were issued to the army, forbidding the officers to use press gangs to force men into service. In the military academies, cadets were no longer to be subjected to the sadistic bullying that had been a hallmark of these institutions. Above all, the army was to become a more efficient and more economical fighting machine. There was no longer room for such extravagances as Frederick William's pet regiment of tall grenadiers, comprised exclusively of men of unusual height: The giants were reassigned to other units or mustered out.

Civilians were hopeful that a new era was beginning. Frederick opened public granaries to keep down the price of bread and established a government department

Drawn up in regimental groups known as inspections, Prussian cavalry *(right)* and infantry *(overleaf)* officers display exhaustively detailed uniforms in a late-eighteenth-century painting. Stern discipline, ceaseless drilling, and an efficient infrastructure of supply developed the army that Frederick had inherited from his father into the dominant military force in eighteenth-century Europe—able to accomplish complex maneuvers in battle that would have reduced any other troops to chaos. Frederick himself wore the sober and functional "Prussian blue" coat of an infantry officer to the end of his life.

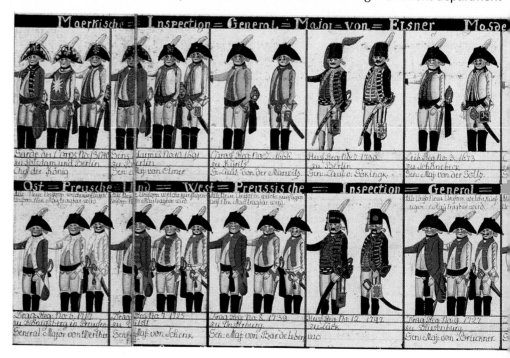

of trade and industry to encourage manufacturing and foster commercial growth. Civil liberties were to be extended. The use of torture by the judiciary was forbidden, except in cases of high treason. Greater freedom of the press was introduced, "for if gazettes are to be interesting," explained Frederick, "they are not to be under constraint." Nevertheless, although greater license was permitted in newspaper debates on spiritual and secular matters, the censors were still permitted to pass their pencils over material that might prejudice national security. As for religion, the king's Hohenzollern ancestors had always espoused a policy of toleration—how better to encourage new settlers into their underpopulated lands?—and Frederick confirmed his subjects' right to freedom of conscience.

It was his wish that Prussia be seen to embrace all the best principles of the Enlightenment. To enhance the kingdom's intellectual stature—and his own—Frederick reorganized the academy established by his grandfather, installing the French scholar Maupertuis as its head and inviting the cream of the Continent's intelligentsia to Berlin, although not all came. To bring the fruits of Prussia's scholarly endeavors to the outside world, he sponsored a new journal of literature, politics, and philosophy, to which he would, on occasion, contribute his own compositions.

Nevertheless, the king's initial encounter with his European neighbors would be military rather than intellectual. Before the first year of his reign was over, he had launched into war, against the judgment of his most senior advisers. He marshaled his troops, made conspicuous military preparations, and marched into the neighboring, Austrian-held province of Silesia, a large region that was not only richer in economic resources than any existing part of his realm but strategically important as well. It was also a territory that his Hohenzollern forebears had once claimed—albeit with little justification—as their own. Yet his motives, as he confessed in a letter to a friend, were not restricted to reasons of state: "My youth, the fire of passion, the

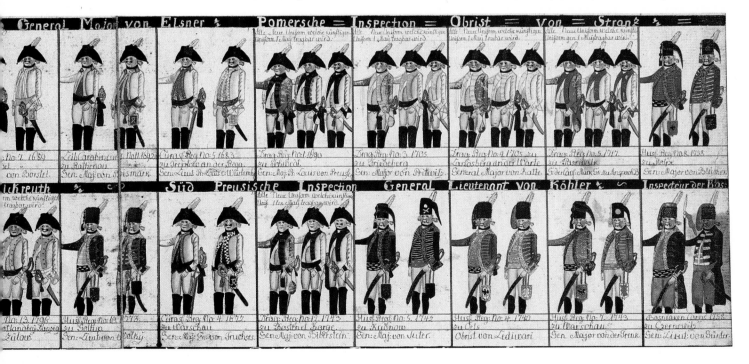

thirst for glory, yes—to conceal nothing from you—even the taste for novelty, in short a secret instinct has torn me from the jaws of quietude. The satisfaction of seeing my name in the newspapers and later in history has seduced me."

As well as nourishing the royal ego, the war against Austria had broader military and political implications. Austria itself, and all of central Europe, was in a state of instability. The Hapsburg emperor, Charles VI, had died without a male heir, bequeathing the rule of Austria, Hungary, Bohemia, and the southern Netherlands to his daughter, Maria Theresa. Her sex barred her from ruling in Germany as Holy Roman empress in her own right, but she could share the crown with her husband if he were elected emperor. Strong interests elsewhere in Europe were unwilling to assent to this arrangement and had their own reasons for stirring up a certain amount of turmoil. France felt most secure when the German states were weak and divided among themselves: It wanted to see its old rival Austria, currently the strongest force in central Europe, undermined, and hoped to keep it at loggerheads with the other important German powers—Bavaria, Saxony, and Prussia itself. Prussia, in turn, looked forward to achieving greater power at Austria's expense.

Frederick's conquest of Silesia was achieved with relative ease. The Austrian forces offered little resistance, and the indigenous population was not entirely against a change of masters. Silesia's large Protestant majority had never felt comfortable under the rule of Austria's Roman Catholic monarchy, while the Catholic community, well aware of Frederick's policy of religious toleration, saw little to fear from the takeover. Following Prussia's momentous defeat of the Austrian army at the battle of Mollwitz, Frederick offered to negotiate an agreement with Maria Theresa. He promised he would support her claims to the succession, and defend her territories from attack, so long as she recognized his conquest of Silesia. Unconvinced of his sincerity, she spurned his overtures, and he turned to the French for support.

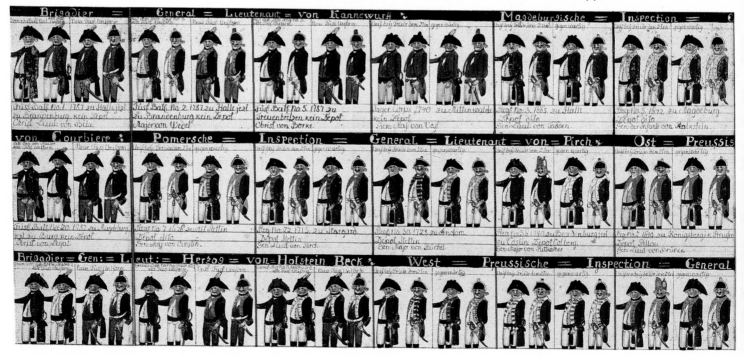

France and Prussia made uneasy allies. Neither trusted the other: The French did not want Frederick too strong or too confident, and Frederick in turn felt France had far too much power in central Europe as things stood. Nevertheless, they worked together, at least on the surface, to bend Austria to their will. Even as they planned joint attacks on Maria Theresa, however, Frederick's agents were courting her with diplomatic overtures, first negotiating a clandestine agreement, and then breaking it in time to allow Frederick to achieve a decisive victory over her army at Chotusitz. For the moment, she had no choice but to acknowledge Prussia's hold over Silesia.

But conflict would go on for another three years. Maria Theresa made fresh efforts to regain Silesia, bolstered by new allies. Britain now entered the fray to support her claims, as a means of pursuing its ancient rivalry with France; Saxony, conscious of Frederick's covetous gaze, also took her part. Prussian morale began to crack. The French were trounced by their old cross-Channel foes in a north German campaign, and they supplied little concrete assistance to Frederick. His war chest emptied, his supplies ran low, and his troops grew weary. Meanwhile, the Austrian alliance gained strength, and Frederick—once the aggressor—now found his own province of Brandenburg under threat. Reports suggested that even Russia was now about to enter the conflict on the enemy's side, and that Berlin itself would soon be attacked.

Adversity seemed to inspire Frederick. He stirred himself and drove his army to fresh efforts. An elaborate deception lured the Austrian army across the mountains from Bohemia to Silesia. Once there, they were pounced on by Prussian troops.

Driven back to Bohemia, the Austrians sought to retaliate by cornering Frederick's army in the valley of Soor and launching an ambush of their own. This time they were undone by Frederick's willingness to break the conventional rules of war by launching a cavalry attack uphill. After a day of hard fighting, in which Frederick's horse was shot from under him, the Prussians once again won the day. A few weeks later, undermined further by defeats in Saxony, Maria Theresa sued for peace. On Christmas Day of 1745, her envoy signed the Treaty of Dresden, acknowledging Prussia's possession of Silesia and ending Prussia's involvement in the war. The acquisition of this well-endowed province increased Prussia's territory and its population by more than 30 percent at a stroke, and its new king, with his formidable army, was acknowledged by all Europe as a force to be reckoned with. At home, Frederick's jubilant subjects rewarded their sovereign with the title Frederick the Great, the name by which he would one day be known across the Continent.

At home again, the king resumed the energetic program of reforms he had launched early in his reign. Frederick had no doubt of his priorities. A state newly important on the world stage needed a strong army. His father had laid the groundwork, leaving Frederick to test the Prussian war machine in the field. Now he was ready to profit from that experience. Like his father, he channeled three-quarters of all state revenues into the army, improving training and discipline and more than doubling the size of the military through an intense recruitment program. On the civil side, he initiated judicial reforms to speed up and simplify legal proceedings, in hopes—thwarted—of making justice affordable for even the poorest of the realm.

Criticism, however well informed or well intentioned, was rarely welcomed. The king made it clear to those under him, generals and civilian ministers alike, that he was in command. In war he would give the orders and develop the strategy; in peace he would exercise direct control over every department of state and chamber

In a portrait painted in 1745, Maria Theresa, arch-duchess of Austria and queen of Hungary and Bohemia, stands in solitary splendor beside a table crowded with her multiple crowns. Only twenty-three when she became ruler, Maria Theresa abandoned her youthful pursuits—riding, dancing, and music making—and immersed herself in affairs of state. Although unschooled in politics, she possessed a stubborn character and deep religious faith, which enabled her not only to secure her claim to her hereditary lands but also to reign over them for four decades, until her death in 1780.

of provincial government, oversee the treasury, and conduct diplomacy himself.

Petitions and information would flow up to him, and decisions—which he alone would make—were to be handed down on everything from the wording of foreign treaties to the purchase of cloth for military uniforms. Even the most senior advisers rarely had the royal ear: All requests, and all responses, were to be put in writing and channeled through the appropriate bureaucrats. Officials were to ensure that every document was concise—or face dismissal. And however senior their status or impressive their expertise, they were denied autonomy: "You have no right of initiative whatever," Frederick told one Provincial Chamber that had made a decision without consulting him. "All matters must be reported to me directly."

He began work in the early morning, kept up a relentless pace through the day, and demanded that his staff do so too. Couriers arrived at regular intervals, and five secretaries sorted the contents of their pouches into the appropriate portfolios. Even when the king made one of his periodic—and strenuous—inspection tours of the realm, the royal cabinet office packed up its pens and sealing wax and went along.

Acting as the king's eyes and ears, the cabinet secretaries wielded considerable, if covert, power. By the manner in which they wrote a précis or rearranged the contents of a file, they could manipulate royal decisions, influence expenditure, make or break a political career. But, although Frederick relied on his bureaucracy, he did not necessarily trust it. "The more civil servants, the more thieves," he opined, and ventured a guess that 99 out of 100 public officials were corrupt. As his father had done, he set his bureaucrats to spy upon one another, maintained secret communications with his senior officials' underlings, assigned several different minions to work—unbeknownst to one another—upon the same tasks, and used the knowledge thus gleaned to keep the whole elaborate hierarchy under his firm control.

The highest echelons of the civil service, like the upper ranks of the army, were staffed largely by the Junkers. Frederick was well aware that his control depended on their cooperation. Even after a century of increasingly centralized rule by the Great Elector and the Prussian kings, they enjoyed largely untrammeled power in their rural domains. The Junker lands were tilled mainly by serfs with no rights, privileges, or property. Although Frederick passed laws barring masters from punishing peasants with cruelty, he never persuaded the Junkers to free these laborers from their bonds.

And just as the peasants were unable to rise above their lowly station, so too were other classes denied any measure of social mobility. Frederick's system of government required each segment of Prussian society to perform its own clearly defined role. At the top, the Junkers were expected to give military and administrative service, in return for which the king maintained their near-monopoly of top army and civilian posts and also allowed them to maintain their own law courts, which buttressed their authority in the rural areas. The middle class, meanwhile, was expected to develop commerce and do the day-to-day bureaucratic work of running the country. Unlike monarchs elsewhere, Frederick rarely ennobled these commoners as a reward for meritorious service, and he even tried to keep aristocrats from selling their estates to wealthy burghers. Marriages between the classes were similarly frowned on.

No aspect of life in his kingdom was too insignificant to attract the attention of a ruler who described himself as the "first servant" of his state. But a pace and volume of work that would have exhausted other mortals seemed only to infuse Frederick with energy. In the hours when he was not perusing official documents or touring the far reaches of his realm, he devoted himself to intellectual pursuits. He designed his palace of Sans Souci as the ideal residence for a philosopher-king, with a well-equipped library, and retreated there to produce a stream of works on history and statecraft. Foreign scientists, scholars, and men of letters—including Voltaire—were entertained at dinners spiced with elevated and often malicious conversation.

Meanwhile, outside Prussia's borders, the cauldron of politics was coming to a boil. Frederick's old antagonist, Maria Theresa of Austria, was gaining strength, and in Wenzel von Kaunitz, she had a chancellor who was openly determined to regain Silesia from the Prussians. At the same time, in the northeast, Russia was emerging as an ever-more-threatening rival. Conscious of these dangers, Frederick signed a new agreement with Britain, in 1756, upon which the French, on the principle that any ally of their enemy across the Channel was France's enemy as well, overcame their antipathy to the ruling Austrian house of Hapsburg and negotiated an alliance with Maria Theresa. The Saxons, who had taken Austria's part during the latest hostilities with Prussia, hesitated to abandon their neutrality until August, when Frederick marched his army over the border and seized their capital at Dresden.

Frederick claimed his action was purely defensive: The Saxon frontier was only thirty miles south of Berlin. The rest of Europe saw it as the start of further Prussian expansion. To the east, Elizabeth, empress of Russia, buried her mistrust of France and joined the anti-Prussian alliance. Frederick's enemies had their individual reasons for entering the fray. Austria hoped to regain Silesia, lost to Prussia eleven years before; Russia saw a chance to expand westward and to annex East Prussia; France perceived the war mainly as a continental extension of a more important conflict, its struggle with Britain, which was raging even in the colonial territories of North America and India. Within months, Maria Theresa's envoys would persuade Sweden and some southern and western German principalities to join the cause. Whatever their private motives, and however tenuous their common purpose, the continental powers were united against Prussia. Frederick's war became a fight for survival.

The prolonged hostilities, which came to be known as the Seven Years' War, would be a hard test of Frederick's generalship. He had made a careful study of ancient and modern writers on military science, and had evolved a number of strategic and tactical theories of his own. After his baptism of fire in the Austrian conflict at the beginning of his reign, not even the most carping critics could dismiss him as an armchair warrior. The army that he had so zealously improved and expanded during a decade of peace was now devoted to him. One of his officers compared him with a Scottish chieftain, as much a father as a commander to his warriors. Others remarked on the magnetism he exerted when he addressed the troops, his blue eyes blazing with passion, his voice stirring them to ever-greater heroics on his behalf.

He was acutely aware of his own symbolic importance to the soldiery, and he liked to appear before them in the same unchanging garb: a simple, increasingly shabby army greatcoat in the color the world now knew as Prussian blue, creased riding boots, and an equally wrinkled pair of breeches, saddle-worn and black with age. He lived in a tent at the center of the army's encampment and rose before dawn to inspect the troops before turning to piles of state and military paperwork.

The theater of war would encompass many different, and often difficult, terrains. Central European roads were frequently uneven, deeply rutted, and punctuated with oceans of mud. It was often impossible to tell where the roads gave way to open field—and when they did, these often hid swamps and bogs that could force entire

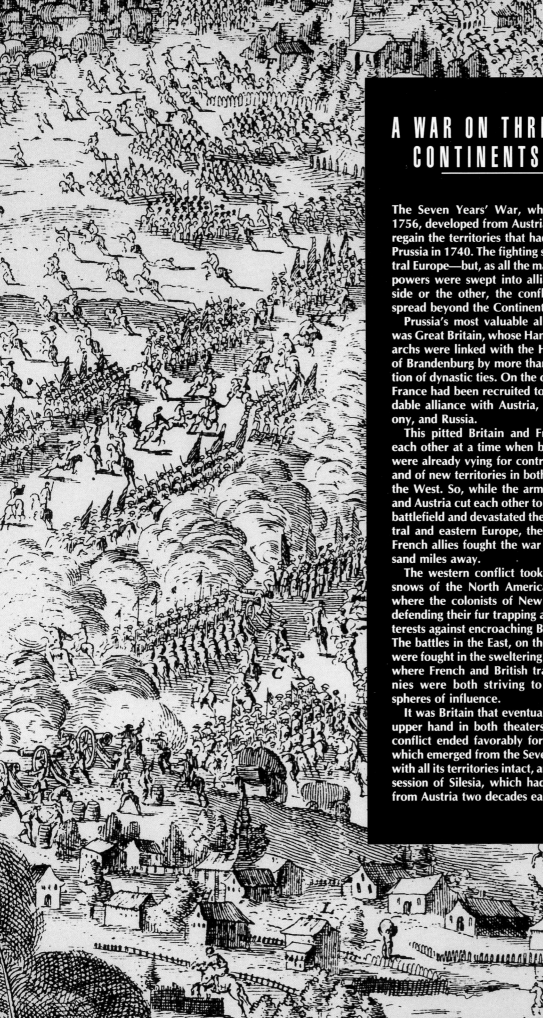

A WAR ON THREE CONTINENTS

The Seven Years' War, which began in 1756, developed from Austria's attempt to regain the territories that had been lost to Prussia in 1740. The fighting started in central Europe—but, as all the major European powers were swept into alliances on one side or the other, the conflict inevitably spread beyond the Continent.

Prussia's most valuable ally in the war was Great Britain, whose Hanoverian monarchs were linked with the Hohenzollerns of Brandenburg by more than one generation of dynastic ties. On the opposing side, France had been recruited to join a formidable alliance with Austria, Sweden, Saxony, and Russia.

This pitted Britain and France against each other at a time when both countries were already vying for control of the seas and of new territories in both the East and the West. So, while the armies of Prussia and Austria cut each other to pieces on the battlefield and devastated the lands of central and eastern Europe, their British and French allies fought the war several thousand miles away.

The western conflict took place in the snows of the North American continent, where the colonists of New France were defending their fur trapping and fishing interests against encroaching British settlers. The battles in the East, on the other hand, were fought in the sweltering heat of India, where French and British trading companies were both striving to widen their spheres of influence.

It was Britain that eventually gained the upper hand in both theaters of war. The conflict ended favorably for Prussia, too, which emerged from the Seven Years' War with all its territories intact, and still in possession of Silesia, which had been seized from Austria two decades earlier.

An allegorical engraving *(inset, left)* shows European kingdoms engrossed in billiards as they try to win the lands they covet on a table marked with a map of the continent. Amid the diplomatic and strategic complexities of the deadly game, Frederick the Great's tactical skills were displayed at their most brilliant in the Battle of Leuthen on December 5, 1757 *(background on these pages and on page 61)*—and played a critical part in Prussia's survival.

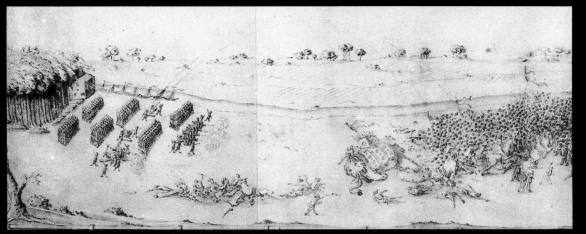

At the Battle of Plassey in June 1757, a small and disciplined British force *(left)* commanded by the gifted East India Company officer, Robert Clive, routs a milling horde of warriors incompetently led by the young nawab of Bengal. Clive profited by his victory to replace the nawab with a ruler sponsored by the British, thus counteracting the entrenched influence of the French in southern India.

An English engraving of 1797 shows British infantry, commanded by General James Wolfe, scaling the precipitous heights to the Plains of Abraham on September 13, 1759, and attacking the French garrison of Quebec under General Montcalm. The British capture of Quebec, capital of New France, justified their heavy commitment of men and money to the American campaigns. The French had invested fewer resources, trusting that victory in the European theater would save their North American colonies from defeat. But in 1763, the Treaty of Paris made France cede to Britain all her territories east of the Mississippi.

armies into time-consuming detours. The northern plains of Brandenburg, Saxony, and Silesia were traversed by two strategically important rivers—the Elbe and the Oder—but these were separated by tracts of heath and forest. In the fields, the wheat grew almost seven feet high, allowing whole regiments to slip through unseen. After the summer rains, the fields released clouds of vapor, giving even more cover.

Such difficulties, however, did not deter Frederick: The first year of the war saw him triumph over the Saxons, and in the spring of 1757, he felt able to invade Bohemia at four different points, winning his way to the gates of Prague before an Austrian onslaught drove him off. The autumn brought new setbacks. Russian and Swedish forces had invaded his Baltic territories, and the French had defeated his only allies, the German Protestant troops commanded by the English duke of Cumberland and paid by the British. Frederick did, however, acquire a brilliant cavalry commander, thirty-six-year-old General von Seydlitz, nicknamed the Horsed Hurricane, who helped him win a victory in just ninety minutes at Rossbach and who pursued the retreating Franco-German forces out of the territory.

Although Prussia was increasingly surrounded by hostile and numerically superior forces, Frederick took the offensive. He exhorted his troops to challenge the Austrian army—three times the size of his own—wherever they might find it, firing them with calls to valor, reinforced by well-chosen threats to Prussian military pride. He promised that if any cavalry regiment failed to attack when ordered, he would have it dismounted immediately after the battle and turned into a garrison regiment. "If any infantry battalion so much as begins to waver, it will lose its colors and its swords, and I shall have the braid cut from its uniform."

His soldiers loved it. In December 1757, they rewarded the warrior they called "Old Fritz" with a spectacular victory on the snow-covered battlefield at Leuthen, repelling wave after wave of enemy assaults, and demonstrating the success of Frederick's carefully crafted and unconventional tactics. Six thousand Prussians were killed, injured, or captured, but the Austrians suffered five times as many losses. The king, pleased, spent the night with his troops, sleeping on straw in a commandeered house in the village.

The next two years brought serious reverses. A clash with the Russians at Zorndorf, on the banks of the Oder River near Frederick's old prison at Küstrin, resulted in hideous carnage and no outright victory for either side. Frederick lost 12,000 troops at one blow, more than a third of his army. In August 1759, his army was again cut to pieces by the Russians, this time fifty miles downstream at Kunersdorf. Drained of men, money, and morale, Prussia feared for its survival. The king was forced to violate his aristocratic code by promoting bourgeois soldiers into the officer corps and drafting boys from the cadet academies to swell the ranks. Prisoners of war were impressed into the

Clad in her dead husband's coat and hat, the destitute widow of a Prussian soldier begs money for herself and her baby, in an engraving made in 1764. Sights such as this became commonplace after the Seven Years' War, in which 180,000 Prussian soldiers had died, many as a result of wounds that had been inadequately treated in Frederick's makeshift field hospitals. The state gave no support to the dependents of ordinary soldiers, and as officers were—in theory, at least—forbidden to marry, their wives could not claim a widow's pension. Even retired veterans who had survived the conflict could expect little more than an annual pittance.

In a 1780 engraving, Berliners stroll in the city's center; the tree-lined avenue named Unter den Linden stretches away in the background. The Opera House with its Corinthian portico on the left and the baroque palace of the king's brother Henry *(right)* were created by Frederick the Great and his architect Knobelsdorff, who from the 1740s onward sought to develop Berlin into a capital worthy of the rising Prussian state. Foreign visitors remarked upon the wide straight streets and clean modernity of the city, but the French writer Madame de Staël, visiting in 1813, regretted the absence of any "traces of ancient times" among the new buildings.

Prussian army, and agents were sent to scour central Europe for fresh cannon fodder.

Two important victories raised Prussian hopes in 1760. When Frederick was surrounded on three sides by 90,000 Austrians at Liegnitz, he deceived the enemy by leaving campfires blazing before deserted tents, stole away in midnight darkness, then pounced on the unwary enemy and smashed them in a battle of little more than two hours. At Torgau, on the edge of the Elbe, Frederick was hit by a cannonball in the chest and was saved only by the thick fur lining of his coat. He lost more soldiers than the Austrians but overcame near-impossible odds to win the day.

The wheel of fortune turned again, however, in the next year. The contenders fought a war of attrition, and although the army managed to survive, the battered economy nearly did not. Further miseries were heaped on Frederick when he lost the support of his British allies after a change of government at Westminster. In a letter to one of his few female friends, the king confessed: "I tell you, I lead a dog's life." "It has aged me so much," he said, "that you would scarcely recognize me. My hair is completely gray on the right side of my head. My teeth are breaking and falling out. My face is as deeply folded as the flounces of a lady's skirt, my back is bent like an archer's bow, and I go about as gloomy and downcast as a Trappist monk."

The new year of 1762 brought optimism. The Russian empress had died, and her successor, Peter III, admired Frederick the Great. Russia withdrew from the Austrian alliance to make a separate peace with Prussia in May; Sweden soon followed suit. Encouraged—and helped by forces from his new Russian allies—Frederick was soon on the offensive, driving the French army back across the Rhine.

The last theater of war was Silesia, where the Austrians and Prussians were evenly matched, with 80,000 troops on each side. But the surviving contenders' appetite for combat was by now more than sated, and in February 1763, Prussia, Austria, and Saxony agreed to peace, restoring the borders to the 1756 positions.

Prussia had come of age, and Frederick was acclaimed as the leader of a major European power, a formidable fighter who had secured his kingdom's survival against all the odds. But the realm had paid a price. Thousands of houses had been destroyed, uncountable numbers of horses and livestock had been lost, and many regions, especially east of the Elbe, had been devastated by war. As many as 500,000 out of a prewar population of about four million had been killed, captured, or forced to flee. The currency was weak, and prices for land, food, housing, and manufactured goods climbed ever higher. The situation was exacerbated by an international economic crisis, a widespread squeeze on credit emanating from Amsterdam bankers. In Berlin, finance houses and merchants went bankrupt; nobles and burghers alike faced ruin. But Frederick set to work repairing the shaken economy. Though physically drained by the war, he threw himself into a program of wide-ranging expansion and reform, picking up projects interrupted by the war and launching fresh initiatives.

The realm that had come into his hands in 1740 had been an underdeveloped and underpopulated country, blighted by poor soil, an unkind climate, inadequate communications, and a paucity of mineral resources. Conquest had brought him the booming region of Silesia, with its mines and factories, and given him control over the Oder River—one of Europe's busiest trade arteries. In all territories, he fostered commercial ventures, opened mines, and sponsored land reclamation. He gave

Sections of ivory flutes from Frederick's large collection are visible in their elegant box.

Written in Frederick's own hand, the music for "Solo for Flute" (above) typifies his compositions, which were unoriginal though often charming.

landowners financial compensatation for war damage and helped revive agricultural production. He built towns and invited foreign farmers and artisans to settle the less populous parts of his kingdom. Prussian officials were sent throughout Europe to offer prospective immigrants incentives: travel expenses, exemption from military service, land and livestock for farmers, commercial privileges for entrepreneurs. Miners, dairymen, silkweavers, metalworkers, and porcelain-makers were particularly encouraged by the king, but they were not always welcomed by the native population.

To place the state economy on a firmer footing, he set up a royal bank and a stock exchange in Berlin, government departments to oversee forestry and the mining industry, and an overseas trading company as well—although the latter was nearly strangled in infancy by the corruption of its principal officers. The king also interested himself in new manufacturing industries, and the Crown became a major shareholder in porcelain and cutlery factories. Prussia may have won its status as a great power on the field of battle, but Frederick was convinced that industrial and commercial expansion was the only way to maintain that position.

Frederick raised funds for these endeavors from several sources. The largest sums were raised by the "contribution" tax levied on the peasants, who made up 95 percent of the population. Other revenues came from farm rents on his extensive estates, timber sales from his forests, profits from the royal mint and the factories and saltworks wholly or partly owned by the Crown, land taxes, a levy on town dwellers, road and bridge tolls, and customs and excise duties on grain, leather, sugar, beer, firewood, and other necessities. These revenues paid for the king's civil administration, his royal court—a relatively spartan establishment by the standards of the day—and the maintenance of the Prussian army. The share of expenditure devoted

A WARRIOR'S MUSICAL SANCTUARY

Although Frederick the Great's love of music dated from his childhood, it was not until he was allowed his own household that he could escape his father's intemperate embargoes on artistic activity.

Frederick lived in a wide variety of residences during the course of his reign as king of Prussia. But it was in the voluptuous music room of the little Sans Souci palace near Potsdam, which had been built to his own design in 1747, that he at last created a haven where he could indulge his taste for music with his friends and the musicians he employed.

A flutist of considerable skill and sensitivity, Frederick was a prolific composer as well. Toward the end of his lifetime he would play night after night through his repertoire of 300 concertos, accompanied by his court musicians *(right)*. With the onset of extreme old age and the loss of his front teeth, he abandoned the flute and turned to the piano instead.

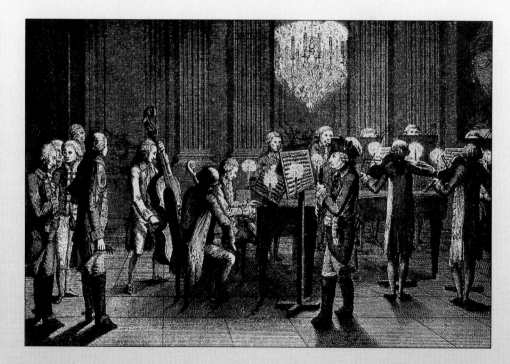

to the last of these declined dramatically in the latter half of the reign: Prussia remained an emphatically military state, but its formidable forces now accounted for only 50 percent of expenditure instead of the 75 percent it absorbed at the beginning of the reign. The other German states looked on with fascination: Prussia might be the least prosperous among them and the poorest in resources, but its king managed to keep its coffers overflowing and kept a stock of bullion hidden away in case of war.

The wealthiest Prussians now were those who had been in the right business at the right time, such as arms manufacturers and the makers of uniforms. Dealers in luxury goods also waxed fat, selling jewelry, fine furniture, and art objects as a hedge against inflation. Nobles complained that it was impossible to buy a suitable dwelling in Berlin; all the best houses had been snapped up by newly rich burghers with ideas above their station.

While Frederick was bullying his subjects into economic growth, he kept a constant weather eye on the power struggles taking place beyond his frontiers. The Russians were flexing their muscles. They had defeated the Turks in southeastern Europe and controlled the weak and crumbling state of Poland, which lay between Russia's borders and the heart of Frederick's realm. Frederick feared that his powerful Russian allies might eventually combine with Austria against him; Maria Theresa, in turn, worried about the growing Russian presence in the Balkans, now that the Turkish threat had been dispelled. Neither of the two monarchs wanted war.

Frederick offered a solution: that a large tract of Polish territory be divided among the three powers. At first, his fellow monarchs demurred. Russia spoke of the need for Poland to keep its territorial integrity; Austria wanted more land to compensate for the loss of Silesia but felt qualms about the arrogant carving-up of a neighboring kingdom. But, as Frederick argued, all Europe knew that Poland was on the point of tumbling into anarchy. In 1772, Poland was partitioned.

To Frederick fell the region known as West Prussia. Its acquisition gave him a vital strategic link between the heartland of his kingdom and the distant province of East Prussia. He took charge of his new possession with characteristic vigor, surveyed it himself, and pronounced it "a very good and advantageous acquisition."

Nevertheless, the king was uneasy. His distrust of Austria had been heightened by a brief war between 1778 and 1779 over the disputed inheritance of the Bavarian electorate. And when Russia, in her search for allies to fight the Turks, chose Austria over Prussia, the aging Frederick marshaled his energies for one last initiative. In

Painted near the end of his life, Frederick's bent figure and lined face betray the broken health and disillusionment that dogged him after the rigors of a lifetime's soldiering. Despite the gout and asthma that increasingly disabled him, he never abandoned the tasks he set himself. He died at seventy-four from a chill caught while reviewing troops in the rain. Future generations would remember him affectionately as portrayed here—the stooping, careworn father of the nation.

1785, he persuaded the rulers of fourteen German states to join forces in the League of Princes. Frederick, the most powerful among them, stood at its head.

His fellow monarchs had no doubt that he was a lion among them; his own people reserved the right to differ. The absolute dedication to the service of the state that he had sworn when first he took Prussia in his charge remained constant, but the development of that state—and the autocratic manner of its royal servant—did not endear him to all its inhabitants. The Junkers may have been loyal to him through his guardianship of their interests, but the members of the ambitious middle classes chafed at his carefully fostered caste system, and the peasantry—mostly serfs—had little to thank him for. He had held all but the most blue-blooded subjects in contempt and confided to a friend that he was "tired of ruling over slaves."

But the slaves, it seemed, were also tired of him. When he died, at the age of seventy-four, in August 1786, his people received the news in silence. The French observer Count Mirabeau described the scene in Berlin: "No face which did not show relief and hope, not one regret, not one sigh, no word of praise. This, then, was what became of so many battles won, so much fame, a reign of almost half a century so full of so many great deeds. All were longing for it to end; all congratulated themselves that it was over."

Frederick had been, as his old friend and correspondent Voltaire had perceived, a potent but unstable amalgam of the old ways and the new. He had been in love with the idea of modernity and progress, but in practice he had ruled his state autocratically. Building on the foundations of his Hohenzollern predecessors, he had brought his realm firmly out of the Middle Ages and on to the threshold of the modern world—yet not across it. His military conquests and economic policies would give Prussia a central place in the coming Industrial Revolution, but his dynastic obsessions and aristocratic elitism confined him to an era that was fading fast. He may have preferred French writers to those who shared his heritage, but he never sensed the direction in which their Enlightenment was inexorably moving: He did not perceive the winds of revolution blowing through France, nor would he see the outcome.

His personal domination of the state apparatus may have ensured the achievement of his desired ends, but it also sowed the seeds of that state's decline. Childless, he bequeathed the throne to his unremarkable nephew, Frederick William II, who was to reduce the state to near-bankruptcy with his expensive military adventures, while demonstrating none of Frederick's capacity for single-handed implementation of power. Unaccustomed to autonomy, the bureaucratic grandees would fall into confusion or fight among themselves for control of the machinery of government. The kingdom Frederick had so zealously built up would survive for almost another century, until the German states united, but the old order over which he had presided was passing away. Command of the civil service was to become no longer the sole preserve of the nobility. Professionalism and education would become more important qualifications for steering the state than high birth. A new, increasingly confident clique of administrators would take control, and instead of dancing to the monarch's tune, they themselves would set the agenda for the Crown.

Twenty years after the old king's death, it was an enfeebled Prussia that allowed Napoleon to lead a French army through the gates of Berlin. Even in his moment of triumph, the conqueror would confess that if the formidable old warrior Frederick had been alive on that day, France's victory would never have been possible.

THE PACIFIC ADVENTURE

3

On January 30, 1774, after defying tempestuous Antarctic seas, blizzards, and dense fog, a lone British exploration ship, the 500-ton *Resolution,* confronted an impenetrable and mountainous ice field that seemed to stretch into infinity. Reluctantly, the order was given to come about. At that precise moment, a sixteen-year-old midshipman, George Vancouver, clambered onto the end of the bowsprit, flourished his cap, and shouted, *"Ne plus ultra!"*—"None farther!" Ever after, it was to be his vainglorious claim that he had ventured farther south than any other man on earth. And so, technically, he had. But, as Vancouver and all his fellow crewmen acknowledged, the real honor belonged to their captain. On this day, Commander James Cook had sailed his ship to the southernmost ocean limits, down to a latitude of 71° 10' S. In so doing, he had all but solved the puzzle that had challenged scientists and scholars for more than a millennium: the mystery of *terra australis incognita,* the "unknown southern land."

The existence of this fabled realm—a continent supposedly girdling the bottom of the world—had first been proposed in the second century AD by the Alexandrian astronomer Ptolemy, who argued that antipodes—or "balancing feet"—must exist to provide a counterweight to the landmass of Eurasia. Over the centuries, hypothesis had hardened into dogma; and between the 1560s and 1770s, at a cost of many hundreds of lives, European navigators had persistently searched for the Southern Continent, which was popularly believed to be a paradise of lush forests and fertile valleys, with millions of inhabitants. Now, through Cook's endeavor, the search was at last drawing to an end.

Beyond the enormous ice field confronted by the *Resolution* there might be an extensive landmass, but it could not possibly be a paradise—only a region of icy desolation, forever cloaked in snow. And if any dreams of a southern continent lingered on, these were to be shattered just one year later when Cook continued his voyage east of Cape Horn and into the lower latitudes of the South Atlantic. There, he found only an icebound island, which he called South Georgia, and frozen coastlines, which he named South Thule and Sandwich Land. Not a single tree was to be seen in this savage territory; the only living things encountered were penguins in teeming tens of thousands.

Although Cook had demolished the last possibility of finding a habitable continent at the bottom of the world, the quest for *terra australis incognita* had been successful in another way. As the primary inspiration for all oceanic exploration in the eighteenth century, it was to lead to the eventual opening-up of the Pacific, a region that accounted for almost one-third of the entire earth's surface and an area greater than all the land in the world combined.

The first crossing of the ocean by a European—the daring Portuguese navigator

A Maori warrior, his face lavishly tattooed, stares rapt with curiosity out of this drawing by Sydney Parkinson, the artist who accompanied the celebrated English explorer James Cook on his earliest travels in the South Seas. As white adventurers reached the Pacific in force during the late eighteenth century, pursuing knowledge, wealth, and territory, encounters between Europeans and the native peoples became increasingly frequent and often proved puzzling to both sides.

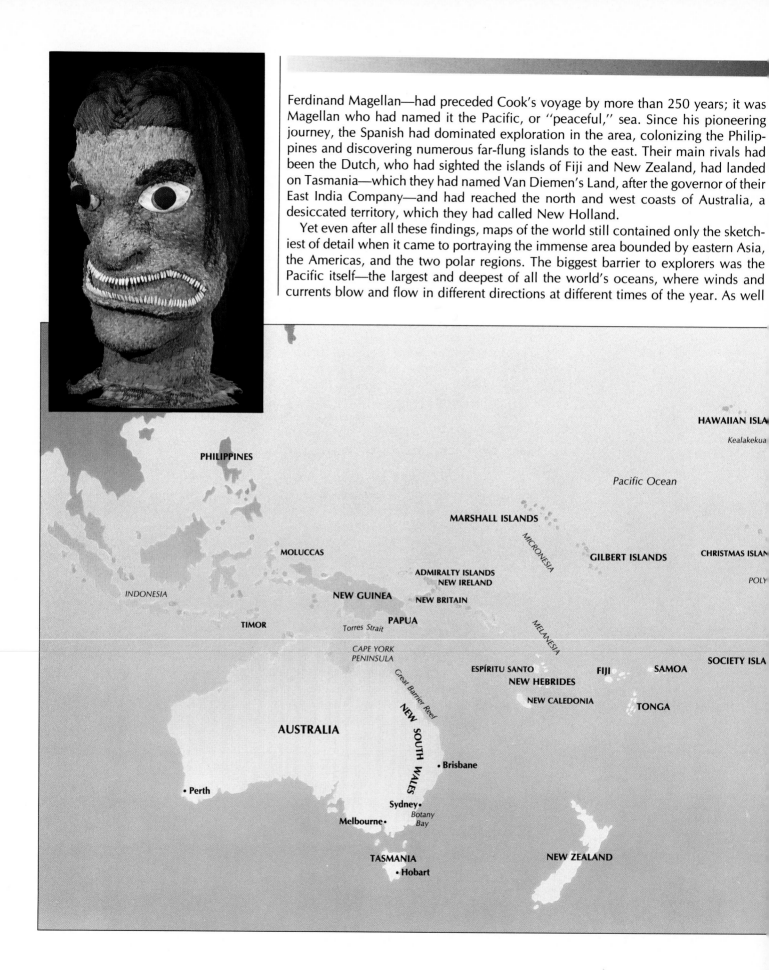

Ferdinand Magellan—had preceded Cook's voyage by more than 250 years; it was Magellan who had named it the Pacific, or "peaceful," sea. Since his pioneering journey, the Spanish had dominated exploration in the area, colonizing the Philippines and discovering numerous far-flung islands to the east. Their main rivals had been the Dutch, who had sighted the islands of Fiji and New Zealand, had landed on Tasmania—which they had named Van Diemen's Land, after the governor of their East India Company—and had reached the north and west coasts of Australia, a desiccated territory, which they had called New Holland.

Yet even after all these findings, maps of the world still contained only the sketchiest of detail when it came to portraying the immense area bounded by eastern Asia, the Americas, and the two polar regions. The biggest barrier to explorers was the Pacific itself—the largest and deepest of all the world's oceans, where winds and currents blow and flow in different directions at different times of the year. As well

HAWAIIAN ISLA

Kealakekua

Pacific Ocean

PHILIPPINES

MARSHALL ISLANDS

MICRONESIA

GILBERT ISLANDS

CHRISTMAS ISLAN

MOLUCCAS

ADMIRALTY ISLANDS
NEW IRELAND

POLY

INDONESIA

NEW GUINEA

NEW BRITAIN

TIMOR

PAPUA

Torres Strait

MELANESIA

CAPE YORK
PENINSULA

ESPÍRITU SANTO

FIJI

SAMOA

SOCIETY ISLA

NEW HEBRIDES

Great Barrier Reef

NEW CALEDONIA

TONGA

AUSTRALIA

NEW SOUTH WALES

• Brisbane

• Perth

Sydney•

Botany
Bay

Melbourne•

TASMANIA

NEW ZEALAND

• Hobart

CALIFORNIA

San Diego•

MARQUESAS ISLANDS

MOTU ISLANDS

EASTER ISLAND

as the hazards of storms and shipwreck, the Pacific also presented the eighteenth-century mariner with unparalleled problems of distance. Here, as Magellan and his successors discovered, one might sail for two months without ever sighting land. In the face of such prolonged periods at sea, crews could suffer between 40 and 75 percent losses from scurvy, the disease caused by lack of vitamin C found in fresh fruit and vegetables.

Furthermore, European navigators were handicapped until the 1770s by want of a device for determining longitude at sea—the measurement of how far east or west they had voyaged. Because of this lack, some islands had been inaccurately charted in the sixteenth century, which meant that after nearly two centuries of exploration, the map of the Pacific was still like some nightmarish jigsaw puzzle in which pieces were continually being misplaced or lost altogether.

Largely through the efforts of a handful of British and French explorers, the eighteenth century would see most of the major missing pieces finally located. Although they faced the same hazards as before, their voyages were made easier by improvements in navigation—notably the chronometer, a new device for determining longitude. Western governments, moreover, were increasingly willing to finance expeditions that might help them harness the huge strategic and commercial potential of the South Seas. By the end of the century, European traders, whalers, and missionaries had reached every corner of the Pacific in the wake of the explorers, and Australia had become the home of about 5,000 men and women of British stock.

The very first migrants to the South Pacific had not even encountered the sea. These were the Aborigines of Australia, a race of uncertain Asian origin, who had arrived on foot during the Pleistocene epoch 40,000 years ago, at a time when the level of the Pacific had been so greatly lowered by an ice age that a fragile land bridge had come into being, stretching from New Guinea to the empty southern continent of Australia. Thousands of years later, the massive ice cap of the last great glaciation had thawed; when the waters rose, Australia had been isolated from Asia, and, in the southeast, Tasmania had been cut off from the main landmass.

The climatic changes of this time had left much of the Australian continent stricken with perpetual drought. As a result, the stranded Aborigines had to maintain a seminomadic lifestyle, ranging over enormous tracts of territory in search of food. During eons of prehistoric isolation, while the wildlife of this land evolved in its own unique direction, the Aborigines developed a civilization that resembled no other in the Pacific region.

By the eighteenth century, there were perhaps 750,000 Aborigines on mainland Australia and about 5,000 more in Tasmania. Ostensibly, they were among the most backward people in the world. The Aborigines had no conception of agriculture. Their temporary homes were no more than branches crudely heaped into cones; their tools were limited to sharp stones, wooden mallets, and curved wooden dishes with which they carried water and dug for termites and other food. Except in the cooler south, they went completely naked. The men had bushy beards, which they occasionally shortened by singeing. Some wore a six-inch bone drilled through the nose, and the great majority practiced scarification on their arms and thighs. Polygamy was not unusual; and, in fact, some men had as many as thirty wives. Women were treated strictly as chattels.

Culturally, though, the lives of the Aborigines were rich and complex. Each tribe had its own mythology and its own distinctive styles of art, including carved totems, body decoration, and paintings on either bark or stone. While they lacked a written language, they preserved a wealth of folklore, not only in stories handed down from one generation to another but also in songs, some of which contained hundreds of verses and built up intricate word pictures through the use of vivid imagery.

Above all, they had developed exquisite skills in the art of hunting. They could reproduce perfectly an enormous range of bird and animal calls, read the faintest sign of movement in undergrowth or dust, or pick up a trail by their acute sense of smell. A fisherman would stand poised with his spear beside a water hole for hours at a time; a stalker could freeze in midstep and stand motionless on one leg for half an hour, waiting for his prey to venture within striking range. They had invented a number of ingenious weapons, including the woomera, or spear-thrower, which enabled them to propel a spear more than 325 feet; and various kinds of throwing sticks and boomerangs, which were effective up to a distance of 165 feet. Less subtly, they also burned bushland to drive out kangaroos and anteaters, and set fire to hollow trees in order to smoke out possums and lizards.

In many ways, the Aborigines had achieved a oneness with nature, adapting to the forbidding environment as completely as the creatures upon which they preyed. This oneness far transcended their day-to-day physical needs. They were also bonded spiritually to the land through their belief in the Dreamtime, a period when supernatural beings moved over the earth and gave it form and life. The Aborigines regarded themselves as descendants of these mythical creators, and they lived in a state of permanent communication with the world about them, a world in which

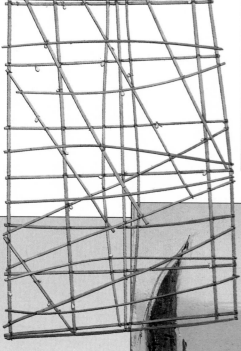

A Micronesian chart *(below),* marks the position of the Marshall Islands with shells and indicates the wave patterns of the surrounding seas with shaped wooden rods.

In a scene captured by William Hodges, the artist on Cook's second voyage, canoes ply the Tahitian waters. The small, single-hulled outrigger *(near right)* was for short offshore trips; the larger double-hulled canoe *(far right)* was for carrying cargo between the islands.

every feature of the landscape—each tree, each rock, each water hole—contained the spirit of their ancestors.

Thousands of years after the Aborigines had come to terms with their vast, barren territory, other migrants followed them out of Asia. But the later voyagers were seafarers, and the homes in which they settled were the small, lush islands that dotted the Pacific. The colonists, who would be known as Polynesians, had neither compass for fixing directions nor astrolabe for ascertaining latitude. They were illiterate and knew nothing of metals or even of the wheel. Yet they possessed such extraordinary nautical skills—based on an extensive knowledge of ocean currents, of the year-round positions of stars, of prevailing winds, and of the habits of migratory birds—that they were eventually able to cross 9.3 million square miles of uncharted waters. Starting from the islands of southeast Asia, the Polynesians had begun moving in an easterly direction sometime around 2500 BC. By the eighth century AD, they were the most widely dispersed people on earth, having colonized virtually every habitable speck of land within a roughly equilateral triangle bounded by the Hawaiian Islands in the north, by New Zealand almost 5,000 miles to the southwest, and by remote Easter Island in the southeast.

The Polynesians—a Caucasian people, with sturdy physiques, light brown skin, and straight or wavy hair—were by no means the only seafarers to have begun spreading eastward from southeast Asia a few thousand years ago. Two other distinct races had started to occupy Pacific islands during the same epoch. A predominantly Mongoloid people, slightly built, with yellow-brown skin and straight black hair, inhabited

The Earliest Explorers

For centuries before the first Europeans came, the people of the Pacific had been traveling vast distances across the ocean, finding and settling new islands. Using the most rudimentary of stone tools, the natives of the South Seas fashioned tree trunks into strong, lightweight canoes in a range of sophisticated designs. Sections of wood were literally sewed together to build craft that could hold scores of passengers; horizontal beams and double hulls enhanced stability. Whether fleeing from enemies or seeking more living space and land, whole villages would put to sea in these vessels. Taking all their goods and livestock, they would journey thousands of miles to settle new islands, which had been discovered by small advance parties.

SHIPS FOR UNCHARTED SEAS

Such arduous expeditions as Cook's required special ships. It surprised many observers that, with all the vessels at their disposal, Cook and the Admiralty decided to use converted colliers. Yet these stalwarts of Britain's coal trade, in which Cook had first learned his seamanship, proved ideal for the task. Robust, broad, and relatively flat-bottomed, boats such as Cook's first ship, the *Endeavour,* and his second, the *Resolution,* could carry large amounts of supplies and equipment in their holds, stay upright in rough seas, and navigate safely both in shallow creeks and estuaries and across treacherous coral reefs.

During her life as the *Earl of Pembroke,* Cook's first ship (top), the *Endeavour,* leaves her home port of Whitby, in Yorkshire. A sketch (center) of his second ship, the *Resolution,* shows the broad, flattened hull that made the boat so stable and so easy to steer in shallow waters. A plan (right) shows the extra deck for the *Resolution,* demanded by naturalist Joseph Banks for his party. The changes were not practical, and Banks pulled out of the expedition.

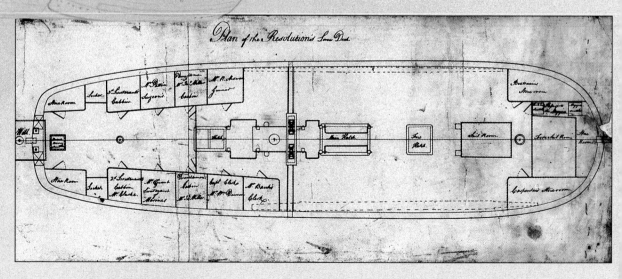

Micronesia—"small islands"—a region due east of the Philippines and Moluccas, made up largely of atolls. Another group, of Papuan origin, mostly thickset, dark-skinned, and curly-haired, fanned out from New Guinea into the neighboring region of Melanesia—"black islands"—composed mainly of large and medium-size volcanic islands in archipelagos lying northeast of Australia.

But of all the pioneer explorers of the Pacific, the Polynesians were by far the most prolific. By the eighteenth century, their mid-Pacific triangle, named Polynesia—"many islands"—by French intellectual Charles de Brosses, was populated by several million people. The largest settlements were at its apex, on eight Hawaiian islands, which had an estimated 300,000 inhabitants. On the eastern side of the triangle, in an archipelago of spectacular beauty, about 80,000 lived on the Marquesas Islands; and, on the western side, about the same number of people occupied the hundred-odd islands of Tonga and Samoa. The most concentrated population, however, was at the tropical center of the triangle: on the fertile Society Islands. One of these, Tahiti, furnished its 40,000 inhabitants with a self-regenerating supply of natural riches.

By this time, the great age of Polynesian exploration had long since passed. These peoples were no longer sea-farers, but fishermen-horticulturalists who had withdrawn into myriad self-contained communities. Most were strong and healthy; as far as is known, they had never experienced a plague like the Black Death, which had decimated Europe, or any major endemic disease. They were also relatively free from stress; food and possessions were distributed more or less equally, and their lives were undisturbed by any abstract ideas or religious teachings that might promote self-doubt or guilt. But placation of malevolent deities was a constant requirement, involving elaborate and often violent rituals. Tribal wars—fought with clubs, spears, and slings—were frequent; and on some islands, there had emerged a powerful priesthood, which practiced infanticide and human sacrifice.

Although their tribal groups had different mythologies, all Polynesians believed in a supreme being—a creator of life—and in numerous lesser gods, most of them hostile. They also believed in an afterlife and revered their ancestors. Some built temples, usually no more than stone platforms raised in clearings. But religious wars were unknown, and the people had no concept of hell to strike fear into them.

They were also without any formal legal code, being limited in their actions simply by centuries-old taboos. Major violations of these traditional prohibitions were met with death, but by and large, communities were so closely knit that disgrace and shame—shared by the entire family of a miscreant—were sufficient deterrents to antisocial behavior.

On the more fertile Pacific islands, life was mostly placid and pleasurable, except

Designed by Yorkshire clockmaker John Harrison, the chronometer taken by Cook on his second Pacific voyage allowed truly accurate timekeeping—and, thus, navigation. By comparing the time of day at his location with the time of day in Greenwich, England, Cook could work out his point of longitude. Since the earth rotates 360 degrees during every twenty-four-hour period, each hour's time difference represented a 15-degree difference in longitude. Earlier timepieces had been affected by extremes of temperature, but Harrison's chronometer was able to keep time with impressive exactness under all weather conditions.

Joseph Banks, the British naturalist who accompanied Cook on his first voyage, stands among souvenirs of the trip—including a Maori cloak, an elaborate feather headdress, and, at his feet, a Polynesian adz. A wealthy amateur, Banks saw himself as the ultimate gentlemanly tourist, saying contemptuously of the grand tour of Europe: "Every blockhead does that; my grand tour shall be one round the whole globe." His insistence on traveling in style and comfort, accompanied by a retinue of servants, could make him a difficult companion, but despite his eccentricities, Banks showed himself to be a serious scientist of considerable ability. He later served for many years as the president of London's distinguished scientific body, the Royal Society.

for tribal conflicts, which were invariably marked by acts of great cruelty and ferocity. On Tahiti, for example, food was plentiful and the climate so balmy that everyone could enjoy an outdoor existence all the year around. The inhabitants lived from day to day, responding to their natural needs and desires—passing the time eating, sleeping, fishing, bathing, surfing, dancing and singing to the music of flutes and drums, and, not least, making love without inhibition.

But not all the Pacific islanders were blessed with a perfect climate and such easy living. On the outer fringes of Polynesia, less temperate climes saw the emergence of stockier, more vigorous breeds: Most notable were the Maoris, who, as skilled farmers, had thrived and multiplied on Aoteoroa—"the land of the long white cloud"—now known in the West as New Zealand. The Maoris had been late settlers there; probably they had not arrived in great numbers until the thirteenth or fourteenth century. By the eighteenth century, their population had reached 200,000 and was divided into numerous rival tribes, concentrated mainly on the warmer and more northern of two large, rugged islands.

No other people in the Pacific more jealously guarded their tribal territories. Permanently geared for war, the Maoris fortified their hilltop villages with walls and trenches and trained all their young men in the use of spears, clubs, and throwing sticks. In action, their ferocity was greatly accentuated by loud war chants and by the curvilinear tattoos that lavishly colored their faces and torsos. Sometimes the combatants made slaves of prisoners of war; sometimes they practiced ritual cannibalism.

The European encroachment upon the self-contained worlds of the Pacific islanders was spurred by a travel book. Its author was William Dampier, the buccaneering son of a Somerset farmer, who had become, in 1688, the first Englishman to set foot on Australian soil. In 1697, after his return to England, he made his name by writing *A New Voyage round the World,* a brilliantly entertaining account of his experiences. He told of how he had eaten flamingos' tongues in the Cape Verde Islands, of how he had escaped from a desert island in the Indian Ocean, and how he and his fellow pirates had plundered from Mexico to the Philippines. Such revelations greatly stimulated British interest in the South Seas. One conse-

A portrait of Philibert Commerson, who accompanied Louis Antoine de Bougainville on his expeditions in the South Seas, hints at the great French naturalist's intensity and determination. An inveterate collector, Commerson brought back to Europe some 5,000 species of plants, most of them never before recorded. Despite this frenetic botanical research, Commerson still found time to observe the peoples that the expedition encountered and to marvel at their sexual freedom. Such license was not permissible for Europeans, however; when it was discovered that Commerson's devoted "manservant" Jean Baret was in fact his mistress, Jeanne Baret, the two were made to occupy separate cabins for the rest of the voyage.

quence of the new curiosity was a demand for exotic travel books, which was met by more and more fanciful accounts of the Pacific. In 1719, Daniel Defoe's *Robinson Crusoe* appeared, based on the true story of Alexander Selkirk, a Scottish sailor who had been marooned off the coast of Chile and rescued by Dampier's ship four years later. In 1726, Jonathan Swift's best-selling satire *Gulliver's Travels* took its hero on a voyage throughout the Pacific: to Lilliput, a mythical land of little people, said to lie northwest of Tasmania, and to Brobdingnag, an imaginary realm of giants, somewhere in the vicinity of Japan.

In the meantime, the quest for a prosperous, teeming *terra australis incognita* intensified. It came to be monopolized by Britain and France as they entered into imperial competition around the globe. The governments of both countries were being urged by merchants and entrepreneurs to find and exploit this elusive land. Now, more and more frequently, appeals were heard from scientists, naturalists, and humanists eager to gain greater knowledge of the Pacific world. A new spirit of scientific inquiry had begun to take hold—a spirit evinced by the proliferation of natural history societies in western Europe, by the monumental works of the Swedish botanist Carolus Linnaeus, and by research being promoted in Paris by the French Academy of Sciences and in London by the Royal Society, which, during the first quarter of the century, had gained new vigor under the presidency of the celebrated physicist Sir Isaac Newton.

The most forceful advocate of Pacific exploration was Charles de Brosses, who, in 1756, published his *History of Navigation to the Southern Lands*. He outlined the advantages of building up a comprehensive inventory of the earth's animal and vegetable life, and argued that in the process it might be possible to advance newly discovered peoples by giving them the benefit of European knowledge.

Most significant, Brosses aroused political opinion by stressing the strategic importance of the South Pacific. France, he proposed, could take the initiative by establishing a South Atlantic base in the Falkland Islands, which, being located just off Cape Horn, would enable his country to control access to the South Seas. Another base might then be planted in the western Pacific and used as a springboard for securing the great Southern Continent.

By the time his book appeared, the Seven Years' War had erupted, precluding immediate action on his proposals. But once the war had ended in 1763, both Britain and France renewed their interest in the South Pacific. For the vanquished French, the acquisition of a huge new colony in the Southern Hemisphere would compensate for the territorial losses they had sustained on the North American continent. For the British, it was no less critical to take command in the region and so to maintain their supremacy over the high seas.

It was remarkable, however, that a private individual made the first move toward implementing Brosses's plan. Louis Antoine de Bougainville, a thirty-four-year-old Parisian aristocrat, was determined to help his humiliated nation regain its self-respect and prestige. He had no naval command experience and no financial support from the bankrupt French government. Nevertheless, with money raised from wealthy relatives, he purchased and outfitted two small ships and, on September 15, 1763, set out to colonize the uninhabited Falkland Islands.

Ordinarily, such an amateur enterprise would have been doomed from the start. But Bougainville was no ordinary adventurer. Cultivated, sagacious, and fearless, he was commanding a naval expedition in the sure belief that he had learned enough

The meticulous paintings of the young British artist Sydney Parkinson bring to life the exotic flora of the Pacific. Employed by Joseph Banks to accompany him on Cook's first expedition and to record his finds, Parkinson was never to see England again, dying on the voyage home. While in the Pacific, however, he had prepared over 1,300 paintings and sketches of the region's plants, including *Hibiscus rosa-sinensis (right),* whose vibrant red blooms often adorned Polynesian girls; Australia's *Melaleuca quinquenervia (far right, top),* known as the paperbark because of the wafery bark with which Aborigines stuffed their children's pillows; and *Myrmecodia beccarii,* a plant whose bulb is home to ant colonies and butterfly larvae.

about seamanship from books and from his observations while on active duty during the war. His self-confidence proved justified. In February 1764, he took possession of the Falkland Islands, leaving behind, in the charge of his cousin, a small colony of Acadians—French Canadians who had been expelled from Nova Scotia by the

British. He did not envy them their new home, describing the islands as having "a vast silence and a sad and melancholy uniformity."

A British expedition the following year made a reconnaissance of the Falklands but did not notice the Acadians' small fort. A more successful voyage in 1767 added Pitcairn Island and the Admiralty Islands to Britain's growing list of newly discovered Pacific territories. The most fruitful British expedition of this time was led by Captain Samuel Wallis, who, on June 18, 1767, came to a Polynesian island of such mountainous grandeur and such an abundance of fruit and flowers and fresh water that he gave it the most honored of all royal names: King George III. Later explorers would know it as Tahiti, largest of the group that is now called the Society Islands.

Initially, the Tahitians proved hostile. They came out in hundreds of canoes to pelt the *Dolphin* with stones; in these early skirmishes, one native was killed and another wounded. But peace was soon established, after which the Englishmen found themselves being treated with extraordinary friendship, especially by the young women of the island, who were willing to accept iron nails as payment for their favors. Indeed, this particular exchange became so popular that Wallis was compelled to limit shore leave to deter his men from stripping every nail and spike from the *Dolphin's* timbers. Even then, his order was defied by some men, who judged the delights of Tahitian maidens well worth the risk of a flogging.

After a month in these seemingly idyllic surroundings, Wallis set sail for home, reaching Plymouth on May 18, 1768. The Admiralty was impressed by his achievement in sailing for twenty-one months without losing a single man. Less enthusiasm, however, greeted his glowing account of an island paradise. They noted its possible usefulness as a base for future expeditions. But its discovery had taken them no nearer their ultimate target: the great landmass of *terra australis incognita*.

Meanwhile, as the British evaluated Wallis's discoveries, the French were already in the Pacific, systematically exploring with two ships: a twenty-six-gun, 615-ton frigate, *La Boudeuse,* and a 535-ton storeship, *L'Étoile*. This expedition, prepared with the assistance of Brosses and members of the Academy of Sciences, was more scientifically oriented than any previous voyages. Besides approximately 300 crewmen, its personnel included a number of expert researchers, the most notable of whom were the distinguished naturalist Philibert Commerson, intent on observing flora and fauna, and the astronomer Pierre Antoine Véron, on board to study new ways of determining longitude.

Once again, Bougainville was responsible for France's taking the initiative. In 1766, he had been ordered to sail to the Falklands and formally hand over the islands to Spain. Both Britain and Spain had objected to his French settlement, protesting their prior claims; and, out of political expediency, the French had chosen to yield in deference to their Spanish allies. Bougainville had reluctantly agreed to the assignment, but only after shrewdly proposing that he should turn loss into gain—by sailing on from the Falklands to acquire colonial outposts in the Pacific and to probe for the Southern Continent.

Bougainville surrendered the Falklands on April 1, 1767. After stopping at Rio de Janeiro for fresh provisions, his ships entered the Pacific via Magellan's narrow and tortuous channels and finally, on April 4, 1768, made their first landfall. Ten months after Wallis, they had arrived at Tahiti.

Whereas the British had been merely enthusiastic, the French were positively rhapsodic about the enchantments of Tahiti and of its people, who came out to meet them in fruit-laden canoes. Even Bougainville, so often scathing in his descriptions of newly visited lands, was lavish in his praise. He compared the island to the Garden of Eden and noted that it had "surely the most fertile soil in the universe." Commerson was no less extravagant in his praise. Everything he saw confirmed his belief in the theories of the French philosopher Jean-Jacques Rousseau, who, twenty years earlier, had propounded the idea that people in their primitive state were basically good and that only organized society corrupted them. In Tahiti, Commerson later wrote, he had discovered "man in his natural state, born essentially good and free from all prejudice, unsuspiciously and unremorsefully following the gentle impulses of an instinct that remained sure because it had not degenerated into reason."

The Frenchmen found the natives hospitable beyond belief. All their appetites were fully met; the young women did not even demand nails for their favors. To be sure, the explorers were the victims of continual pilfering—a major problem throughout their brief visit. But, as Bougainville observed, theft was almost unknown among the islanders themselves. It was just that "curiosity for new objects excites cupidity in them."

During a stay of only thirteen days, the French remained largely unaware of the darker aspects of Tahitian culture. Their overall impression was that of a paradise of natural, sensual humanity, where people lived in a state of blissful innocence. And so the European legend of Tahiti was born. Utopia had been found.

From Tahiti, Bougainville continued the

Sydney Parkinson's hasty sketch of a leaping kangaroo shows his attempts to depict the animal's hopping legs and reflects the bemusement European observers felt on seeing the Australian marsupial and its peculiar—but astonishingly swift—means of propulsion. "To compare it to any European animal would be impossible," wrote a baffled Joseph Banks, "as it has not the least resemblance of any one I have seen." The kangaroo was one of the few animals encountered by Cook's expedition to be recorded by the naturalists, who were primarily botanists and, thus, far too busy identifying and cataloging the hundreds of new plant species they were finding.

search for the Southern Continent, sailing west to Samoa, to Espíritu Santo, and, unknowingly, to the fringes of the Great Barrier Reef on the uncharted east coast of Australia. His ships often confronted severe storms, and in the New Hebrides, they came under attack from hostile islanders. Provisions were so low that the crew ate a pet dog and a rat. Scurvy became rife, and soon they had to contend with an additional malady—venereal disease, picked up from islanders who had been infected by other Europeans. In later years, both the British and the French would blame one another for having introduced syphilis to Tahiti.

It was remarkable that Bougainville's ships lost only seven men on a voyage of two years and four months. In March 1769, he returned home to national acclaim. After a series of military defeats, the French at last had a triumph to celebrate: They had surpassed the British in exploring the South Pacific. Véron, making lunar observations by a new, more complex technique, had pinpointed islands with greater accuracy than had been achieved before. Commerson had brought back some 5,000 species of plants, two-thirds of them new to Europe. Moreover, besides numerous artifacts, Bougainville had returned with a real live Tahitian: Aotourou, brother of a chieftain, was idolized by Parisian society, but he became homesick after eleven months and died of smallpox on the return voyage.

In April of 1769, only one month after Bougainville's triumphal homecoming, a 410-ton British discovery vessel dropped anchor in Tahiti's palm-fringed Matavai Bay. The ship was an awkward-looking craft, a former North Sea collier, only 105 feet long, with a top speed of a mere eight knots. But it was supremely well equipped for Pacific exploration and commanded by a resolute Yorkshireman: Lieutenant James Cook, who was making the first of three epic voyages that would be infinitely more productive, in terms of discoveries and contributions to science, than all previous expeditions combined.

France's lead in the Pacific was about to end almost as soon as it had begun. On this voyage of discovery, Cook would sight, survey, and exactly locate hundreds of landfalls hitherto unknown to Europeans. He would chart the 2,350 miles of the coastline of New Zealand, make the first exploration of Australia's more inviting eastern shores, and, by sailing home through the Torres Strait, confirm once and for all that Australia was a separate island from New Guinea. Cook's subsequent voyages would complete the broad picture of the Pacific, enabling cartographers to make the first near-comprehensive maps of the region, and would establish finally his reputation as the greatest navigator of the century and the most efficient South Seas explorer of his time.

Cook's achievements were all the more astounding in the light of his humble background. The son of a Yorkshire laborer, he had worked as a farm hand and grocer's assistant before going to sea as an apprentice in the coal-shipping trade. He was twenty-seven years old when he joined the navy as a mere able seaman. Yet, within twelve years, he had so impressed the lords of the Admiralty with his skills in seamanship and surveying that he was made a lieutenant and given command of a major Pacific expedition.

His appointment caused considerable surprise. Unlike the leaders of previous British expeditions, Cook was virtually unknown to his countrymen. He had sprung from the lower ranks of society purely on the strength of his own endeavors: studying astronomy and mathematics in his spare time, developing his rare navigational skills

In engravings based on lost drawings by Sydney Parkinson, a priest of the Society Islands *(right)* wears a ceremonial headdress made of basketwork and feathers; Maori warriors of New Zealand *(below),* stick out their tongues to warn off intruders; and naked Australian Aborigines *(opposite)* advance into battle. The poses of these Aboriginal fighters resemble those of Greek and Roman art, suggesting the engravings are not too literal a representation. How closely they follow Parkinson's originals is unclear.

on coal ships in the treacherous waters of the North Sea, earning distinction by his meticulous charting of the Saint Lawrence River in preparation for the British assault on the French at Quebec, and then confirming his reliability by his precise charting of the whole length of the rugged coast of Newfoundland.

The proclaimed purpose of Cook's first expedition was to observe from Tahiti the transit of Venus across the face of the sun. This rare astronomical event, due to occur in June 1769, was also to be viewed from stations at Hudson Bay, in North America, and at the north cape of Norway; by comparing the separate readings, the Royal Society hoped to be able to determine the earth's distance from the sun. The British Admiralty had agreed to support the society's plan, but, in providing a ship and a captain of their own choice, they intended not so much to support scientific endeavor as to promote the British Parliament's territorial ambitions. Once the stargazing had been completed, Cook's instructions were to proceed south from Tahiti, exploring for about 1,250 miles in search of the Southern Continent. If unsuccessful, he was to turn west and investigate the east coast of New Zealand, all the while cultivating the friendship of any islanders he encountered and taking possession of all newly discovered territories in the king's name.

For this purpose, Cook was given a bark-rigged, three-masted collier identical to those on which he had first gone to sea. It had been renamed the *Endeavour* and radically renovated for the conditions it would meet in the Pacific. The ship had to accommodate seventy-one officers and crewmen, and twelve marines, as well as eleven civilians. Among the civilians were the Swedish botanist, Daniel Solander; an astronomer, Charles Green; and, most conspicuous, the naturalist Joseph Banks—a wealthy young aristocrat (later to be president of the Royal Society), who, having contributed £10,000 to the cost of the adventure, was able to insist on bringing along four servants, a private secretary, and a young artist protégé by the name of Sydney Parkinson.

It was a measure of Cook's leadership qualities that, given such a motley company, he was able to maintain discipline and relative harmony on an around-the-world voyage lasting almost three years. Standing more than six feet tall, with piercing eyes and a composed demeanor, Cook exuded an air of authority and commanded respect with his total professionalism and steadfast character. He could certainly be a firm disciplinarian: In order to keep scurvy at bay, he insisted that his men consume quantities of vegetables—pickled cabbage ad nauseam. But he was never known to be unfair or unfeeling; and these same qualities were to be of no less value in his dealings with the South Sea islanders.

Unlike Wallis and Bougainville before him, Cook made a prolonged visit to Tahiti—a three-month stay during which he explored the interior, charted the coast, and traveled to the neighboring islands, naming the entire group the Society Islands. He was so effective in overcoming initial hostility that many islanders were in tears when he finally took his farewell. He came to know the Tahitians well, though not as intimately as did his crew, half of whom were eventually infected with venereal disease. Cook recognized where the responsibility lay. The disease, he noted in his journal, "may in time spread itself over all the islands in the South Seas, to the eternal reproach of those who first brought it among them."

In New Zealand, Cook encountered sterner opposition. Twice his marines had occasion to fire their muskets, and at least four Maoris were killed in skirmishes. But again he succeeded in establishing friendly relations with local groups. He spent six months accurately charting the coastline of both islands, and by the time he left, he

was able to make a detailed description of the land and its "strong, rawboned, well-made" inhabitants. Cook also ventured the opinion (a rare misjudgment on his part) that it would not be difficult for foreigners to settle this land because the Maoris were too divided among themselves to offer any serious resistance.

At this point, having completed his assignment in twenty-one months, Cook could have set sail for home without exploring farther. Instead, he headed northwest toward the still-undiscovered east coast of Australia. Approximately three weeks later, on April 28, 1770, he dropped anchor in an inlet on the south side of present-day Sydney. Two naked Aborigines attempted to defend their territory. But gunfire soon forced them to flee, and Cook and his companions became the first Europeans to set foot on Australia's eastern shore. They named the place Botany Bay because more than 200 unknown plants were collected there.

From here, Cook sailed almost 1,900 miles along the eastern coast of Australia. Unknowingly, on the way, he passed inside the Great Barrier Reef, where the Endeavour struck coral and subsequently was laid up for six weeks for major repairs. The unexpected delay allowed time to explore inland and make the first real contact with the Aborigines. Cook later wrote: "They are an inoffensive race, in no way inclined to cruelty. They may appear to some to be the most wretched people on earth, but in reality they are far happier than we Europeans. For they live in tranquillity. The earth and the sea furnish them with all things necessary." He also took a favorable view of the land. It was "well diversified with hills and plains," and he thought that the soil might be suitable for breeding sheep.

This was a more inviting Australia, quite unlike the arid regions that had been so cursorily condemned by Dutch explorers. On August 22, 1770, after rounding Cape York Peninsula in the extreme north, Cook paused at a little offshore island to hoist the Union Jack and formally declare possession of the entire eastern coast in the name of King George III. He called this vast territory New Wales—soon to be amended to New South Wales.

A woman of Vancouver Island, off the southwest coast of Canada, stares suspiciously out from beneath a hat made of basketwork and decorated with a whaling scene. Cook's search for a northwest passage between the Pacific and the Atlantic oceans led him as far north as Alaska and the Arctic Circle, and in 1778, he and his companions spent some days with the inhabitants of Vancouver Island, the Nootka Indians. The visitors appreciated their hosts' hospitality and admired their music and art, but one English observer noted that the Nootka were beyond any doubt "the dirtiest set of people I have ever yet met with."

It was not until July 1771—almost two years and nine months after leaving Plymouth—that the *Endeavour* arrived back in England. More than one-third of her crew had died in the course of the voyage, most of them victims of malaria and dysentery contracted in the Dutch East Indies on the homeward run. Cook was commended for his success in combating scurvy. The Admiralty stated its approval of his conduct and, in due course, promoted him to commander. Yet he received no great public acclaim. Instead, the press lionized Banks and Solander, who had brought back so much of concrete interest: 1,000 new species of plants, 500 skins of birds, 500 fish preserved in alcohol, countless insects, and a fascinating assortment of native artifacts. Items they had been unable to bring back had been captured in a collection of 1,300 paintings and sketches by the young artist Sydney Parkinson, who had succumbed to dysentery on the last leg of the voyage.

Cook appeared impervious to the lack of recognition. Already he was planning a second Pacific voyage, to search for the Southern Continent. He had proved that, aside from the great island of Australia, no continental landmass existed in the tropical and temperate zones of the South Pacific. But theorists still argued that *terra australis incognita* might lie in the vast, uncharted regions to the south and east of New Zealand. He aimed to eliminate this possibility. At the same time, as he noted, he had the ambition "not only to go farther than anyone had been before, but as far as it was possible for man to go."

The Admiralty provided him with the *Resolution,* another converted collier. His orders were to penetrate as far south as possible toward the undiscovered pole. Again, he was to be accompanied by a civilian team: two naturalists, two astronomers, and one artist. And for the first time, he was to have the benefit of a chronometer, the newfangled invention of Yorkshire clockmaker John Harrison, which at last enabled navigators to calculate a ship's longitude with complete accuracy.

Cook sailed from Plymouth on July 13, 1772. He returned three years later, having completed the most exhaustive of all South Pacific explorations: two enormous crisscrossing sweeps, which took him three times to New Zealand; twice to Tahiti and the Friendly Islands (Tonga); to Pitcairn and the Tuamotu Islands; and deep inside the Antarctic Circle. He had discovered as many as thirty new islands and, most important of all, had explored the high-latitude waters of the South Atlantic to end all dreams of a habitable southern continent. Remarkable, too, was the fact that he had sailed the *Resolution* almost 70,000 miles without losing a single man to scurvy.

This time the magnitude of Cook's achievements was officially recognized. He was congratulated personally by King George III, made a fellow of the Royal Society, and promoted to the rank of captain. At forty-six, he was famous and financially secure, and yet he was still eager to get back to sea.

His goal this time was to discover whether or not a northwest passage existed across the north polar seas between the Atlantic and the Pacific. For 200 years, Europeans had dreamed of finding such a passage to replace the long and costly trade route to Asia via the Cape of Good Hope. Previously, English explorers had made the quest only from the Atlantic side, through Hudson and Baffin bays. Now, for the first time, Cook was to seek such a seaway from the Pacific side. The Admiralty provided two ships for his expedition: the old *Resolution*, hastily and poorly fitted, and another collier, the 330-ton *Discovery*.

He sailed on July 12, 1776, on what was to be a four-year voyage—the longest of his three great circumnavigations. Once at Tahiti, he headed directly north, and on December 24, 1777, after crossing more than 1,000 miles of open sea, he discovered uninhabited Christmas Island. Approximately three weeks later, on his continued northern course, he was startled to come upon three large volcanic islands that appeared on none of his charts. To his even greater surprise, the inhabitants not only spoke a Polynesian dialect similar to Tahitian but also prostrated themselves before him in homage. He had become the first European to reach an island of the great Hawaiian group.

Unaware that the Hawaiians had mistaken him for the reincarnation of Lono, their god of plenty, Cook admired the islanders for their hospitality and wrote that "no people could trade with more honesty . . . they even abandoned their efforts to steal." Two weeks later, having named the group the Sandwich Islands after the first lord of the Admiralty, he hastened northeastward toward the coast of North America, finally taking shelter on the seaward shore of what is now Vancouver Island, British Columbia. There, the expedition had to remain for a full month while the structurally weak *Resolution* underwent extensive repairs.

After trading with friendly Nootka Indians, Cook resumed his survey of the North American coast. He followed the shoreline as far as southern Alaska, but then seemingly endless headlands compelled his ships to veer westward. On June 15, he reached the Aleutian Islands, where he met the Inuit, or Eskimos. Then, sailing north again, he approached the narrow stretch of water dividing Asia and America, known as the Bering Strait after Vitus Bering, the Danish navigator who had discovered its existence nearly fifty years earlier. Thick fog had prevented Bering from sighting the North American shore, but Cook was able to see both continents simultaneously. He went on to enter the Arctic Circle, but finally, as on his Antarctic voyage, he was brought to a halt by an impenetrable wall of ice. His hope of finding a northwest passage had come to an end.

Returning to the Sandwich Islands, Cook now came upon the group's largest island, Hawaii. More than a thousand crowded canoes put out to welcome his ships in Kealakekua Bay, together with many hundreds of swimmers who swarmed around "like shoals of fish." Again the captain was presumed to be the great god Lono who, according to Hawaiian legend, would arrive one day, bearing wonderful gifts. But this time, for some unknown reason, the island chiefs gradually came to have doubts about his divinity. For two weeks they treated him as an honored guest; then, pressingly, they began to inquire when he planned to leave.

Sensing the change of mood, Cook departed as soon as his ships could be made ready. But he ran into a gale and was compelled to return to Kealakekua's safe anchorage a week later to repair the *Resolution*'s foremast. He did not meet a second joyful welcome. Instead, a series of ugly incidents was sparked by the Hawaiians' persistent pilfering. Finally, the theft of the *Discovery*'s cutter prompted Cook to take drastic action. Fuming, he went ashore with armed marines on February 14, 1779, intending to hold the local chieftain hostage until the missing boat was returned.

Cook was on the beach, about to escort the compliant chief into a small boat, when a crowd gathered with spears and stones. Threatened by a dagger-wielding Hawaiian, the captain fired his double-barreled musket, missing his assailant but killing a bystander. In the ensuing fracas, Cook turned to issue an order to his men offshore. At that moment, he was stabbed in the back of the neck; then, prostrated in the Pacific shallows, he was repeatedly clubbed and stabbed by the crowd. Four marines were also killed before the rest were able to escape. Subsequently, Cook's body was hacked to pieces and burned.

No other eighteenth-century explorer would approach his achievements. After his three epic voyages, lasting a total of ten years in all, very few territories remained to be discovered in the Pacific. In the words of Charles Darwin, the outstanding naturalist-explorer of the century ahead, the Yorkshire laborer's son had "added a hemisphere to the civilized world."

In 1768, after leaving his newfound Tahitian paradise, Louis Antoine de Bougainville had written in his journal: "Farewell, happy and wise people. Remain always as you are now." But the people of Tahiti would never be the same again; nor indeed would any of the Pacific societies, once they had been exposed to the influences of Western civilization. And largely as a result of Cook's explorations, such exposure became commonplace by the late eighteenth century.

First came the commercial invasion, as British and North American opportunists sought to expand trade with China. In Europe and America, there was now a huge demand for Chinese silks, brocades, porcelain, and tea, but in China there was very little appetite for Western goods with which these luxuries could be exchanged. Then the would-be traders found that the Pacific offered products that did appeal to Asian tastes: pearls, tortoiseshell, coconut oil, sweet-smelling sandalwood, and trepang, a popular delicacy otherwise known as the sea cucumber.

After the traders came the hunters—British, American, and French whalers scouring the Pacific from the Aleutians to the Antarctic. It was a profitable business: A sixty-five-ton whale could yield more than one ton of whalebone for corsets and hooped skirts; and in London, that harvest alone could fetch enough to finance a

OMAI OF THE ISLANDS

Brought to London in 1774 by Captain Tobias Furneaux, the master of the *Resolution's* companion ship, the *Adventure*, the Polynesian Omai took high society by storm. Welcomed by the aristocracy and by writers such as Dr. Samuel Johnson, Omai became a much sought-after guest. He impressed everyone with his intelligence and dignity, seeming to embody the ideal of the "noble savage" promoted by the influential French philosopher Jean-Jacques Rousseau. The adulation continued even after his return home with Cook's third expedition, when Omai became the subject of a play entitled *Omai, or A Trip round the World.*

In a portrait by Sir Joshua Reynolds, Omai cuts an imposing figure with his flowing robes, swirling turban, and haughty, classically inspired pose. That the leading society portraitist of the day painted Omai is testimony to the Polynesian's celebrated status in London.

At the height of his London success, on July 17, 1774, Omai is presented by the naturalists Daniel Solander and Joseph Banks to the king and queen. Omai greeted King George III, it was reported, with the words "How do King Tosh?" His Majesty was too intrigued to object to this unconventional form of address and even gave Omai a generous pension.

voyage to the South Seas and back. In addition, the same creature would yield more than two tons of oil, in great demand for domestic and street lamps. Meanwhile, fur hunters wrought a veritable holocaust in the sub-Antarctic where they clubbed to death millions of seals within a few decades. Similarly, in the North Pacific, Russian and American adventurers reaped rich commercial rewards in the form of seals, whales, walruses, and sea otters—animals that had previously been killed by the indigenous peoples only for food.

In the process, the whalers and sealers also disrupted Pacific communities with alcohol, violence, and disease. Often they brought with them escaped convicts, navy deserters, and ruthless mercenaries, and most disastrous, they introduced ailments—influenza, smallpox, measles, tuberculosis, and cholera—against which Pacific islanders had built up no immunity. In consequence, there began a catastrophic decline in the population of the region.

Following the traders and the hunters came those in search of souls. The London Missionary Society led the way, landing its first Protestant representatives on Tahiti in 1797. Within a generation, more than 100 British, French, and American mission stations were to be established on Pacific islands. Apart from opposing cannibalism, infanticide, and ritual sacrifice, which were by no means widespread practices, their work was confined largely to combating the social problems—drunkenness, disease, slave labor—which their own countrymen had created. Meanwhile, they strove with remarkable success to impose an alien code of laws and morals that conflicted with local cultures.

As early as 1772, in his *Supplément au Voyage de Bougainville*, the French philosopher Denis Didérot had warned the Tahitians that the Christians would eventually enforce acceptance of their own customs and values. "One day, under their rule, you will be almost as unhappy as they are." And so it happened. The missionaries effected a radical transformation of life on Tahiti. Within two decades, many islanders were wearing European-style clothes, and almost all were attending church on Sunday. Regular working hours—mainly spent gathering coconuts for export—were established. Singing and dancing were discouraged; women cropped their long hair; even the weaving of flower garlands was banned. Above all, extramarital sex was condemned. A people who had once taken for granted the pleasures of free love were now firmly shackled by Christian guilt.

To be sure, there were many Europeans who gave generously to the Tahitians and other Pacific societies. But this also had ill effects. Presents of firearms made tribal wars much more destructive; and, having been supplied with iron tools and clothes, island groups quickly lost their traditional skills in making cloth from the bark of trees and implements from

An early-nineteenth-century ceramic figurine, based on a celebrated contemporary portrait by Nathaniel Dance, commemorates Captain James Cook, the greatest explorer of his age. News of his death, at the age of fifty, inspired scores of plays and poems lauding his life and achievements. More concrete recognition of Cook's feats came from the British navy, which granted his widow an annual pension of £200.

In a 1799 painting by Robert Smirke, English officers and clergy look on as the kneeling Tahitian chief Pomare cedes land to members of the London Missionary Society. While many Europeans envied the people of the Pacific their natural state, the Nonconformist missionaries saw them as damned souls in need of salvation. By organizing industry and modernizing agriculture, the missionaries helped to increase the prosperity of the native population. At the same time, however, rigidly disciplined work practices did not come easily to the islanders, and the strict Protestant moral codes that the missionaries introduced, with prohibitions on alcohol and "wanton" dancing, were to prove burdensome to a newly "civilized" people.

stone and bone. Increasingly, they became dependent on the generosity of foreigners; and once drawn into the vortex of Western influence, there was no escape. Cook himself acknowledged the damage that the introduction of new aspirations had done to the islanders' gentle, if monotonous, lifestyle. He wrote, after his last visit to Tahiti:

> *They cannot be restored to that happy mediocrity in which they lived before we discovered them, if the intercourse between us should be discontinued.*

Over the long term, however, the fate of Pacific societies was not completely bleak. A number of them, notably the Hawaiians, the Tahitians, and the Tongans, achieved an equilibrium, albeit uneasy, between the negative effects of the Europeans—erosion of traditional culture and religion—and the positive—increased economic and trading opportunities. And although Western-made weapons were now the arbiters of intercommunal disputes, the Western countries themselves were still, for the most part, too preoccupied with events nearer home to take over actual government of their Pacific territories. When, in the nineteenth century, the United States, France, and England did impose their rule over Polynesian islands, they would usually find it expedient to do so with the involvement and support of local leaders.

The people who resisted the European intruders most successfully were the fierce and stubborn Maoris. The acquisition of firearms from whalers and traders increased fatalities in their intertribal conflicts, but it also enabled them to fight more effectively against the white man. When Britain finally annexed New Zealand in 1840, they were still strong enough to keep limited possession of their lands and fisheries.

But the oldest civilization in the South Pacific had the ability neither to adapt nor to resist. The 755,000 Aborigines of Australia and Tasmania had no permanent settlements to emphasize their claim to the land, no charismatic leaders or tribal councils to represent their interests, no culture that readily commanded the foreigner's respect. Quite simply, they were regarded as Stone Age primitives, barely above the animal kingdom. As such, they would be powerless in shaping their country's future.

In 1781, when the American colonies finally won their war of independence against Britain, they also unwittingly set in motion the events that led to the end of the Aborigines' independence. For more than a century, Britain had used its American colonies as a destination for convicts serving sentences of seven years or more. But now, with the wartime suspension of transatlantic deportations and a sharp rise in the prison population, British penal institutions were overcrowded to the breaking point.

The British government had ignored Cook's favorable report of the land he had called New Wales. But now, ten years later, his findings were reexamined. New Zealand was among the territories considered for a penal settlement, but the British government rejected this location on the grounds that the Maoris were too hostile. Eventually, Joseph Banks, now a celebrated and knighted scientist, lent telling support to the nomination of Botany Bay. The matter was settled.

The choice appealed for a number of reasons. The natives there were relatively timid and apparently few in number. The land was so distant that, to Europeans of the time, it was akin to putting undesirables on another planet. There were also strategic arguments for establishing a British base in the area, but their strength is hard to evaluate since, in the end, Botany Bay was to become a penal settlement and nothing more.

The "First Fleet"—eleven ships under the command of forty-eight-year-old Captain Arthur Phillip—set sail for Botany Bay on May 13, 1787. On board were 443 sailors and 200 marines, the latter responsible for guarding 736 convicts, of whom about one-third were women. Thirty of the marines were accompanied by their wives. In addition, approximately twenty-five children—offspring of both the marines and the female convicts—embarked on the eight-month voyage.

Apart from the exclusion of murderers and rapists, the convicts had been chosen virtually at random. Among them were a few trained carpenters and bricklayers, and several with limited farming experience, but the overwhelming majority were petty criminals with no useful skills. They included pickpockets, shoplifters, forgers, and swindlers. They ranged in age from a nine-

Convicts condemned to transportation are ferried away from England's shores to a waiting ship, which will take them to Australia, on the other side of the world. Behind them in Thomas Rowlandson's cartoon, a gibbet with hanging bodies reminds the beholder that, however unhappy the lot of the transported criminal, it might be much worse under the brutal legal system of the day. When the American colonies rebelled against British rule in 1775, it was no longer possible to ease the pressure on Britain's overcrowded prisons by transporting convicts across the Atlantic. Australia seemed to offer a solution to the crisis in the British penal system.

year-old chimney sweep, found guilty of stealing some clothes and a pistol, to an eighty-two-year-old rag dealer, condemned for perjury. All had been sentenced to a minimum of seven years' penal servitude.

In view of the appalling overcrowding, it is remarkable that only forty-eight people died on the 14,300-mile voyage—a loss partly offset by a number of births en route. The survival of so many was largely because of the humane command of Captain Phillip, a naval officer of honesty and integrity. Upon arrival, he also had the wit to recognize immediately that Botany Bay, with its stony soil and open aspect, was entirely unsuitable for his settlement. A few miles to the north, he located an infinitely more desirable site—"the finest harbor in the world." It was almost landlocked and offered both fresh water and apparently rich soil. In 1770, Cook had named it Port Jackson; Phillip now chose what he termed a "snug cove" within the harbor and called it Sydney, after Britain's home secretary of the time.

The First Fleet landed at Sydney Cove on January 26, 1788. They came with plants, seeds, and livestock—but without the farming expertise to make effective use of them. As a result, they faced years of near-starvation. Crops failed on sandy soil far less fertile than first imagined; sheep died of an unknown infection; cattle escaped into the wild; and most of the other animals—cows, pigs, and poultry—were butchered faster than they multiplied.

It was to be almost five years before the penal colony became self-supporting. In the meantime, scores of people died of scurvy, and hunger drove others to theft and violence. With daring fair-mindedness, Captain Phillip put prisoners and guards on equal rations—much to the resentment of the latter. In the end, fairness gave way to harsh measures. One man received 1,000 lashes for stealing crops; six marines were hanged for breaking into the public stores. Here was no story of bold pioneering; only one of self-interest, cruelty, apathy, and despair. The sense of hopelessness was expressed most forcefully by the octogenarian Dorothy Handland. She hanged herself from a tree at Sydney Cove—the first recorded suicide in the colony.

In 1790, the Second Fleet arrived at Port Jackson. It brought comfort to the first settlers to know that they had not been abandoned. But, contrary to Phillip's forecasts, the advent of these reinforcements did not signal the end of the famine. One ship, carrying two years' worth of supplies, had been abandoned after striking an iceberg. The others merely delivered more mouths to feed. Of the 1,038 convicts who had left Britain, one-quarter had died at sea, and half of the rest were helplessly ill upon arrival. In similar fashion, a Third Fleet, arriving in 1791, brought no relief—only some 1,600 prisoners (including 144 prostitutes), who were all too emaciated to be put to work immediately.

That year, however, did see a major breakthrough in the struggle against starvation. A certain James Ruse, one of the few convicts with previous farming experience, produced a healthy crop of wheat and corn on a plot of land at Parramatta, a dozen miles west of Sydney. By the end of the following year, Parramatta had become the principal center of agricultural development. More than 1,000 public acres were under cultivation there, as well as about 500 private acres—land granted by Phillip to retired marines and sailors, and to convicts who had been pardoned as a reward for good behavior. Free enterprise had begun.

From the beginning, Phillip had sought to establish harmony between the Aborigines and the Europeans. But the Aborigines remained deeply suspicious, rejecting his every approach; and their mistrust mounted as the settlers encroached farther and farther upon their hunting and fishing grounds. Within eighteen months of the Sydney Cove landing, smallpox was decimating the harbor tribes. Those survivors who chose not to retreat into the arid interior were condemned to what seemed to them a spiritual death, living subserviently in the white man's shadow.

Unlike the Polynesians, the Aborigines were fundamentally incapable of adapting to the white man's world. When they lost their tribal territories, they lost their raison d'être, their place in the seamless universe of their ancestors. The fate of approximately 300,000 Aborigines on the mainland was to be dispossessed of their inheritance, stripped of their culture, and forced into marginal existence on the fringes of white society. For the 5,000 darker Aborigines in Tasmania, there was no future at all. In the first two decades of the next century, they were to be hunted down like animals until only a few hundred remained. The rest would be exiled to an island reservation, and by 1876, not one full-blooded Tasmanian Aborigine would exist.

However, the white man's inhumanity was by no means reserved exclusively for the Aborigines. Over a period of seventy years, more than 160,000 convicts were transported to Botany Bay; and many of them suffered unspeakable hardships and tortures, especially under the authority of the New South Wales Corps, a specially raised military police force, which had arrived with the Second Fleet to relieve Phillip's marines. Known as the Rum Corps, this force established a lucrative trade monopoly based on their control of imported rum, the most valuable commodity in the colony. From 1792 until the corps's disbandment in 1809, its officers were the effective rulers of Australia, acquiring vast estates and great personal wealth. The

Two views of Sydney painted sixteen years apart show a settlement transformed. The penal colony of 1788, in a watercolor by Lieutenant William Bradley *(below)*, is little more than a cluster of huts along the water's edge. However, Edward Dayes's 1804 engraving *(opposite)* shows a thriving seaport. Attracted by the opportunities the continent offered, many immigrants now arrived of their own free will. No longer a home only to convicts and their guards, Sydney had become the focus for Australia's industrial and agricultural growth.

most prominent among them was Captain John Macarthur, who founded a highly efficient farm and, in 1797, helped to lay the foundations of a great wool industry by crossbreeding hardy English sheep with the abundantly coated Spanish merino.

More immediate prosperity was achieved with the discovery that nearby coastal waters were rich in whales. It was akin to striking oil. The result was a commercial stampede that ensured a permanent white presence in the region. By 1800, there were more whalers than convicts in Sydney.

Yet even at the end of the eighteenth century, Australia was still a landmass of uncertain shape and size, known vaguely as New Holland, with European possession established only in a relatively tiny southeastern corner. The event that was to change this was the voyage of Matthew Flinders, a twenty-seven-year-old British naval officer. Spurred on by reports of a French expedition into Australian waters, the British Admiralty agreed to set up a similar voyage, proposed and commanded by Flinders. Far outstripping his French rivals, Flinders charted all of the southern coast of Australia in 1802 and, in the following year, completed the first circumnavigation of the entire continent, charting the great majority of its coastline.

From this point on, the British claim to Australia was never seriously challenged. Flinders's discoveries not only determined the political future of the colony but also its pattern of urban development. He had charted the best harbors around the coasts, and by the mid-1830s, they had all become major new settlements—Hobart in Tasmania, Brisbane in the east, Perth in the southwest, and finally, Melbourne in the south. The embryo of a new nation had been formed.

AMERICA INDEPENDENT

On the first July morning of 1776, a grim-faced group of men gathered inside the sweltering statehouse at Philadelphia. They were the representatives of the thirteen British-owned colonies in North America, who had come together from the leafy uplands of New England and the humid swamplands of South Carolina, from the craggy Allegheny Mountains of West Virginia and the sophisticated cities of the eastern seaboard. The reason for their presence in Philadelphia was a session of the colonies' fledgling government, the Continental Congress. The resolution awaiting them was the most momentous and dangerous they had ever debated—that all American colonies should declare themselves independent of their mother country, Britain, and thereby terminate one and a half centuries of rule by a king and a parliament more than 3,000 miles across the sea.

The atmosphere in the statehouse and the surrounding countryside was tense. The American settlers had been at war for more than a year with their colonial masters; so far, their ill-trained, impromptu army had somehow managed to hold at bay the professional war machine of King George III. Now came the ominous news that, just sixty miles away, a British army of 30,000 was massing for an attack on New York.

All day long, the delegates debated the resolution, and on the following day, they approved it. Two days later, on July 4, they affixed their signatures to a document explaining the reasons for their break with Britain. Known as the Declaration of Independence, it defined, in a few simple but eloquent phrases, the great principles on which the decision had been made: "We hold these Truths to be self-evident, that all Men are created equal, that they are endowed by their Creator with certain inalienable Rights, that among these are Life, Liberty and the pursuit of Happiness."

With these words, colonies hitherto divided by differences of geography, temperament, and religion took the first formal step toward becoming a united nation. There was to be no turning back. As the delegate from Pennsylvania, Benjamin Franklin, put it: "We must all hang together, or assuredly we shall all hang separately."

And hang together they did, finally surmounting not only the military opposition of both the British and those Americans who sided with the British, but also the postwar economic and political obstacles that stood in the way of a workable, constitutional republic.

The spectacle of an entire people successfully asserting its right to choose its own government was one that sent political reverberations across the Atlantic and throughout the kingdoms of the Old World. Ironically, the country in which these tremors were to manifest themselves most violently was France, where members of the same ruling class who had helped the Americans overthrow their British masters were in turn swept away by a popular revolution.

Erect in the saddle, the commander in chief of the American forces, George Washington, points the way to victory over British redcoats at the Battle of Princeton, in a painting by John Trumbull. The Virginia country gentleman emerged as an inspiring leader and above all a patient and persistent soldier. Avoiding battle wherever possible, he stretched Britain's superior forces until, after six and a half years of fighting, he and his French allies seized the opportunity to inflict the decisive defeat that would end the war and secure independence for the United States of America.

The Declaration of Independence severed a link between Britain and America that dated back to the year 1607, when 104 English settlers landed on the east coast at the southern end of Chesapeake Bay and established a base on the James River at a site they named Jamestown. Their pioneer settlement was a commercial initiative launched by a group of British entrepreneurs known as the London Company. Thirteen years later, another small band of settlers landed 500 miles to the north, at Plymouth, in Massachusetts Bay Colony. This time the motivation was spiritual rather than economic; the voyagers were Puritans, a sect of zealous reformists, who had fled England to escape persecution at the hands of the established Anglican church.

Other religious refugees followed. Catholics put down their roots in Maryland, and Quakers in neighboring Pennsylvania—one of the so-called middle colonies. Their arrival added to the already rich mix of people who had made America their home: the Dutch in New Amsterdam (later New York); the French in Canada, more than 600 miles north of Jamestown; and the Spanish in Florida, more than 600 miles south.

Life for the earliest settlers had been a grim struggle against disease, hardship, and Indians, who were resentful and fearful of the land-hungry intruders. However, with

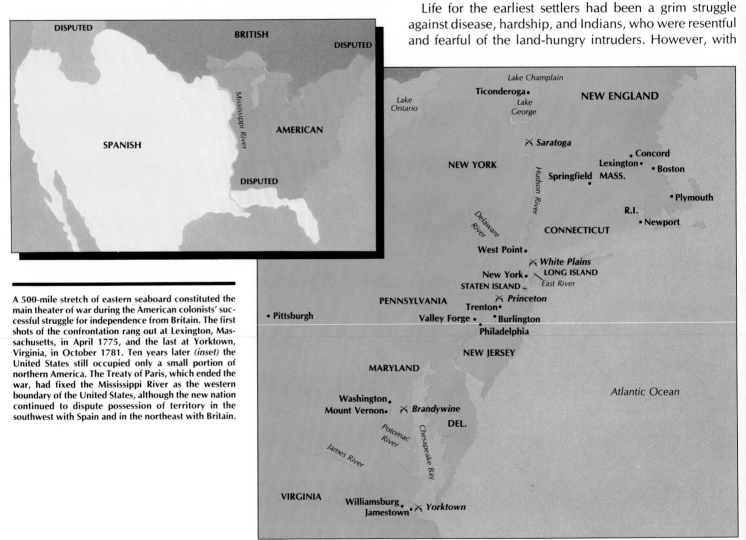

A 500-mile stretch of eastern seaboard constituted the main theater of war during the American colonists' successful struggle for independence from Britain. The first shots of the confrontation rang out at Lexington, Massachusetts, in April 1775, and the last at Yorktown, Virginia, in October 1781. Ten years later *(inset)* the United States still occupied only a small portion of northern America. The Treaty of Paris, which ended the war, had fixed the Mississippi River as the western boundary of the United States, although the new nation continued to dispute possession of territory in the southwest with Spain and in the northeast with Britain.

America's first political cartoon employs the image of a segmented snake to represent the colonies' disunity in 1754. It was devised and published in his own *Pennsylvania Gazette* by the brilliant philosopher and scientist, Benjamin Franklin. Using the slogan Join, or Die, he urged the colonies to band together in a defensive alliance against the French and the Indians. That summer he succeeded in persuading delegates at an intercolonial congress in Albany, New York, to set up a grand council, which would have the power to override individual colonies' assemblies in matters of defense. But the Albany Plan of Union was rejected by Americans and British alike. The assemblies saw it as a threat to their independence and the British as a threat to the authority of King George III.

each new generation prosperity had increased, and with it the population. In 1688, just 200,000 people lived in the British-owned American colonies, but by 1750, that figure had risen to more than 1.5 million. In the north, earning their living from farming, fur trading, and shipbuilding, the inhabitants of the four New England colonies were still predominantly English and Puritan. In the agricultural middle colonies, there was now a rich mixture of races, cultures, and religions, including recent arrivals from Germany and northern Ireland. And in the southern colonies, the families of the first planters had become a landed aristocracy, living off the tobacco, rice, and cotton plantations, which were worked by slaves shipped from Africa.

The colonies had also developed an embryo system of grass-roots democracy; every town had its council, and every colony had an elected assembly, which passed the laws that governed it. As time went on, it had become more likely that the members of these assemblies would be smartly dressed merchants and planters than roughly clad farmers or frontiersmen, but even so, representation was still more broadly based across the social classes than in the British Parliament.

Each assembly was, in theory, subject to the authority of a colonial governor and his council of ministers, who had the right to veto new laws on behalf of the British government. However, governors very rarely exercised that right, since they depended on the assembly for their salaries and, in some cases, for their jobs. Even the governor's right to appoint judges and other officials had been eroded by the assemblies, some of which would withhold the governor's salary if they disagreed with his choice. Thus the colonial assemblies had achieved virtual autonomy in domestic politics, while the British Parliament took an active interest only in matters of America's foreign policy and trade.

Britain's main preoccupation had always been to ensure that the American colonies continue to benefit its economy by producing essential raw materials and consuming British-made goods. Britain had maintained its grip on trade by requiring that all goods brought in or out of American ports be carried in British ships. In theory,

Americans who wanted to buy or sell in European markets could do so only through British middlemen, who skimmed off a fat commission. However, these restrictions had usually been bypassed, partly because customs officers had been open to bribes and partly because American seamen and merchants had become expert smugglers.

The event that altered Britain's attitude toward the colonies was its victory in the Seven Years' War. Fought between 1756 and 1763, this global conflict had seen the British and the French lock horns on every continent where they had outposts. In America, the colonists had taken the side of their mother country, and in the dense forests and lakes of the northwest, colonial militiamen had fought with great success alongside regular British redcoats and friendly Indians. Under the terms of the 1763 Treaty of Paris, Britain received Canada from the French and Florida from France's Spanish allies. It was a development that, in the eyes of a senior French diplomat, Charles Gravier, Comte de Vergennes, was bound to have significant consequences.

"The English colonies," he said, "relieved of all menace to their frontiers, will stand no longer in need of the assistance of the mother country. Should the latter attempt to shift onto the colonies any part of the cost of imperial defense, the colonies will retort by declaring their independence."

Few more accurate predictions have ever been made by a politician.

The Seven Years' War had drained King George's treasury. As soon as it was over, the British government began to disband regiments and cut down on the costs of the navy. At the same time, it argued that although the immediate threat of French attack had gone, British soldiers were still needed in America—both to garrison the newly acquired territories and to protect the existing colonies. In the same year that the Treaty of Paris was signed, the northwestern Indians went on the warpath, encouraged by French fur traders. They slaughtered and burned all along the Canadian frontier, capturing virtually every fort in the area. The colonial militia was unable to master them, and in the end, it was British regulars who put down the uprising.

To the government back in London, it seemed reasonable to ask the colonists to pay for this kind of protection. In order to raise the money from them, the British Parliament in 1764 passed what was known as the Sugar Act, essentially a revival of

In the eighteenth century, the million and a half inhabitants of Britain's American colonies included frontiersmen, who lived hard and simple lives in little log cabins *(far left)* built on land hacked from the wilderness; and citizens of fast-growing metropolises such as New York, with its bustling port *(near left)*, paved streets, and population of 13,000. Outside the towns could be found neat, prosperous farms *(right)*, and large, elegant mansions *(above)* with extensive landholdings that were a match for many a lordly estate in the mother country. The colonies had also proved fertile ground both for academic institutions such as Princeton *(overleaf, left)*, one of several North American universities, and for religious communities such as the Moravians' magnificent settlement *(overleaf, right)* at Bethlehem, Pennsylvania.

an earlier law that had never been enforced. Among other measures, the Sugar Act imposed a three-penny tariff on every imported gallon of molasses, the raw material for rum. This time the British made it clear that they not only intended to collect the tax, but that they would be supporting the revenue men's cutters with the full firepower of the Royal Navy.

What most angered the colonists was the open admission of the British government that the tax had no foundation in trading policy but was merely a means of raising revenue. The persuasive American polymath Benjamin Franklin traveled to London to suggest an alternative: the creation of an American bank, which would make loans to the colonists and pay the British troops with the interest. But his proposal fell on deaf ears. A year later the British government passed the Stamp Act, imposing a tax on all legal documents, newspapers, and playing cards and requiring them to carry tax stamps. Violators of this legislation, as of the Sugar Act, were to be denied the right to a trial before a jury of fellow Americans. Instead they were hauled before an admiralty court, where cases were tried solely by a sitting judge, who not only determined the size of the fine but also received five percent of it as commission.

The Massachusetts Assembly protested vehemently, followed by its counterpart in Virginia, which passed five resolutions condemning the acts. They objected not just to the economic disruption that the acts would cause, but to the principle of a parliament imposing a direct tax upon a people who were not even represented in it. Publishers, lawyers, and others who were to be directly affected instigated mass discontent. "No taxation without representation" became the rallying cry throughout the colonies. Mobs rioted in the streets of New York, Newport, and Philadelphia, pillaging property. In Boston, the mob hung an effigy of the official in charge of implementing the Stamp Act, the distributor of stamps, on a tree, which forever afterward was known as the Liberty Tree. Representatives of nine colonies met at a Stamp Act conference in New York and drew up petitions requesting the king and both houses of the British Parliament to repeal the offending act. Meanwhile, towns along the coast stopped local merchants from importing British goods by threatening to boycott their shops.

On February 13, 1766, Benjamin Franklin appeared before a committee of the

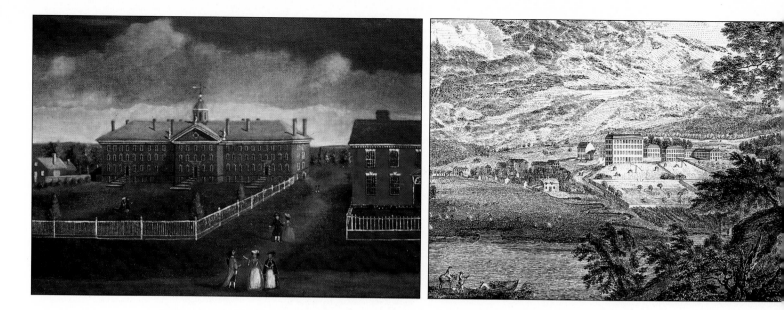

House of Commons in London. This time he was not making suggestions but issuing a protest. He argued that the British Parliament had no right to tax subjects who were not represented among its members. He also warned that any attempt to enforce the Stamp Act might lead to a rebellion. Among his supporters was the influential William Pitt, the politician who had masterminded Britain's victory in the Seven Years' War. But the most powerful voices in his favor were those of the British merchants who were suffering financially because of the American boycott.

Eight days later, Parliament repealed the Stamp Act. When the news reached America, the colonists rang bells, threw firecrackers, shot off muskets, and even broke a few windows. Their rejoicing, however, was premature; on March 4, the British Parliament passed the Declaratory Act, asserting its right to impose laws on the colonies "in all cases whatsoever."

Political infighting in London now returned Pitt to power. But he was no longer the man he had been. Disabled by gout and depression, he was unable to control his fellow ministers, and into the void slipped the artful Charles Townshend, chancellor of the exchequer. Instead of seeking to pacify the Americans, Townshend set about devising more ingenious methods of extracting money from them. Without consulting Pitt, he introduced a series of parliamentary acts imposing import duties on glass, lead, paint, paper, and tea. Some of the proceeds were to be used to cover the cost of colonial garrisons, but the rest were to pay the salaries of the colonial governors and judges, thereby making them independent of the colonial assemblies.

The new acts inflamed American opinion. Mobs rioted again, and after customs officers had been attacked in Boston, two regiments of British infantry were dispatched across the Atlantic as protection. In May 1769, the Virginia legislature, known as the House of Burgesses, approved a motion that Virginians could be taxed only by other Virginians; when the furious governor dissolved the House, the members simply moved to the nearby Raleigh Tavern. There they agreed to stop importing all British goods. Other colonies soon followed their example, and by the end of the year, British exports to the American colonies had fallen by more than one-third.

With tension high and tempers short, bloodshed was almost inevitable. It came early in February, when a Boston Loyalist who had been acting as a customs informer fired into a crowd besieging his house and killed an eleven-year-old boy. Then, on March 5, there occurred the incident that came to be known as the Boston Massacre. It began with a mob baiting a British sentry near the Boston statehouse. When other soldiers came to his assistance, the mob threw stones and hunks of ice at them. A soldier fell. The others opened fire—in self-defense, they claimed—killing three men instantly and wounding eight others, two of them mortally.

At the ensuing trial, the officer of the guard and four of his men were acquitted of murder; two other soldiers were found guilty, but only of manslaughter. It was not a popular verdict. Ironically, on the very same day the shooting took place, the new British prime minister, Frederick Lord North, who had taken over from the ailing Pitt, was introducing a motion to repeal most of Townshend's duties. The one tax he retained was the duty on tea, which he kept as a matter of principle.

It was tea that brought the crisis to a head. In 1773, Lord North introduced an act allowing the financially ailing British East India Company to ship tea via Britain to America without paying any British import duties. With only American import tax to pay, this meant the company's tea would undercut all other available teas in America, including the large stocks that had been smuggled in from Holland. Also, in the eyes of the angry colonists, it set a precedent for the British government to set up similar monopolies as and when it pleased.

When the first East India Company tea arrived in Boston, the citizens refused to handle it and demanded that it be sent back to England. The governor refused to allow this until export duty had been paid. The impasse was resolved by the Boston Tea

In *The Cricketers,* painted by Benjamin West in 1763, five young American gentlemen converse at the edge of an English cricket field. Like many young men from well-to-do colonial families, they had come to Britain to finish their education. The two Allen brothers, James, seated on the extreme left, and Andrew, standing in the center, were studying law at London's Inns of Court. The other three, Ralph Wormeley, seated between the brothers, Ralph Izard, holding the bat, and Arthur Middleton behind him, were all at Cambridge University. When war came, however, the friends were divided. The two on the left became Loyalists; the two on the right joined the Continental Congress; and Andrew Allen, who started as a Patriot, went over to the British after the Declaration of Independence.

Party, a demonstration organized by the Massachusetts Assembly that culminated in colonists boarding the tea ships and emptying their cargoes into the harbor.

Angered, the British Parliament passed the Coercive Acts—known in America as the Intolerable Acts—closing the port of Boston and severely curtailing the powers of the Massachusetts Assembly as a reprisal for its part in the Boston Tea Party. The Assembly responded by organizing a conference to discuss united action. The First Continental Congress met at Carpenter's Hall, in Philadelphia, on September 5, 1774; all thirteen colonies were represented except Georgia, whose assembly members were afraid that if they sent representatives to the Congress, the British might refuse to support them in their war with the Creek Indians.

Those delegates who did gather in Philadelphia set up a continental association to prevent all American trade with Britain. Merchants who flouted the boycott, either through commercial considerations or pro-British sympathies, could expect severe haranguings or in some cases physical attacks.

As the gulf between Britain and her colonies grew, so too did the division between those Americans, known as Patriots, who backed the rebel cause and those who supported King George III, known as Loyalists or Tories—a reference to the British parliamentary party. The Loyalists came from a range of places and classes. Some were wealthy merchants and landowners, hostile to any disruption of their comfortable lifestyle. Others were ordinary citizens who resented being drawn into a war. But many were simply proud to be British, and disinclined to give in to what they saw as the illegitimate and unconstitutional pressure being exerted by the Patriots.

As the mood in the colonies grew more martial, and towns began to raise their own regiments of Minutemen—so called because of their readiness to fight at a moment's notice—greater pressure was brought to bear on the Loyalists. Some were forced to swear oaths of allegiance to the Patriot cause; a number were imprisoned; some were tarred and feathered; others had their land and goods confiscated and were driven out of their communities.

Lacking both the numbers and the fervor of their Patriot neighbors, out-and-out Loyalists were faced with the choice of fighting or fleeing. Many of them fought; more than 50,000 Loyalists threw in their lot with the British troops, and in every area there were others who were prepared to act as spies. In New York, the Loyalists provided

Stamps indicating the payment of duty ranged in value from a halfpenny, as above, to a pound. The Stamp Act's repeal made them obsolete; a contemporary cartoon *(right)* shows bales of unused stamps, sent back from America, piled up near a British dock. Past them files a funeral cortege, solemnly bearing the coffin of "Miss Ame-Stamp, born 1765 died 1766."

15,000 volunteers for the British army and raised 8,000 for a Loyalist militia: The total was more than the city managed to provide for the Patriots. Others preferred to flee. Over the next seven years, about 80,000 Loyalists were to leave America, most of them settling north of Lake Erie, where they founded English-speaking Canada.

By April 1775, the line separating Loyalists and Patriots had been clearly drawn. As British soldiers enforced the Coercive Acts in Boston, the Massachusetts Assembly set up what amounted to a revolutionary government just outside the city. In the face of this defiance, the British commander in chief, General Thomas Gage, was ordered to assert the king's sovereignty by force. The war was on.

The fighting in America was to last for more than six years, during which time redcoats and Patriots were to join battle as far north as Quebec, Canada, and as far south as Charleston, about 1,000 miles down the coast in South Carolina. Most of the major confrontations, however, took place along a 300-mile stretch of the eastern seaboard between Boston and Philadelphia. Here the population was at its densest and anti-British feeling at its most intense. Indeed, it was around Boston that hostilities began, with the Patriots inflicting damaging losses on the British in the first two encounters of the war.

The first of these took place on April 19, 1775, on the village green at Lexington, about ten miles inland from Boston. The night before, General Gage had sent out a force of 700 infantrymen to seize military supplies that he knew the colonists had been collecting in the town of Concord. But a Boston silversmith named Paul Revere set out to raise the alarm. The next morning, the British had gone as far as the village of Lexington when they encountered a small band of about seventy Patriot militiamen. The British commander, Major John Pitcairn, ordered them to lay down their arms and disperse, upon which the militiamen's leader, Captain John Parker, gave the order to dismiss. His men obeyed, but kept hold of their weapons. "Damn you!" yelled Pitcairn. "Why don't you lay down your arms?"

Nobody could say for certain what happened next. Pitcairn later told Gage, "I gave directions to the troops to move forward, but on no account to fire, or even attempt it without orders." Parker is said to have been equally restrained. "Don't fire unless fired upon," he ordered, "but if they want a war, let it begin here." Nevertheless,

An Indian kneels to George III in this obelisk erected by Bostonians to thank their king for repealing the Stamp Act.

In introducing his Stamp Act, George Grenville, first lord of the treasury, hoped each year to recoup about £60,000 of the £350,000 it cost to keep a British army in North America. But the act, which imposed a duty on every document from newspapers to playing cards, aroused opposition throughout the colonies. At the Stamp Act Congress in New York, American politicians launched a boycott of British goods as a protest. Hit by this embargo, British merchants pressured Parliament into repealing Grenville's clumsy piece of legislation.

A ROYAL TAX RESISTED

somebody disobeyed. "I saw, and heard, a gun fired," said Paul Revere. "Then I could distinguish two guns, and then a continual roar of musketry."

Judging by the casualties, it seems more likely that the British fired first. They killed eight Americans outright and wounded another ten, one of them Parker, who died later. Among their own ranks they suffered only two slight wounds: a graze on a private's leg and another on the flank of Pitcairn's horse. As the surviving American militiamen withdrew, the British pressed on the remaining few miles to Concord, where they found that the Patriots had spirited away most of the military supplies. They spent the rest of the morning frustratedly searching and burning houses, while armed Americans were gathering simultaneously on the hill above the village.

The two sides exchanged fire briefly in Concord, after which the British made off at full speed back to Boston. Near Lexington they were joined by a relief column of 1,000 grenadiers, but this did not mean they were home free. Hard on their heels came the Americans, and others waited all along the road ahead. For ten miles, the colonists harried the British, sometimes sniping at them from behind hedges, sometimes rushing in to fight hand-to-hand. By the time the British soldiers got back to Boston, 73 had been killed, 174 wounded, and another 26 were missing. On the American side, there were 45 wounded and 49 dead.

The events at Concord and Lexington served as a call to arms throughout the New England colonies. As the Massachusetts Assembly ordered its militiamen to lay siege to the British garrison in Boston, so too did British ships begin to arrive in Boston with the first of extra troops requested by Gage. The boat that arrived on May 25 contained no fewer than three major generals, one of whom was the extrovert John Burgoyne.

His reaction to Boston under siege was typical of the dismissive attitude initially adopted by the British. "What!" he said. "Ten thousand peasants keep 5,000 king's troops shut up! Well, let us get in and we'll soon find elbow room."

On June 17, the British duly launched a naval bombardment against the American positions on top of the hills overlooking Boston. They followed this with an infantry attack, but to their horrified astonishment, the redcoats found themselves advancing headlong into devastating volleys of musket fire. In the end they took the American defenses at bayonet point. But the cost was terrible. They had suffered more than 1,000 casualties, against the Americans' 400.

This hollow victory, known as the Battle of Bunker Hill, drastically altered British perceptions. Before he sent his men to Concord, General Gage had written of the Americans: "They will undoubtedly be lions whilst we are lambs, but if we take the resolute part they will undoubtedly prove very meek." After Bunker Hill he wrote:

Part craftsman, part man of action, the Bostonian Patriot Paul Revere shows the more contemplative side of his nature in this portrait by J. S. Copley. An engraver and silversmith by trade, Revere became famous for a heroic ride on the night of April 18, 1775, when he set out on horseback to warn the rebel leaders John Hancock and Samuel Adams of oncoming British troops. Dodging redcoat patrols and rousing every household with his cry "To arms! The British are coming," he arrived just in time to escort Hancock and Adams away to safety from the village of Lexington.

Dawn rises over the village green at Lexington, on April 19, 1775, as British redcoats open fire on colonial militiamen. This record of the opening shots of the war was drawn at the scene a few days later by Connecticut militiaman Ralph Earle and engraved by another, Amos Doolittle. The engraving shows one Patriot still shaking his fist defiantly, while his comrades fall back, leaving behind their dead and wounded. The British commander, Major John Pitcairn, directs the fire from his horse. Among the fallen lay old Jonas Parker, who had refused to retreat when ordered and was bayoneted on the ground; and young Jonathan Harrington, who crawled more than 100 yards to die on his own doorstep, in front of his wife and son.

"They showed a conduct and spirit against us they never showed against the French, and everybody has judged them from their former appearance and behavior."

In addition to this newly won respect from their foes, the Americans also had two new cards up their sleeve. The first was a cache of artillery and other weapons seized during their daring capture of Fort Ticonderoga, a key British outpost controlling the route between New York and Canada.

The second was a leader. Two days before Bunker Hill, the Second Continental Congress had appointed a forty-three-year-old Virginia aristocrat and plantation owner as commander in chief of its Continental Army. His name was George Washington.

Several factors commended Washington to the Congress. First, he was a long-established member of the Virginia House of Burgesses, and the New England-based Patriot leaders were anxious to spread revolutionary fervor into his colony, which was the largest of the thirteen. Also, he was as experienced as any soldier in America; although he had never actually won a battle, he had fought with distinction in the Seven Years' War, had served as aide-de-camp to a British general, and had commanded the Virginia militia. In so doing, he had fallen in love with soldiering. He once wrote to a friend, "I heard the whistle of bullets, and believe me, there is something charming in the sound."

But it was not just his political and military standing that fitted him for the job. A

tall, dignified man, he possessed a single-minded tenacity and a calm confidence that inspired men when all seemed lost. These qualities, rather than any tactical genius, were to be at the root of his achievements as commander of the Patriot army.

During the next eight and a half years, he was to endure hardships that would have destroyed a lesser man. When he took over command of the army, his forces amounted, in soldiering terms, to a ragbag of farmers, clerks, and backwoodsmen, whose immediate allegiance was to their own colony's militia rather than any continent-wide army. They were employed on contracts of a year or less, and expected to be rewarded for their services not just with money but with land; privates had been promised 100 acres, colonels 500 acres. However, the reality of the situation was that, far from receiving regular wages and generous property handouts, the men of the Continental Army were seldom paid and often hungry.

The problem was that the Continental Congress did not have the power to impose a tax throughout the colonies. It could only pass on requests for money to the individual assemblies, who found it hard enough to raise money for guns and ammunition, let alone food and wages. Even when they did pay the soldiers, it was usually with the near-worthless paper money authorized as currency by the Congress; this was frequently refused by tradesmen and tavernkeepers, who preferred to be paid in gold and silver coins. The resulting discontent among the troops meant that there was a constant hemorrhaging of fighting men from the American ranks, with very few signing on for a second term of employment. "Such a dirty, mercenary spirit pervades the whole that I should not be at all surprised at any disaster that may happen," wrote a pessimistic George Washington at the start of 1776.

By contrast, the troops they were fighting against were truly professional; for although King George III had been unable to raise enough volunteers in Britain, he had hired approximately 30,000 experienced German mercenaries, known to the Americans as Hessians, since most of them came from the state of Hesse-Kassel.

Washington knew what he was taking on. He was leading an ill-equipped, undisciplined collection of irregulars, devoid of naval support, against an established world power, backed up by a fleet that could move unopposed up and down the coastline. On the day he took up his command, his prognosis was pessimistic: "This will be the commencement of the decline of my reputation."

But for all the inferiority of his forces in both numbers and organization, their one great advantage over the enemy was maneuverability. They could travel light, launch lightning raids, and then melt back into the countryside, where food and shelter would be forthcoming from Patriot supporters. It was a tactic their opponents never came to terms with. As one British officer wrote: "Never had the British army so ungenerous an army to oppose; they send their riflemen five or six at a time, who conceal themselves behind trees etc. until an opportunity presents itself of taking a shot at our advance sentries, which done they immediately retreat."

In addition to being plagued by snipers, the British also faced the huge logistical problem of ensuring that they were constantly within reach of supplies. Since most Americans refused to trade with them, they were forced either to carry around their food and ammunition in cumbersome supply trains, or else to take care that they never strayed too far or too long from their coastal bases. Furthermore, there was no guarantee of provisions arriving from Britain; ships took between two and three months to complete the 3,000-mile journey, and every voyage was at risk from

DRAFTING LIBERTY'S CREED

In a painting by John Trumbull, the committee that drew up the Declaration of Independence stands before the president of Congress, John Hancock. They are *(left to right)*: John Adams, Roger Sherman, Robert Livingstone, Thomas Jefferson, and Benjamin Franklin.

A messenger on horseback reads a copy of the declaration to a rejoicing crowd. On a wall to his right, a citizen posts a sign reading "America Independant. 1776."

On August 23, 1775, King George III officially proclaimed the colonists rebels and warned that they would be punished as traitors. The more radical of the American politicians seized the opportunity to make a clean break with the mother country and selected a committee to draw up a declaration of independence that would formally sever ties with England.

The chief drafter of this document was a thirty-three-year-old Virginia resident named Thomas Jefferson. A brilliant advocate and scholar, Jefferson filled his declaration with the egalitarian and humanitarian ideals of Enlightenment philosophy. After seven days of debate, Congress adopted this draft with only one major alteration: Jefferson, although he was a slave owner himself, had included a denunciation of the slave trade; Congress decided to remove it—out of deference to the delegates from the South, where the economy was dependent on slave labor.

storms, pirates, and other mishaps. This constant concern with supply lines was to hinder British mobility of thought and action throughout the war. Nerves and resources were further stretched by the necessity of protecting Loyalist communities. This often required large garrisons to be left in dangerously isolated locations; frequently, the difficulty of supplying these bases required that they—and their unfortunate inhabitants—had to be abandoned to the Patriots.

Weighed down by these conflicting burdens, the British commanders consistently failed to take positive action. Washington took full advantage of his opponents' sluggishness when, on the night of March 4, 1776, he ordered the cannon that had been captured the previous summer at Ticonderoga to be deployed on top of the cliffs overlooking the British fleet in Boston harbor. The casualness that was to become a hallmark of the British war effort had left this vantage point unfortified; the next morning, the British awoke to find an artillery battery pointing down at them and realized they had no choice but to evacuate. They set sail for Halifax, in Nova Scotia, taking with them 1,000 Loyalist supporters, who gazed in numbed distress as their hometown disappeared from view; most of them never saw Boston again.

Thwarted in Boston, the British now decided to concentrate their energies on an all-out assault against New York. While the Patriot leaders were debating the Declaration of Independence in Philadelphia, a force of 30,000 British troops—among them the newly arrived Hessian units—massed on Staten Island, from which they could see the city of New York. Against them, Washington could only muster 15,000 men, and these were weakly deployed in two locations, on Manhattan and Long islands. Swift naval action from the British could have cut off the two halves of the American army, but again the dilatory approach of a British commander, this time General William Howe, meant the loss of a vital opportunity.

Finally, on August 26, the British made their move. Their fleet made a diversionary attack on New York, while their army stormed the American flank in Brooklyn. Despite a stirring speech from Washington—"Quit yourselves like men, like soldiers, for all that is worth living for is at stake"—the Americans were heavily defeated, losing 1,000 dead and 2,000 captured. It was only under cover of a thick fog that Washington, in a desperate nighttime operation, managed to ferry the survivors across the East River to safety.

He had learned a valuable lesson. Never again would he adopt the strategy of digging in against a bigger and better-equipped enemy. From now on, the war followed a new pattern as Washington adopted a policy of tactical flight, avoiding confrontation with the redcoats wherever possible and biding his time until the opportunity presented itself to inflict a major defeat.

The British unwittingly assisted by pursuing him with their customary caution. After a minor setback at the village of White Plains, Washington was able to fall back, fight, and fall back again through New Jersey until he retreated over the Delaware River, still ahead of the chasing redcoats.

November 1776 was Washington's darkest hour yet. Casualties, disease, and desertion had reduced his strength to about 6,000 men, and with most of his soldiers' one-year contracts due to expire at the end of the year, it seemed as though American resistance was about to fade away completely.

But with only a week to go before the majority of his army was due to disband, Washington launched a daring counterattack that gave the colonies new heart. On a freezing Christmas night, with a force of just 2,400 men and a battery of only eighteen guns, he crossed back to the north bank of the icy Delaware, braving swift currents, swirling ice floes, and a snowstorm that raged until dawn. The next morning, just after daybreak, he took the enemy garrison at Trenton by surprise, capturing 1,000 Hessians who had been sleeping off the previous night's festive excesses.

A punitive British force arrived in the area a week later, led by the experienced Lord Cornwallis. Defeat looked certain for Washington, but on the night before the battle, he hit upon a desperate ruse. Leaving just 400 of his men around blazing campfires, he and the rest of his forces slipped away under cover of darkness. Traveling by a side road, with the cannon wheels muffled by cloth, they circumvented Cornwallis's entire force and the next morning appeared ten miles away at Princeton. Here they launched a surprise attack on the British garrison and routed three regiments before making good their escape.

These two successes saved Washington's army from extinction. Volunteers began to appear in his camps again; furthermore, it was now possible to equip them, since money, arms, and ammunition were beginning to arrive from France. This was in large measure a result of the efforts of Benjamin Franklin, who for much of the past year had been in Paris, canvassing support from Britain's old cross-Channel enemies.

The Patriot victories left the redcoats with only a handful of bases in the middle colonies, the biggest of which was New York. In 1777, the British turned their attention instead to the north, where they launched a campaign to drive the Patriot forces out of the Hudson Valley and to reestablish control of the vital strategic corridor between New York and Canada. General Burgoyne was ordered to recapture Fort Ticonderoga and then push south, while at the same time another British force, under General Barry St. Leger, was to move east, trapping the Americans in pincers.

Burgoyne set out from Canada that summer with 138 guns and almost 8,000 men, of whom 400 were Indians from the Iroquois tribe. Use of Indian allies was more frequent on the British side than the American. They were an effective means of spreading terror among the civilian population, but at the same time, they could be a liability because they would frequently disobey orders and every so often would carry out atrocities that turned uncommitted Americans against the British cause.

Burgoyne succeeded in taking several forts, including Ticonderoga, but the deeper he got into enemy territory, the more isolated he became. With no army threatening their rear, the Patriot forces, led by Benedict Arnold and Horatio Gates, were able to use the dense forest cover to launch ambushes on Burgoyne's vanguard. To make matters worse for Burgoyne, news came that the eastward-traveling prong of the British pincer had been summarily snapped off, with the rout of St. Leger's troops about 100 miles away. General Howe, his only other potential rescuer, was even farther away, in Philadelphia. Burgoyne decided that his only option was to try to smash through the now rapidly encircling Patriots.

His attempt came to an end on October 17, at Saratoga. Completely surrounded and heavily outnumbered, Burgoyne surrendered his entire army, which had been reduced to 5,700 men. It was the first great American victory.

After the triumph at Saratoga, other countries, which had doubted that the Patriots were capable of winning, came out in open support of the Americans. Those nations that had suffered in the Seven Years' War now took delight in seeing the victor humbled. France took the lead in February 1778, officially recognizing American independence and establishing a military alliance with the thirteen colonies. The

French provided supplies and later ships for the daring John Paul Jones, an American sea captain who was already causing havoc within British territorial waters. Spain joined in, too, attacking British supply ships where it could, while the Russian empress Catherine the Great united Russia, Holland, Prussia, and the Scandinavian kingdoms in the League of Armed Neutrality, designed to protect their merchant ships from British interference. This altered the whole nature of the war. What had begun as a confrontation between a king and a troublesome section of his subjects now became a full-scale international conflict, with Britain pitted against half the world.

Elated New Yorkers, after hearing the first public reading of the Declaration of Independence, rush to Bowling Green at the foot of Broadway and topple the two-ton lead statue of King George III, before melting it down to make musket balls. This French etching of the event, which took place on the evening of July 9, 1776, is one of many imaginative re-creations produced in Europe to satisfy curiosity about the American Revolution. In fact, Broadway did not resemble an Italian street, and the king's statue not only was much larger than shown here but also portrayed him on horseback.

Parliament met in London in a mood of deep anxiety. Eventually it was agreed to offer the colonies total self-government, provided they remained the king's subjects. But too much blood had been spilled for any compromises to be made. The Americans would accept nothing short of total independence.

Their goal was brought nearer by the news that a French fleet, which had sailed from Toulon in April, had now begun active operations against the British. This was the help that the Americans needed most. Previously, the Royal Navy had held undisputed control of the coast; it had been able to blockade any port it chose and to transport British troops at will. As news of the approaching fleet reached them, the British evacuated Philadelphia and fell back to New York.

Washington gave chase, and after an indecisive battle at Monmouth, in which only his personal intervention prevented a large-scale retreat, he redeployed his men in a line of forts designed to prevent any future British incursions inland. The rest of the war in the northern and middle colonies now became something of a stalemate, although the Patriots did suffer a setback when their once-lauded General Benedict Arnold, embittered by political sniping and beset by money problems, attempted—unsuccessfully, as it turned out—to betray the vital West Point garrison to the British.

In July 1780, the promised French army arrived on American soil. Until now, the Patriot forces had been poorly equipped and trained in comparison to their opponents. The newcomers dramatically changed the balance. France had provided an expeditionary force in the grand European tradition. Every one of its 5,000 men had been issued two shirts and two pairs of shoes. They had 106 heavy cannon and 16

The young French volunteer the Marquis de Lafayette points out to General Washington his army's privations at their winter quarters in Valley Forge, Pennsylvania. Washington had fallen back on this strong defensive position after losing Philadelphia to the British in 1777. But the winter proved unusually harsh, and the situation was made worse both by the inability of Congress to supply enough clothes and blankets and by the hard-heartedness of the local farmers, who ignored their penniless compatriots and sold their produce instead to the enemy. One-quarter of the 10,000 men died. "Their feet and legs froze so hard they turned black and had to be amputated," wrote Lafayette. Yet the shared sufferings strengthened the soldiers' determination, and the army that emerged from Valley Forge turned out to be more effective than its predecessor.

mortars, as well as ample ammunition and a field hospital with folding beds and seventeen health officers. They had a printing press, and what was more, they gladdened the hearts of local merchants by paying their bills in gold coins.

For the moment, the French were to spend more time shopping than fighting, as the focus of the war now shifted more than 600 miles to the south, where the British, after an unsuccessful first two years, had gained control of Georgia and South Carolina and now sought to expand their territory.

During the winter of 1780-1781, after a series of bitter encounters, the Patriot backwoodsmen began to get the upper hand. Employing a hit-and-run style of combat, they enticed the experienced British commander, Lord Cornwallis, deep into Virginia, allowing American units to move in behind and cut him off from his troops in the rear. With resistance building around him and an American contingent snap-

ping at his flank, he headed for Yorktown, at the mouth of the York River. Here he waited, confident that the British fleet would soon arrive from New York, either to rescue him or to bring reinforcements.

It was just the opportunity Washington had been waiting for. Early in the war, he had concluded that his main priority was to keep his fragile and sometimes mutinous army together, and to fight only when he was assured of victory. Now, at last, a large British force had put itself into a position where it could be trapped. Here was the chance to end the war at a single blow.

He moved swiftly, joining with his French allies in a land and sea operation that combined flair with flexibility. On August 20, while a portion of his troops launched a diversionary attack against New York, Washington dispatched the rest of his French and American forces hell-for-leather to blockade Yorktown. At the same time, the French fleet was adhering to its schedule. On September 5, Cornwallis's last chance of a sea escape disappeared when the French ships inflicted a comprehensive defeat on the British fleet, which had been kept in New York by Washington's fictitious raid. Cornwallis sent a hurried note to his commanding officer in New York: "This place is in no state of defense. If you cannot relieve me, you must be prepared to hear the worst."

In the course of the next four weeks, Washington's engineers busied themselves constructing artillery emplacements and fortifications. By the start of October, everything was ready, and the bombardment began. For ten days the guns pounded the British lines of defense, while infantrymen charged through the breaches. On October 19, when there was virtually nothing left to defend, and no ammunition left to defend it with, Lord Cornwallis surrendered Yorktown and the remnants of his army. Next day, the young French General

Lafayette wrote: "The play is over. The fifth act has just ended." He was right. The British still had soldiers in America, but their resources were hopelessly stretched, and public opinion back home was now firmly against the war. Yorktown had been the last straw. The Americans had won.

A temporary peace was negotiated, following which diplomatic bargaining began in earnest, involving France and Spain as well as Great Britain and America. Spain, with France's support, wanted to restrict the amount of territory the Patriots acquired, not relishing the prospect of a strong competitor next door to its own American territories. Britain, however, adopted a more generous stance, hoping to pave the way for good trade relations with its former colonies. The American delegates therefore decided to countermand Congress' orders and sign a preliminary treaty with Britain without first having obtained French approval. Piqued, the French foreign minister Vergennes remarked that "The British buy peace rather than make it." Only the strenuous efforts of Benjamin Franklin prevented an open breach between America and France.

Finally, on September 3, 1783, another Treaty of Paris was signed, twenty years after its predecessor. Under its terms, Britain formally recognized the independence of its former possessions in America, which were now no longer to be called colonies but states. The new nation stretched from Georgia north to the Great Lakes. Its western frontier was fixed at the Mississippi River, thereby opening up an immense and—if its Indian inhabitants could be subdued—highly valuable area of new territory west of the Allegheny Mountains.

By contrast, America's allies fared less well. Under a separate treaty, signed on the same day in Versailles, the Spanish regained Florida, which had been seized by the British during the Seven Years' War, while the French acquired the Caribbean island of Tobago, two islands in the Saint Lawrence River, and insignificant trading posts in Africa and Senegal—a small return for a war that had left France with a deficit as onerous as the British debt that had helped bring about the war in the first place.

Two months later, as the last British troops left New York, a weary George Washington retired to Mount Vernon, his Potomac River estate, having first submitted to Congress his record of expenses, maintained meticulously throughout his eight and a half years of service. The general's wish, he said, was to spend the rest of his days living the life of a country gentleman. He wrote to Lafayette, who had returned to France: "Envious of none, I am determined to be pleased with all; and this, my dear friend, being the order for my march, I will move gently down the stream of life, until I sleep with my fathers." But it was not to be. He had guided the nation through the stormy seas of war, but there were still dangerous political rapids to be negotiated.

During the fighting against the British, Congress had hammered out an embryo national constitution, under the terms of which money could be requisitioned from state assemblies for the purpose of national defense. Now, though, it became obvious that the provisions of this constitution—known as the Articles of Confederation—would need refinement if they were to provide an adequate basis for effective peacetime government, since they failed to give Congress the power to collect taxes, to regulate trade, or to pass laws that were binding on all thirteen states. The nation was still just a federation of former colonies—and near-bankrupt former colonies at that.

The war had left the country with raging inflation and huge debts. Dissatisfaction stalked the land. Most of those Americans who had fought for the Patriot cause had been sent home unpaid and unrewarded, save for warrants entitling them to land in the new western territories, where massed Indian tribes waited to repel white settlers. Those Americans who had fought against the Patriot cause had mostly fled the country, taking with them valuable manpower, expertise, and in some cases wealth. Arguments now broke out between states over where boundary lines should be drawn; some even set up customs posts and levied duty on each other's goods. Others tried to pay off their war debts by imposing heavy taxes. Those citizens who did not pay were taken before the courts, and many of them were evicted from their homes, which were then sold to pay off the debt.

A typical victim was Captain Daniel Shays, a Massachusetts farmer and veteran of Bunker Hill and Saratoga, who had served bravely and honorably throughout the entire war, but had since been reduced to such penury that he had been forced to sell most of his possessions, including the beautiful and treasured sword that had been presented to him by Lafayette. In the autumn of 1786, Shays tried to draw attention to the large number of people in the same predicament by leading angry groups of farmers into three courthouses and physically preventing the judges from hearing any cases involving debt.

The state legislature responded by passing a law allowing it to arrest suspected insurgents and hold them without cause. Incensed, Shays fetched guns for his followers and led them against the military arsenal at Springfield. But the angry farmers were no match for trained militiamen. The attack was routed and the rebels fled.

Shays's Rebellion was only one of several such incidents, and conscious of the support these uprisings had aroused, the state legislature granted pardons to all the insurgents, including Shays. In terms of relieving his own suffering he had achieved very little, but in drawing attention to it he had highlighted a fundamental weakness in the structure of American government. A rebellion had broken out within a state, and Congress, the supreme body in the land, had been powerless to intervene.

The situation became so desperate that Washington, now suffering from rheumatism, allowed himself to be coaxed out of retirement in order to preside over a special

Stretching back to the ruins of Yorktown, a line of defeated British redcoats more than a mile long marches to surrender at 2:00 p.m. on October 19, 1781. Their path takes them past the watchful eyes of their vanquishers: on one side of the road, in blue, the neat ranks of the French army; on the other, the buckskin-clad American Patriots. The British commander, Lord Cornwallis, could not bring himself to surrender in person. Instead, he sent his second in command. His men were equally affected. Some wept, and as if unable to believe what had happened, their band played the English popular song "The World Turned Upside Down."

convention in Philadelphia, which was to be dedicated to the creation of a workable constitution. "Without some alteration in our political creed," he wrote, "the superstructure we have been seven years raising, at the expense of so much blood and treasure, must fall. We are fast verging to anarchy."

At the convention, in May 1787, the cream of the country's leadership met in closed session. In the words of Thomas Jefferson, author of the Declaration of Independence and one of the foremost intellectual architects of the Revolution, the men who gathered in Philadelphia were "an assembly of demigods." The problem facing them was of suitably daunting size: how to balance the rights and aspirations of individual and often fiercely independent states with the need for an effective centralized government.

The first to propose a solution were the delegates from Virginia, who put forward a new constitution in which there would be a congress of two houses, with the power to legislate on national issues. The members of both houses would be elected to office, the lower house by the people, the upper house by the members of the lower. In both cases, the number of representatives from each state would be determined by the size of that state's population.

Predictably the smaller states objected, since this would mean that such a congress would be perpetually dominated by their bigger brothers. Led by New Jersey, they proposed the creation of a single house—in which all states had the same number of

representatives—which could raise revenue, regulate trade, and compel all states to obey its decisions. This time the larger states voted the proposal out.

The deadlock continued day after day, and tempers rose in the hot Philadelphia summer. Finally, in July, the delegates from Connecticut, one of the larger states, came up with a compromise. There would again be two houses; in the lower house, states would be represented in proportion to their population size, while in the upper, each state would have the same number of representatives. Members of the lower house were to be elected by the public, members of the upper house, or Senate, by the state assemblies. Their power was to be balanced by that of a president, who could veto their decisions but could in turn be overridden by a two-thirds majority vote in each assembly. The judiciary was to remain independent of both the president and the two houses. Numerous checks and balances were inserted to prevent any one branch of government from extending its authority at the expense of the others. There were innumerable other adjustments to be made, among them a ruling on whether slaves should be included when calculating population size: It was agreed that they should be, but that each slave should only count as three-fifths of a free man. Eventually, with the support of another large state, North Carolina, the compromise was accepted. On September 17, after a celebration dinner at the City Tavern, the delegates went home to submit the Constitution to their state legislatures for ratification.

The country at large was even more divided over the Constitution than the delegates had been. The Philadelphia convention had decreed that the approval of just nine out of the thirteen states was required for the Constitution to be ratified. From the outset it became apparent that even this figure would be hard to reach.

Those who supported the proposed constitution became known as Federalists. They were for the most part younger men, who had no emotional attachment to the colonial past, whereas the Antifederalists tended to come from an older generation, more committed to the concept of state independence and more suspicious of central government. In the end it was the Federalists who won the day. Two main factors contributed to their success. The first was that they won over large numbers of Antifederalists by agreeing to their demand that the Constitution should include a bill of rights, protecting the individual against infringements of freedoms by the federal government. The second was that they had a concrete proposal around which to unite, whereas the Antifederalists could put forward nothing more substantial than their feelings of mistrust. All the same, it was not until June

In an English cartoon of 1782, published during the peace negotiations between Britain and the United States, the symbol of Britain, Britannia, reaches out and asks for a kiss, or "buss," from her errant daughter America, symbolized here by an Indian maiden clad in tobacco leaves. The cartoon's optimism proved unjustified. After the peace treaty of 1783, each side saw the other as a violator of its terms: the British, because the Americans were confiscating Loyalists' property and refusing to pay prewar debts; and the Americans, because the British were keeping soldiers in American frontier posts and refusing to trade on equal terms. Relations improved temporarily in 1785, with a reconciliation between King George and John Adams, the first United States ambassador to Britain.

1788 that New Hampshire cast the ninth and crucial vote in favor of ratification.

The news was greeted with a heady mixture of relief and enthusiasm. The streets of New York, Boston, and Charleston erupted in celebrations and processions, while on July 4 in Philadelphia, a crowd of 17,000 revelers drank toast after toast to the United States of America.

All that was needed now was to find a father figure for the infant nation. Before parting, the delegates at the Philadelphia convention had agreed that their new government should be led by a president, who would be chosen by popularly elected representatives from each state. Their choice was unanimous. The news of their decision reached Mount Vernon in a letter from Senator John Langdon to General George Washington: "Sir, I have the honor to transmit to Your Excellency the information of your unanimous election to the office of the president of the United States of America."

It was not unexpected. Washington had already prepared his speech of acceptance. Despite his private feelings, he knew that it was his duty to take office. On April 30, 1789, in the Federal Hall on Wall Street, in New York, he was sworn in as the first president of the United States. Seconds later, the Stars and Stripes were raised above the dome of the hall.

In the last of a series of allegorical drawings that appeared in *The Massachusetts Centinel* between January and August 1788, eleven upright columns—representing the eleven states that have already ratified the new United States Constitution—support the structure of the nation. Meanwhile, North Carolina rises to join them, and crumbling Rhode Island hovers indecisively. It was not until May 1790 that Rhode Island ratified, more than two years after the first state, Delaware. But even at the time this drawing appeared, the Constitution had already received the nine ratifications that were needed to bring it into effect. While rich and powerful Virginia and New York held back from what they feared would be surrender of their autonomy, New Hampshire provided the critical ninth confirmation.

Not everyone liked the new system. Benjamin Franklin said: "I consent, sir, to this constitution because I expect no better." But the delegates at that momentous Philadelphia convention had recognized that they were fallible. They had provided machinery for amending the Constitution, and the result was that their people continued to live at peace within its provisions. The one exception was to be in the middle of the next century, when the northern states' distaste for southern slavery and other issues smoldering at the time of independence, finally ignited in civil war.

For the moment, though, the Philadelphia delegates could drink a well-earned toast. They numbered among their ranks not only the men who had lighted the torch of the American Revolution, but also the men whose task it would be to keep its glow alive in the years ahead—men such as the most junior Virginia delegate, James Madison, who in two decades would follow in the footsteps of George Washington, the most senior, and take up the presidency of the United States. In the space of just four months, these men had drafted the most successful constitution in history. Theirs was the example that was soon to be copied by many others, and of all the Constitution's words, none were more significant than the first three: "We the People. . . ."

THE CRUELEST TRADE

One morning in 1756, an eleven-year-old African boy and his younger sister were confronted by three strangers who had climbed over the wall of the family compound in Benin (now part of Nigeria), West Africa. The intruders seized the children and took them off into the forest. Two days later, they were forcibly separated, never to meet again. The girl's fate is unknown, but the boy was taken, after a journey lasting many months, to the Atlantic coast, where he was sold to the captain of a British slave ship bound for Barbados.

His name was Olaudah Equiano, and in the account of his experiences published forty years later, he told of his terror at encountering both the sea and the white man for the first time.

I was immediately handled and tossed up to see if I were sound . . . and I was now persuaded that I had gotten into a world of bad spirits and that they were going to kill me. Their complexions, too, differing so much from ours, their long hair, and the language they spoke (which was very different from any I had ever heard), united to confirm me in this belief.

Such was Equiano's introduction to the transatlantic slave trade—a trade that, from its inception in the early sixteenth century until its final suppression in the 1880s, was to transport more than 11 million Africans to a life of servitude and oppression in the New World. During the eighteenth century, the peak period for the slave trade, some seven million men, women, and children were sent to be sold in scores of American and West Indian ports.

The source of this merchandise was the coast and hinterland of what the first

Copper engravings dated 1764 show *(top)* an English slave trader tasting an African's sweat in order to determine his health and *(bottom)* Africans on the shore weeping as some of their loved ones are shipped off to supply a profitable trade that stretched *(opposite)* from India to North America.

slavers called Guinea, a word deriving from the Berbers of North Africa and meaning "land of the black men." Extending south more than 3,700 miles from the Senegal River through modern-day Ghana, Nigeria, Zaire, and Angola, it was a region of sun-seared beaches, mosquito-ridden swamps, and sweltering rain forest.

The slavers found it convenient to divide the region into Upper and Lower Guinea. Lower Guinea began approximately at the Gambia River and was subdivided into four sections, each named after its principal export: from west to east, the Grain Coast (where a spice called grains of paradise was obtained), the Ivory Coast, the Gold Coast, and the Slave Coast—including the Bight of Benin. The main peril facing Europeans was tropical disease, and so great was the death rate among the crews of the slave ships that the Guinea coast became known as "the white man's grave."

But if slaving posed serious risks, it also offered high returns. The trade followed a triangular pattern that allowed each voyage to make a three-way profit. Ships from Europe sailed to Guinea with cargoes of manufactured goods—knives, swords, guns, cloth, and rum were the most popular items—and these were bartered with the local rulers for slaves. The second leg of the triangle, the so-called middle passage, was the long Atlantic crossing to the Caribbean or the Americas. Having sold their human cargo here, the slavers used the proceeds to buy New World products, such as molasses, cotton, and tobacco, that they then took back to Europe.

The Atlantic slave trade brought prosperity to more than the slavers themselves: A host of tradesmen—cutlers, distillers, gunsmiths, iron founders, shipbuilders, sailmakers—also benefited from the commerce with West Africa.

Money was also to be made on the East African coast. During the eighteenth century, many thousands of slaves were shipped out from the ports of Mombasa and Kilwa to the plantations on the French island colonies of Île de France (modern Mauritius) and Bourbon (Réunion).

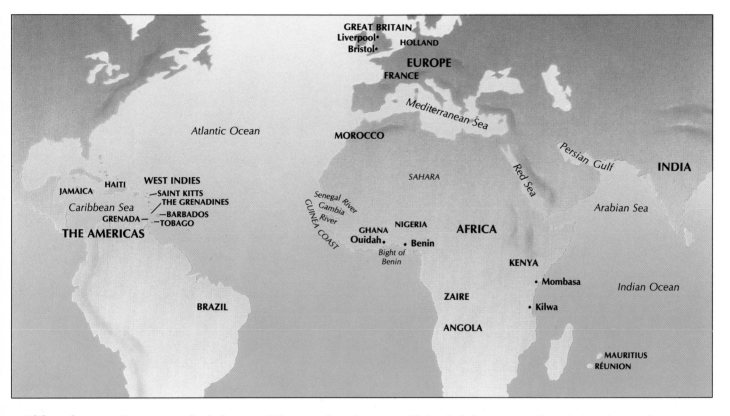

Although some Europeans had denounced the slave trade from the start, it was not until the end of the eighteenth century that it prompted widespread condemnation. Before then, most people in Europe looked upon the Africans as little more than commodities, valuable only insofar as they could be used for the pleasure or profit of their white masters. The popular view was expressed by King Louis XIV of France: "There is nothing that contributes more to the development of the colonies and the cultivation of their soil than the laborious toil of the Negroes."

Others preferred a more high-minded approach, arguing that, since the Africans were heathens, it was a Christian duty to take them from their own benighted land and place them under the benevolent supervision of white owners. The Scottish author, James Boswell, having faithfully recorded the antislavery sentiments of his friend, Dr. Samuel Johnson, went on to record his own proslavery views:

To abolish a status which in all ages God has sanctioned . . . would be extreme cruelty to the African savages, *a portion of whom it saves from massacre, or intolerable bondage in their own country, and introduces them into a much happier state of life.*

Certainly, servile labor in Africa was an institution that had long preceded the appearance of the white man. Captives taken in war invariably became slaves. Others were kidnapped or else enslaved as a punishment for crimes.

Nor were Europeans the first outsiders to come in quest of African slaves. Arab merchants had been transporting their own hu-

In an illustration *(left)* from an 1809 volume of poems calling for the abolition of the slave trade, a mother and children flee their burning village as rival tribesmen search for people to enslave.

man purchases across the Sahara for some 700 years before the European traders arrived in Guinea; over the course of the centuries, more than three million people were exported to Islamic states on the Mediterranean and Red seas, and innumerable others perished on the scorching march through the desert. Slaves from central and East Africa were traditionally shipped to India and the Persian Gulf.

But the scale of this trade was to be dwarfed by the size of the commerce that grew up between Africa and the New World. The ancient institution of slavery in Africa was still flourishing in the eighteenth century. Many African societies measured wealth and rank in terms of manpower rather than territory. So widespread was the practice of possessing bondsmen that there were communities in which virtually every task was performed by slaves.

The status of the domestic African slave was somewhat loosely defined. In most societies, a child born of a slave woman usually became free, and even those offspring who remained legally in bondage would often come to enjoy the same rights and privileges as other free members of the community. Francis Moore, an English slaver who traded on the Gambia River during the 1730s, noted that the domestic slaves of the Africans lived "so well and easy" that it was "sometimes a hard matter" to distinguish them from their owners.

Others even found their way into the upper echelons of government. In the kingdom of Oyo, which at the height of its power in the eighteenth century stretched almost 500 miles north from the Bight of Benin, slaves served as royal bodyguards, messengers, and tax collectors, and three of the most senior were responsible, re-

A wooden figure *(left)* portrays the resourceful Shamba Bolongongo who, despite being the son of a slave, became king of the Bakuba tribe, in what is now Zaire, in 1625.

Carvings on an elephant tusk from central Africa *(right)* show slaves bound and confined.

Armed Africans oversee a column of shackled slaves, known as a *coffle* from the Arabic for "caravan."

spectively, for judicial, religious, and administrative affairs.

The fate of black Africans enslaved in their own societies was usually considerably better than that of those who were transported across the Sahara by Arab and Berber slave traders.

By the eighteenth century, most slaves taken off across the desert ended up in the Muslim lands fringing the Mediterranean. There, the slaves most in demand were boys and young women—the former for training as warriors and administrators, the latter for service as concubines and domes-

tic workers. But many of these unfortunates—adult males and the least attractive females—ended up as slave laborers in the Sudan or in the rock-salt mines of the northern desert.

For Muslims, it was a duty to convert unbelievers, and most slaves accepted the religion of their masters. Although conversion did not automatically lead to emancipation, it was often the start of a better life. Gifted slaves could even rise to great power within the state. Eunuchs were looked upon with particular favor, for, having no dynastic ambitions of their own,

they were likely to be more trustworthy and less susceptible to manipulation than a freeborn nobility.

Under Islamic law, a woman who was taken as a concubine could not be sold once she had given birth to a child by her master, and she became free on her master's death. Moreover, the child itself was free. If the child was male, he could legitimately succeed to the highest office. Mawlāy Ismāīl, for example, was born to a black concubine, yet in 1672 he became sultan of Morocco. He ruled for fifty years, staffing his army, his palaces, and his gov-

A white trader pays an African slave dealer for the slaves who are being herded toward a ship in the background of an illustration for an 1826 anti-slavery poem.

A painting on wood (below) shows a solidly constructed slave fort on the coast of West Africa. Slaves transported from the interior were kept here in preparation for the transatlantic journey.

The configurations of a branding iron identify a particular slave-trading company. Before they were put on the ships, slaves were branded with the sign of the firm that had bought them.

ernment almost entirely with black slaves imported from the southern Sahara.

For centuries, the slave requirements of the Islamic countries were accommodated without any effect on the African bonded labor system. However, in the eighteenth century, the increased demand among European colonists for cheap labor transformed this indigenous social system into an international business. By the beginning of the eighteenth century, slave exports to the Islamic countries were being outstripped by shipments across the Atlantic Ocean. The pioneers of this trade were Por-

tuguese traders, who, in 1505, had begun transporting Africans to the newly founded Iberian colonies in the Caribbean and South America.

The market for this human merchandise remained limited until the middle of the seventeenth century, when the burgeoning of sugar plantations in the West Indies and Brazil had created an insatiable demand for cheap labor. Suddenly, large numbers of European traders arrived in Africa, offering firearms, sugar, pineapples, and other appealing forms of payment, in return for slaves. These dangled riches encouraged

slave owners no longer to view their bonded laborers as indispensable assets, but as salable items.

The profits offered by the trade ensured slavery's rapid expansion, even into African societies where it had not previously existed. In order to step up "production," many of these communities passed new laws whereby criminals and debtors were no longer punished by being imprisoned, but by being enslaved.

The local rulers were the linchpins of the system. They leased the land along the Guinea coast for the Europeans to build

Pitiless white slavers separate an African chief from his wife and child in George Moreland's painting *Execrable Human Traffic*, dated 1789.

slave "factories," and they rounded up the cargoes for the slaving ships. To maintain a steady supply, they used every means possible, from kidnaps to mass attacks on neighboring tribes.

Such expeditions were eagerly encouraged by the white slave traders, who ensured that their partners did not lack for arms. Isaac Parker, an English sailor who accompanied an upriver raiding party from the Nigerian coast in 1765, noted that each of his African comrades' war canoes sported two three-pounder cannon—one in the bow and the other in the stern—and was

filled with pistols, muskets, and cutlasses. Traveling during the day, the kidnappers would storm a village at dusk, rounding up everyone they could see—men, women, and children.

As the slaves were marched from the interior, they were roped or chained together into long processions known as *coffles*, from the Arabic word for "caravan." The Scottish explorer, Mungo Park, joined one such coffle on "a wearisome peregrination of more than 500 miles" through the Gambia River valley. When one woman became too exhausted to go farther, he wrote, there

was a "general cry of . . . 'cut her throat, cut her throat,'" and she was promptly dragged behind a bush and killed.

On their arrival at the coast, the slaves were usually herded into open-air pens known as barracoons. Before putting them up for sale to the Europeans, their captors tried to make them look as young and healthy as possible: Their wounds were treated, their skin was rubbed with palm oil, their hair was cut short, and their nails were trimmed.

They were then paraded before the expert gaze of the slaving skippers and their

MISERIES OF THE MIDDLE PASSAGE

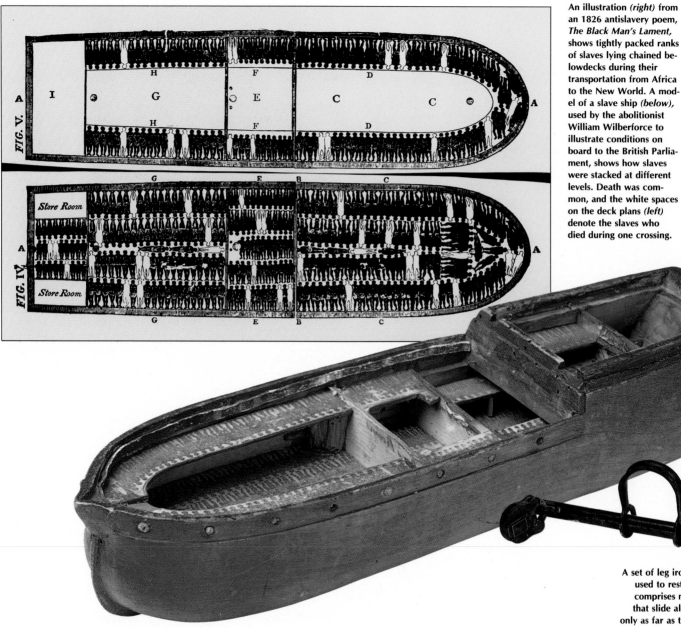

An illustration *(right)* from an 1826 antislavery poem, *The Black Man's Lament,* shows tightly packed ranks of slaves lying chained belowdecks during their transportation from Africa to the New World. A model of a slave ship *(below),* used by the abolitionist William Wilberforce to illustrate conditions on board to the British Parliament, shows how slaves were stacked at different levels. Death was common, and the white spaces on the deck plans *(left)* denote the slaves who died during one crossing.

A set of leg irons *(above),* used to restrain slaves, comprises metal hoops that slide along the bar only as far as the padlock.

doctors. Willem Bosman, a Dutch slaver, wrote: "They are thoroughly examined, even to the smallest member, and that naked too, both men and women, without the least distinction or modesty." Once a price had been agreed upon for those who passed the inspection, they were branded on breast, buttock, or shoulder with the stamp of their new owner and ferried in canoes to the waiting ship.

During their transfer from shore to ship, many slaves threw themselves into the shark-infested waters rather than be eaten by the race of giant cannibals, who, they believed, were lying in wait for them across the sea. An English slave captain, Thomas Phillips, once lost twelve of his consignment in this way, "they having a more dreadful apprehension of Barbados than we can have of hell."

Once aboard ship, the captives would be driven, naked and trembling, into its stifling slave holds for the beginning of a voyage that, depending on the weather, could last up to three months. There was rarely more than five feet of headroom belowdecks, yet this space was divided by ledges for the slaves, who were chained in pairs, and packed, according to one British slaver, "like books upon a shelf."

Infectious disease was the greatest hazard of the middle passage, and a single infected slave could decimate a whole ship. On one voyage in 1780, a British slaver, the *Alexander,* lost 105 of its 380-strong consignment as a result of an outbreak of dysentery. The ship's doctor, Alexander Falconbridge, found the floor of the slaves' quarters "was so covered with the blood and mucus, which had proceeded from them in consequence of the flux, that it resembled a slaughterhouse."

The newspaper advertisement at right announces a sale of "Gambia Negroes" on June 7, 1785, on board a newly arrived slave ship.

GAMBIA NEGROES.
TO BE SOLD,
On TUESDAY, the 7th of June,
On board the SHIP
MENTOR,
Captain WILLIAM LYTTLETON,
Lying at MOTTE's wharf,

A Cargoe of 159 prime healthy young Negroes, just arrived in said ship from the river Gambia, after a passage of 35 days.
The Negroes from this part of the coast of Africa, are well acquainted with the cultivation of rice, and are naturally industrious.

CONDITIONS OF SALE.
To approved purchasers, bonds payable the first of January, 1786, and to those who make immediate payment in cash, rice or any other produce, a proper discount will be made thereon.
ROBERT HAZLEHURST & Co.
No. 44. Bay.

If the weather permitted, slaves were taken up on deck twice a day for meals and exercise—a joyless cavorting enforced by sailors banging a drum and swinging a cat-o'-nine-tails. Many slaves sought release from their torment by trying to starve themselves to death, but such defiance was answered with the whip or, if this failed, with the *speculum oris,* a metal feeding tube that had two movable points for prying open the jaws.

The plight of female slaves during the middle passage was worse even than that of the men. John Newton, an English slaver, who was later to become a leading campaigner against the slave trade, wrote that when the women and girls were taken on to a ship, "naked, trembling, terrified, perhaps almost exhausted," they were greedily watched by the crew and "in imagination, the prey is divided on the spot, and only reserved till opportunity offers."

The conditions of the seamen were scarcely better than those of the slaves. Some captains valued their crews far less than their cargoes, and discipline was harsh. In a single crossing aboard the *Alexander,* all but three of the fifty-man crew were flogged, one so frequently that he threw himself overboard.

As a slave ship drew close to its port of call, its cargo was again oiled and shaved in preparation for sale. Special attention was paid to the sick; it was common practice to disguise sores and abscesses with rust and gunpowder, and to hide evidence of dysentery by stuffing the victim's anus with a fiber known as oakum, made from unraveled ropes.

Once they were ashore, the slaves were paraded through the streets to the marketplace, there to undergo, for a second time,

ORDEALS OF A PLANTATION SLAVE

Illustrations from William Clark's book *Ten Views of Antigua,* published in 1823, show African slaves engaged in the production and refining of sugar, at the mill yard *(top),* the distillery *(middle),* and in the fields *(bottom).*

the ordeal of inspection, auction, and branding. In some parts of the Caribbean, slaves were sold by "scramble." A flat price was agreed upon in advance, and at a given signal, the buyers rushed to grab the "goods" of their choice.

With the business of the sale concluded, it was time for the newly arrived slaves to find out what lay at the end of their grim odyssey. The luckier survivors of the transatlantic journey were chosen by their owners to work as domestics—cooks, maids, gardeners, butlers, footmen. Others, who had failed to attract buyers, were taken all

the way back to Europe, where to possess a black servant, decked out in powdered wig and livery, was considered the height of fashion. But the majority were to remain in the New World, serving the inexhaustible needs of King Sugar.

Work in the cane fields, beginning at first light and lasting until dusk, was punctuated by two short breaks for meals, and the only days off were Sundays and an occasional holiday. Laggards got short shrift. On the Caribbean island of Saint Kitts, noted one observer, it was usual for those who failed to arrive for work at the fields on time to

"throw down the hoe, clap both hands on their heads, and patiently take ten, fifteen, or twenty lashes."

Planting began in July or August and lasted for about six months. Then came another six-month period when the slaves would labor in shifts around the clock, sometimes seven days a week, to cut and process the cane. The worst place to be at this time was the boiling house, where the heat was intense. "Some Negroes," advised a slave manual for West Indian planters, "seem to have been adapted to the boiling house by nature, and will endure being kept at the

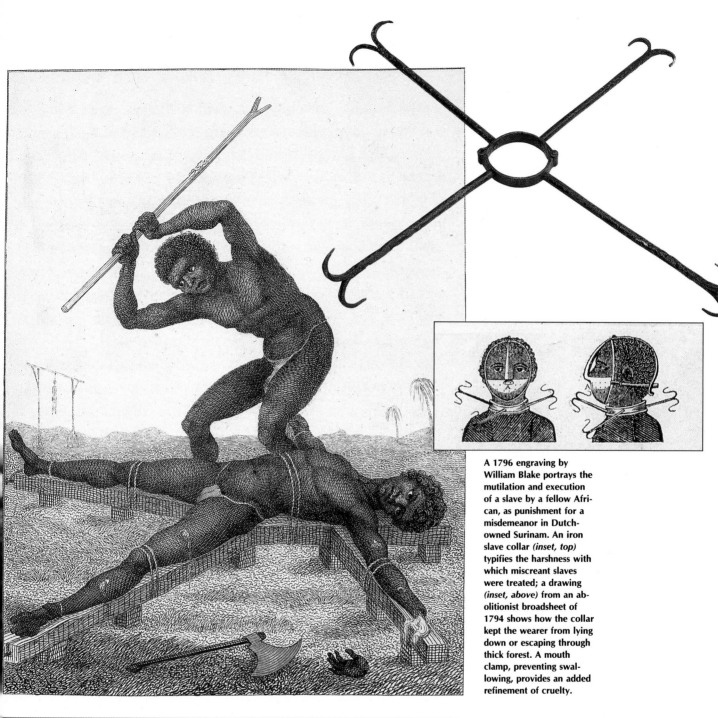

A 1796 engraving by William Blake portrays the mutilation and execution of a slave by a fellow African, as punishment for a misdemeanor in Dutch-owned Surinam. An iron slave collar *(inset, top)* typifies the harshness with which miscreant slaves were treated; a drawing *(inset, above)* from an abolitionist broadsheet of 1794 shows how the collar kept the wearer from lying down or escaping through thick forest. A mouth clamp, preventing swallowing, provides an added refinement of cruelty.

coppers throughout the season without injury; but there are not many who are so happily organized."

At the end of each day, the slaves were marched back to their cabins for food and sleep until the sounding of a conch-shell horn summoned them once more to their labors. They lived, for the most part, in family groups, untroubled by the fact that few slave marriages were legally recognized. The slave owners tended to be indulgent about such relationships, believing that a male slave with a partner was less likely to cause trouble than one without.

Both in and out of working hours, the slaves were at their master's whim. Lord Macartney, governor of Grenada, the Grenadines, and Tobago from 1776 to 1779, felt this arrangement to be largely satisfactory. "The treatment of Negroes," he wrote, "depends much on the temper of the master, whose behavior is greatly regulated by his own interest, connected with the well-being of the slave. . . . I am of the opinion that no more labor is required of slaves than they can well bear."

But a constant complaint of the planters was that their slaves were lazy—and laziness was an offense no owner was prepared to tolerate. The usual punishment was whipping, but overzealous masters might castrate their slaves or burn them alive. Various attempts were made to curb such excesses. The Code Noire, or "Black Code," introduced by the French in 1685, forbade the mutilation or execution of slaves except by the direction of the courts; and a century later, the legislatures of most British colonies set at thirty-nine the maximum number of lashes that could be inflicted at a time.

The trouble was that such edicts were

THE FIGHT FOR FREEDOM

Anne-Louis Girodet de Roucy's 1797 portrait *(left)* shows Jean Baptiste Belley, an ex-slave elected to France's National Convention, with a bust of Raynal, the writer who inspired leader Toussaint-Louverture *(inset)*.

A portrait *(right)* by Sir Thomas Lawrence depicts the kindly features of the British abolitionist William Wilberforce, who carried on a fifty-year crusade against the slave trade. Wilberforce aroused the nation's anger against such cruelties as that shown in the 1791 cartoon at his right, which records a slave in the West Indies being thrown into a vat of boiling sugar because he was too ill to work.

A Maroon *(right)*, from a Jamaican runaway slave community, advances with weapons at the ready.

An 1850 lithograph *(right)* shows Freetown in Sierra Leone, a country created for repatriated slaves.

almost impossible to enforce, and those who found them irksome or inconvenient simply carried on as before. The slaves themselves, unheeded and unrepresented, were left with just two alternatives to passive submission: escape or rebellion. Many slaves tried to flee their masters, but most were recaptured. Some, however, got far enough away to set up their own free communities. The most successful of these was in Jamaica, where, after eighty-five years of guerrilla resistance, the runaways finally won their independence from the island's English rulers.

Other disaffected slaves set their sights on vengeance. They would destroy crops and plot the murder of their owners. A knowledge of plants and herbs, acquired in Africa, was sometimes used to make up a lethal concoction for some particularly tyrannical master. A case in Jamaica involved a fifteen-year-old black female servant who, having poisoned her master's postprandial brandy, stood by his bedside and "witnessed his agonies without one expression of surprise or pity."

The ultimate weapon in the slaves' armory was mass rebellion. In all but the

American South, slaves rapidly came to outnumber the free population, and whites lived in constant fear of black insurrection. The main flash point was the Caribbean, where slaves regularly went on the rampage, burning, looting, and killing.

But it was in only one small area—French-occupied Saint Domingue (present-day Haiti and the Dominican Republic)—that slaves actually succeeded in overturning the regime of their masters. Inspired by the revolution that, in 1789, had swept through France itself, the Saint Domingue rebellion began in August of 1791. Atroci-

ties were freely committed on both sides, and a British visitor to the island was driven to declare that "the most beautiful colony in the world" had been transformed "into a field of desolation and carnage."

The situation was exacerbated by the war that broke out between Britain and France in 1793. Over the next ten years, the island was invaded, first by British and Spanish troops, and then by an army of reoccupation dispatched by Napoleon. However, it was the rebels, under the inspired leadership of Toussaint-Louverture, himself a former slave and self-styled "First of the Blacks," who eventually prevailed.

The Saint Domingue uprising sent shock waves throughout the New World, causing slave owners to introduce even harsher laws than before. But it also gave impetus to the antislavery movement, which argued that violence was the inevitable consequence of black bondage.

The abolitionists, inspired by a mixture of religious and humanitarian ideals, managed to win massive public support, not least in Britain, which, by the end of the eighteenth century, controlled half the Atlantic trade. In 1807, British subjects would be banned from slaving, and by 1818, several other nations, including France, the Netherlands, and the United States, would also renounce the trade.

But many slavers were undeterred, transporting their human cargoes clandestinely where they were unable to do so openly. The fact was that the only effective way to end the slave trade was to end slavery altogether—and that was an objective that still lay far in the future. Not, indeed, until 1888 would the last outpost of New World slavery, Brazil, finally fall before the assaults of the abolitionists.

THE FRENCH REVOLUTION

5 That July of 1789, Paris seethed like a boiling pot. The new National Assembly was in session; a constitution was being discussed; hope and freedom were in the air. But the king would never yield, some said: Was not the city surrounded by foreign troops in the monarch's service? Orators harangued an already nervous population, and rumor swept where their voices did not reach. The king was planning a bloody coup: The people had best look to their own defense.

Governor Bernard Jordan, marquis de Launay, commandant of the royal fortress-prison of the Bastille, was nervous, too. No soldier, he had only eighty pensioners and thirty Swiss mercenaries to defend his charge, and for days he had been looking out in alarm from his eighty-foot-high walls into the agitated streets of the Faubourg Saint-Antoine, the poor district that surrounded the Bastille. For their part, Saint-Antoine's people glowered suspiciously back at him. It was well known that the dungeons in the Bastille were crammed with miserable political prisoners; and besides, they were convinced—wrongly, as it turned out—that the fortress contained bloodthirsty royalist soldiers awaiting their opportunity to fall upon the quarter's unarmed inhabitants.

On July 13, Launay saw smoke rise from burning customs posts around the city, sacked by hungry mobs protesting against a bread shortage. In vain, he begged his military superiors for reinforcements. The next day, as he had feared for weeks, it was his turn to be attacked.

Mobs swarmed through the city that morning, looking for arms for self-defense. The crowd that assembled before the Bastille was relatively orderly; it consisted of ordinary artisans, not ruffians. They sent a deputation to negotiate with the governor. Launay agreed not to open fire. But in a first flush of panic, he had already withdrawn his men from the Bastille's powerful outer walls to a central keep. Now, when he saw the inner courtyard thronged with agitated Parisians, he panicked once more: He ordered his men to shoot.

Their musketry caused heavy casualties among the attackers—although only enough to infuriate the crowd, not to disperse it. At the critical moment, a group of army mutineers arrived with some cannon and pointed them at the Bastille's inner gate. Fear drove Launay to commit his third blunder. With most of the prison's defenses still intact, he surrendered the fortress on the promise of a safe-conduct. On this occasion, he literally lost his head: It was struck from his shoulders by the mob and raised in triumph on a pike.

The people surged into the Bastille, liberating four bewildered counterfeiters, an aristocrat accused of debauchery, and two lunatics. There were no other prisoners, although another notorious debauchee, the Marquis de Sade, had been transferred to another location only ten days before. Sade later discovered that all of his books,

Hauling a commandeered cannon and brandishing spears and pikes, hungry Parisian women march to the palace of Versailles, about ten miles from the city, to demand bread from their king, Louis XVI. The day after their journey—October 6, 1789—they broke into the palace and brought back to the capital not only grain but the entire royal family—the first step along the road toward the overthrow of the monarchy and the eventual execution of the king himself.

pictures, clothing, and furnishings had been looted from his comfortable Bastille cell by the fortress's conquerors.

While some of the attackers set to work with hammer and crowbar to destroy the hated building stone by stone—the job was completed more professionally over the next few months—the rest ranged throughout Paris in an angry tide the city's feeble authorities could not resist. Other heads joined Launay's on the mob's swaying pikes. Paris was out of all control.

Ten miles away at Versailles, King Louis XVI retired early to bed, as was his custom. He was allowed a few more hours of tranquillity before the duc de Liancourt waked him with news of the disturbances. "Is it a revolt?" asked Louis, perplexed. "No, sire," was Liancourt's reply. "It's a revolution."

It seemed a pessimistic analysis: How could a mere street riot threaten 800 years of French monarchy? Yet Liancourt was right. The angry crowd of carpenters and cobblers, locksmiths and cabinetmakers in the Faubourg Saint-Antoine were the leading edge of a great social movement that would cost King Louis first his power, then his throne and his freedom, and finally his life. The Revolution would com-

The birth of Revolutionary France in 1789 posed a challenge to the surrounding countries, most of them ruled by autocratic regimes that were alarmed by the overthrow of a neighboring monarch. Within three years, French troops would attempt to export the Revolution across their northeastern borders, inspired by the radical politician Georges-Jacques Danton's vision of expanding France to her natural frontiers, namely the sea, the Rhine River, the Alps, and the Pyrenees. This forced neighboring countries to take military action, in turn causing France's leaders to put the nation on a permanent war footing against enemies real and imagined, both inside and outside the country. The tightening chain of suspicion, cruelty, and fear would strangle the Revolution by 1794.

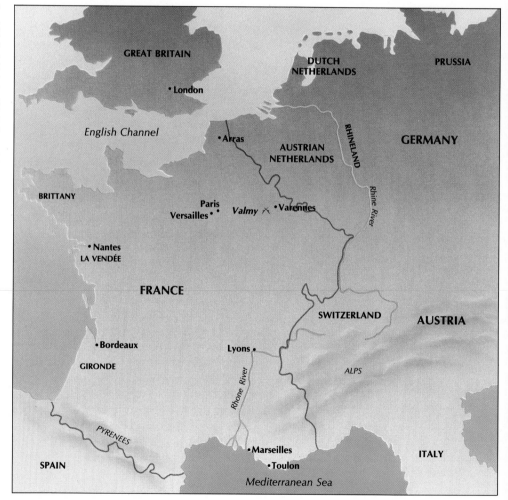

pletely remake France. It would spill across borders and leave the whole old European order either smashed or tottering. And although its light was snuffed out within a span of ten years, the memory of it would serve for the next two centuries both as a beacon to the oppressed peoples of other lands and as a benchmark against which their progress might be measured.

The fall of the Bastille marked the outbreak of the French Revolution; its causes, though, were longstanding. At the time, France was the most powerful nation in Europe, as well as the most populous, but her political system—the Ancien Régime the revolutionaries would excoriate—had been creaking ominously for decades. In theory, the country was an absolute monarchy, run on the strictly centralized lines laid down in the previous century by the talented administrator Cardinal Richelieu. In practice, the system depended heavily on the character of the king, and during the reign of Louis XIV, the glorious Sun King, the monarchy was at its strongest. However, under his successors, the idle Louis XV and the vacillating Louis XVI, royal authority was feebly enforced and often obstructed.

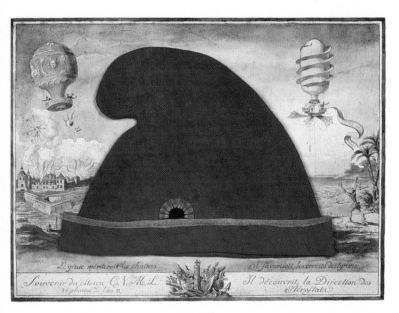

A montage dated 1794 warns scientists not to work for monarchical or counterrevolutionary forces, with the words "The man of genius deserves chains if he approves the crimes of tyrants." As the Revolution progressed, disloyalty to the cause became an increasingly common accusation against people in all walks of life. Here the illustration shows two applications of a scientific invention, one contrary to Revolutionary principles, the other in line with them. On the left, a hot-air balloon is bombing a fortified town, while on the right, another balloon trails a streamer that reads "rights of man" above the head of a freed slave. A red woolen hat of the kind worn to show support for the Revolution forms the centerpiece of the montage.

For royal predominance had been purchased at a high price. The French aristocracy, traditional source of opposition to the king, had been bought off by wholesale grants of privilege, including exemption from taxation. To counterbalance residual aristocratic power, the king had also created a whole new nobility of the robe from his own senior civil servants. But within a generation, the newcomers had joined the old nobility of the sword, with whom many of them had intermarried, and guarded their privileges with equal jealousy.

Among these privileges was the right to extract seigneurial dues from the local peasantry. These feudal tolls and taxes were extracted with assiduous severity, largely through the efforts of the *feudistes,* a professional class whose job it was to unearth—or even to invent—long-forgotten dues.

In addition to supervising affairs in their own immediate localities, the nobility also controlled France's thirteen provincial parlements—appeal courts—and by the mid-eighteenth century had acquired what amounted to a right of veto over royal legislation. Each parlement was determined to uphold its own region's prerogatives, among them, the right to levy customs duty on goods coming in and out of the province. This practice enriched a few officeholders, while stifling the growth of a truly national economy. The parlements made reform impossible; yet reform was clearly essential.

For not only did the whole financial and legal system of the Ancien Régime provoke deep and growing resentment in France's rising middle classes, it was also grossly inefficient. State finances were chronically parlous, and they were put under intolerable strain by the long series of wars

that marked the rivalry among the ruling houses of Europe, each seeking by military means to secure its own patch on the map.

One of these rivalries had even been played out 3,000 miles from Paris, across the Atlantic in North America, where France had helped colonial settlers in their fight against British rule. Victory had been achieved, but the cost of this triumph was a financial crisis of ruinous proportions for the French. By the 1780s, the state was very close to bankruptcy.

There were also powerful political consequences resulting from French participation in the war. The nascent United States was a practical example of the new, liberal ideas of the Enlightenment *(pages 8-13)*, which were widely diffused among the newly educated French middle classes. The example was not lost on observant French citizens, who also noted that the American colonists were rebelling against a government infinitely less oppressive than their own.

While these subversive leavens worked quietly beneath the surface of French society, far out of sight of the sheltered Versailles court of Louis XVI and his unpopular Austrian queen, Marie Antoinette, the king tried to stave off the evil hour of financial catastrophe. In 1787, his capable treasury minister, Charles-Alexandre de Calonne, proposed a series of tax reforms that would at last impose some of the burden upon the landed nobility. But aristocratic protests were too strong for the minister: Louis was forced to dismiss him. When his successor presented a similar plan, the parlements put up a vigorous resistance. In the interest of liberty, as most put it, they refused to recognize the new legislation. The old aristocracy joined in, supported by the Church. Reforms were everywhere blocked, and the conflict between monarchy and nobility became a head-on clash. Louis dissolved numerous parlements, which immediately reassembled in defiance of royal order.

For a time, France was close to open revolt; there were riots in many provinces, as the members of the parlements mobilized the veritable armies of lawyers, clerks, bailiffs, and ushers that depended on the parlements for their living. These servants of the law not only staged their own riots but also rallied still larger crowds of dissatisfied peasants and artisans.

By 1788, the king was forced to act: The treasury was empty, and half of all royal revenues were being used to service the crushing royal debts. Grudgingly, Louis agreed to the parlements' demand that he summon the old Estates General, a three-tiered national assembly of France's clergy, nobility, and commons—the three estates of the realm. The clergy and the nobility were to choose their representatives directly, the commons through a series of elections at local and regional levels. No one was quite sure what the estates would—or could—accomplish: They had last met in 1614. Still, expectations were high.

In some ways, the timing of the great summons could hardly have been worse. The proclamation went out in August; the estates met the following May. In between, one of the century's worst harvests guaranteed that the majority of French people, at one of the most critical moments in the nation's history, would be hungry.

The economic crisis overshadowed the constitutional crisis; there was food rioting, near starvation, and an atmosphere of instability throughout the land. The meeting of the Estates General, which had been engineered by the nobles as a means of protecting their privileges, was now commandeered by agitated middle-class delegates, who saw it as a means of acquiring their own prerogatives.

A portrait by A. F. Callet shows King Louis XVI resplendent in coronation robes that speak of 800 years of unbroken French monarchy. The two ceremonial chains are insignia of the order of Saint Esprit, created by Henry III in the sixteenth century, and the order of Saint Michel, created by Louis XI in the fifteenth century.

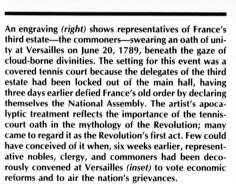

An engraving *(right)* shows representatives of France's third estate—the commoners—swearing an oath of unity at Versailles on June 20, 1789, beneath the gaze of cloud-borne divinities. The setting for this event was a covered tennis court because the delegates of the third estate had been locked out of the main hall, having three days earlier defied France's old order by declaring themselves the National Assembly. The artist's apocalyptic treatment reflects the importance of the tennis-court oath in the mythology of the Revolution; many came to regard it as the Revolution's first act. Few could have conceived of it when, six weeks earlier, representative nobles, clergy, and commoners had been decorously convened at Versailles *(inset)* to vote economic reforms and to air the nation's grievances.

From the beginning, the representatives of the commons, or third estate, essentially the hitherto-silent voice of the French middle classes, took the principal role. They declared they would not take part in any further discussions until, in recognition of its numerical superiority, the third estate was allowed as many delegates as the other two combined. The previous December, Louis had granted them this double representation, on the assumption that voting would be by estate, not by simple headcount. However, this was no longer enough for the third estate, which by now considered itself representative of not just one part of the nation but of the nation as a whole; in June 1789, joined on a tide of liberal sentiment by more than one-half of the clergy and one-fifth of the nobility, the third estate declared itself the National Assembly. After much vacillation, Louis commanded the remainder of the clergy and the nobles to join them—and as a result, he was hailed for his decision by joyful crowds chanting "Long live the king!" But Louis was not yet prepared to become a constitutional monarch. He also ordered royal troops from the provinces to march on Paris, greatly alarming not only the defenseless National Assembly but also the ordinary people of the city.

It was clear that the revolt begun by the nobles had already passed into the hands of the bourgeois delegates of the third estate. Now, in a crescendo of street disturbances, it was the turn of the Parisian lower classes: workers and apprentices, tradesmen and small shopkeepers. These were the sans-culottes—literally, "without knee breeches"—a name proudly adopted from the loose, long trousers the people wore, in contrast to the knee breeches of the wealthier classes. With the fall of the Bastille, Paris belonged briefly to the masses, for all semblance of royal authority over the city vanished. Many of the king's representatives fled; some were murdered. New revolutionary councils took their place, and a citizen militia—soon to be proclaimed as the new National Guard—enrolled itself to defend the Assembly.

As news of the uprising spread along the great royal roads from the capital, provincial towns followed the Parisian example. The countryside, too, where the overwhelming majority of the French population lived, was in wild upheaval: In many areas, peasants marched on the country houses of their aristocratic landlords, burning records of debts and feudal obligations (and occasionally the houses and the landlords themselves). The royal army was itself affected, and few units could be counted on to be reliable.

In the meantime, the Assembly's debates lived up to the excitement of the hour. On August 4, the nobles themselves proposed the abolition of most of their own privileges; and on August 26, the Assembly—now calling itself the Constituent Assembly and charging itself with the creation of a new constitution—issued its resounding Declaration of the Rights of Man and Citizen. "Men are born and remain free and equal in rights," read its first article. The declaration asserted in addition that "The source of all sovereignty lies essentially in the Nation"; Louis thenceforth would be king not of France but of the French people, his power held in strict check by constitutional law.

The declaration was a great step forward for France. The ideas it expounded were not new—rather they were a summation of the thinking of eighteenth-century, even seventeenth-century, philosophers. But it marked the definitive passing of the Ancien Régime, and it was greeted by almost universal enthusiasm—not only in France, and not only by the poor and dispossessed—for written large among the Rights of Man was the sacred and inviolable right to property. The declaration, in fact, offered a

141

The comte de Mirabeau, writer, died 1791.

Jean-Paul Marat, journalist, murdered 1793.

Georges-Jacques Danton, lawyer, guillotined 1794.

The elegant coats and cravats of the leading Revolutionaries, pictured above and opposite, reveal their wearers' middle- and upper-class origins. Two of the most prominent radicals actually came from the aristocracy—Honoré-Gabriel Riqueti, comte de Mirabeau *(above)* and Louis-Philippe-Joseph, duc d'Orléans *(fourth from left)*, who changed his name to Philippe Égalité, or Equality, in keeping with the spirit of the Revolution. But impeccable republican credentials provided little protection for these luminaries, most of whom were consumed by the revolution they had helped to ignite.

template for a constitutional monarchy in which middle-class property owners—who made up the majority of the National Assembly's delegates—could be sure to thrive. The king himself withheld his assent for the declaration, but most of the nobility accepted it willingly enough: Although their feudal rights were lost forever, their property was secure. Nobles who did not accept it either plotted quietly or slipped away into exile.

But there was another class of person altogether, on whom the Revolution had already depended and upon whom it would find itself depending once more—the propertyless sans-culottes, the urban poor of Paris, whose hopes were as high as their bellies were empty. The sans-culottes, too, cheered the declaration, at least for the time being. In October, however, they showed the Assembly that they were not necessarily under its control.

Louis, isolated from Parisian turmoil in Versailles, ten miles away, was tardy in signing certain articles of the developing constitution; a rumor spread that he and his queen had shown contempt for the Revolution at a banquet given for ultraroyalist officers; and flour, as always, was in catastrophically short supply. A housewives' demonstration demanding bread turned into a protest march to Versailles, and by the following morning, 20,000 Parisians had gathered around the royal palace. A few of them broke into the royal apartments, killing some guards. Queen Marie Antoinette managed a narrow escape. The crowd insisted that the royal family return with them to Paris. Units of the National Guard failed to restore order, and Louis yielded. Surrounded by an enormous procession of the poor people of Paris, with a helpless escort of National Guardsmen and his own disarmed bodyguards, the king set off to make his new home in the Tuileries palace, following which all meetings of the Assembly took place in Paris. The so-called March of the Women had turned out to be much more than an admonition to Louis; it was a warning that the sans-culottes—the Paris mob to their enemies, the backbone of the Revolution to their friends—could be neither ignored nor easily managed.

In fact, the Revolution would always have to struggle with a kind of triangular tension. The middle-class men of property who were its leaders needed the support of the urban poor, who were its driving force; but too many concessions to the sans-culottes would eliminate the comfortable social position to which they aspired and which they had in large measure gained. As a counterbalance to both groups, the

The duc d'Orléans, guillotined 1793.

Jacques Brissot, writer, guillotined 1793.

Camille Desmoulins, lawyer, guillotined 1794.

Maximilien Robespierre, lawyer, guillotined 1794.

Louis de Saint-Just, lawyer, guillotined 1794.

great, unseen majority of the peasantry had achieved its own purpose—land reform and the end of feudal obligations—in the first few weeks and had then returned to its traditional conservatism. For assembly-hall politician and street democrat alike, the peasantry was hard to reach, and even harder to radicalize; it would remain a potential source of support for reaction and counterrevolution.

Within the Assembly itself, clear factions were developing. There were no formal parties, but the Revolution had already coined the useful shorthand terms "left" and "right," based on the fact that the more radical deputies grouped together on the left-hand side of the president, whose job it was to chair the Assembly's debates.

Outside the Assembly's debating chamber, a number of recently formed clubs became centers of political activity. Of these, the most influential was the Jacobin Club, so called from its meeting place in the former monastery of the Dominicans of Saint James. Despite the club's radical views, its members were, in general, respectable middle-class professional men who could afford to pay its high subscription fees. They included assemblymen, the most notable of whom was Maximilien Robespierre, deputy from Arras and a successful lawyer, a seemingly emotionless man always impeccably dressed and famously incorruptible. All the club's members thought of themselves as an idealistic elite who could be relied upon to save France. It was an attractive sentiment, and Jacobin clubs by the thousand sprang up throughout the provinces, owing allegiance in general to the parent organization in Paris: It would not be long before the Jacobin Club was as powerful as any other group in the new Revolutionary state.

Constant political ferment was virtually guaranteed by the extraordinary expansion of the press. The first daily newspaper in Paris had appeared as late as 1779; in 1789 alone, with the Revolutionary abolition of censorship, more than 130 new titles were launched, and two years later, the number was around 600. On the extreme left, Jean-Paul Marat's *L'Ami du Peuple* and Jacques-René Hébert's *Le Père Duchesne* used violent and often obscene language to vilify endless and ill-defined enemies of the Revolution; the Jacobin papers were slightly more moderate. Even the king had his defenders among the journalists.

But for all the debate, as the 1790s began, it seemed the Revolution had either achieved or was achieving its main goals. The Assembly worked with a legislative energy unparalleled in French history, reorganizing the country's administration,

From open windows and flagstoned streets, angry Parisians turn their guns on the defenders of the Bastille fortress, as depicted in a crude drawing made by Claude Cholat, a wineshop keeper who took part in the triumphant assault on July 14, 1789. Cholat later received the title of Conqueror of the Bastille, an official honor accorded to 954 of the people who took part in the attack, of whom the youngest was a boy of eight and the oldest a man of seventy-two. Two days after the Bastille's fall, demolition experts moved in, and the fortress that had embodied the autocratic power of the French monarchy was razed. Its bricks were turned into miniature Bastille models and sold as souvenirs.

introducing the beginnings of a modern educational system, and completely overhauling the judiciary. The confused Ancien Régime structure of widely disparate provinces was replaced by a patchwork of eighty-three approximately equal *départements,* inside which scores of new communes—under elected town councils and each with its own small unit of the National Guard—were the basic unit of government. Legal reforms abolished torture and established jury trial in a clear hierarchy of courts and appeal courts presided over by independent judges who were guaranteed security of tenure. The national finances were set in order: All internal customs barriers were swept away, and in place of the gross unfairness and inefficiency of the Ancien Régime's fiscal system, new, easily administered taxes on land, per-

sonal property, and commercial income ensured that every citizen contributed according to his ability to pay.

To meet the government's desperate need for ready cash, the Church's huge landholdings were seized and used as backing for certificates theoretically redeemable against the purchase of the newly nationalized land. A certificate served as a kind of instant currency that paid off the national debt and eased the financial crisis the Revolution had inherited.

For the most part, the Church accepted its losses with equanimity, particularly since the government agreed to provide financial support for clergymen and took over most of the charitable works, including care of the poor, which ecclesiastical lands had ostensibly existed to pay for. But the next stage, the 1790 Civil Constitution of the Clergy, caused an uproar. By its terms, bishops and parish priests were to be elected by secular committees, and only clergymen who took an oath of loyalty to the new constitution might continue to hold religious services. The pope retaliated by suspending all priests who accepted the new arrangements; the outcome was not only a deep division inside the Church but a dangerous level of discontent in France's most strongly Catholic regions.

The long-awaited national constitution, finally promulgated in September 1791, summarized the Revolution's achievements. Much influenced by the example of the new United States, it carefully delineated the separation of power between the legislature, judiciary, and executive branches of government. Full civil rights were accorded to every French citizen. A modest property qualification gave the vote to most adult males. The assembly they would elect had full legislative power, but executive control remained with the king, who was deprived of a permanent veto but given the right, as in Britain at the time, to appoint his own ministers. The transition from absolute to constitutional monarchy was now complete.

Moderate, rational, and derived in large measure from the experience of other nations, the constitution was the blueprint for precisely the kind of state envisaged by the middle-class delegates who had assembled in Paris in 1789. Yet even before it came to a vote, constitutional monarchy in France was dealt a fatal blow—by the king and queen themselves. In June 1791, the royal family—increasingly fearful for their safety—attempted to disguise themselves and fled for the border by night. At Varennes, 140 miles from Paris, they were recognized and forcibly transported back to the capital, where their passage through the streets was observed by silent, hostile crowds. From that time on, Louis was little more than a prisoner in the Tuileries palace; it remained to be seen how well the new constitution could function without the cooperation of its head of state and chief executive.

The elections of October 1791 brought a left-wing majority, dominated for a time by the group of deputies from the Gironde, in southwest France, led by a former pamphleteer and restaurant-owner's son named Jacques-Pierre Brissot de Warville. In the beginning, there was little tension, despite the anomalous position of the king; and although there was much political debate, the new legislature seemed very much to be an assembly of France's most talented men, who could safely be entrusted with the care and maintenance of the Revolution.

France would need their talents. Beyond the borders there were ominous developments. The events in Paris had encouraged a revolt among provinces in the Austrian Netherlands. The Austrian emperor Leopold II was already alarmed at the treatment received by his sister, Marie Antoinette, and was rumored to be planning an armed response; together with the king of Prussia, Frederick William II, he issued a declaration calling upon other European monarchs to help restore the French monarchy. Émigré French aristocrats, many of them military officers, were also known to be urging foreign powers to action.

Many in the Legislative Assembly dreaded the combination of an outside invasion and an internal uprising by aristocrats who had remained in the country; a preemptive French attack seemed the best defense. Others, including Brissot, reckoned that a foreign war would help unite the nation behind the Revolution. True, France's armies were in disarray, with two-thirds of the old officer corps in exile. But the ideas of the Revolution would surely sweep all before them. As Brissot declared, "The picture of liberty, like the head of Medusa, will terrify the armies of our enemies."

Brissot had his way. Although Robespierre spoke out strongly against war, Brissot and his Gironde group were able to form a ministry in March of 1792; the following month, King Louis was persuaded to issue the formal declaration of war, and the Revolutionary armies marched into the Austrian Netherlands.

The result was disaster. The poorly trained French troops panicked at the first sight of the enemy and scurried homeward; the economy almost foundered under the strain of warfare, with food shortages and rising prices creating a dangerous climate of discontent. That summer, Charles William Ferdinand, duke of Brunswick, invaded France, leading the army of Austria's Prussian allies. The duke was a cautious general of the old school who moved slowly and with great deliberation. But nothing, it seemed, could stop him.

In a late-eighteenth-century engraving, country houses blaze and coaches speed their frightened owners to safety in the summer of 1789. Incidents like this occurred all over France as an outbreak of collective paranoia followed the government's collapse, fueled by food shortages and by rumors of invasion forces composed of outlaws, French aristocrats, and foreign troops coming to avenge the overthrow of the old order. Villagers armed themselves and attacked and looted the houses of the local gentry, burning the manorial rolls that detailed their feudal duties.

The summer of 1792 was the Revolution's greatest crisis so far. The Assembly declared a national emergency. Thousands of provincial National Guardsmen flocked to Paris, where they combined with the existing sans-culotte movement to create a popular force beyond the government's power to control. When the duke of Brunswick issued a proclamation threatening dire reprisals for any harm done to the French royal family, Paris was thrown into a state of alarm.

Radicals from the more militant districts forcibly took over the running of the capital from the municipal authorities. A heavily armed crowd descended upon the

Tuileries palace. The king's Swiss guards were casually slaughtered, and Louis and his family had to seek refuge in the Assembly itself, where they listened to a dramatic all-night debate that suspended the monarchy. This was the first decisive step in the king's ousting; his powers now passed to the Provisional Executive Council, in which the Girondists retained their ministry, but the new minister of justice was Georges-Jacques Danton, a Paris lawyer who had been a noted left-wing activist since the early days of the Revolution. Danton was a massive, sensual man, a lover of women and good food, and an inspiring orator with a notorious weakness for obscene language—a complete opposite of the icily calm Robespierre, who had more influence than any other man over the street fighters, but who for the time being chose to remain in the background.

Meanwhile, the invaders still advanced. In Paris, fear led to terrorism: Traitors, or so it was believed, were everywhere, and illegal mass roundups of suspects filled the jails. Unruly mobs of sans-culottes, not satisfied with the mere incarceration of their enemies, broke in and massacred more than 1,000 prisoners; there were more prison murders in the provinces.

While hastily mobilized new units of the National Guard marched off to the front, Danton rallied the country with some of the most memorable speeches in French history, and the Legislative Assembly agreed to dissolve itself. The Assembly was unmourned; it had proven itself incapable of governing in a crisis: Now, the National Convention was summoned. To be elected by full manhood suffrage, it would prepare a new and wholly republican constitution.

Yet the emergency that had destroyed the government, and with it the last hopes of a French constitutional monarchy, was almost over. As the unemployed deputies were returning to their homes, the armies of the Revolution won a momentous victory at Valmy, less than 100 miles from Paris. The battle was little more than a skirmish fought on a misty morning, with only a few hundred casualties. But it was decisive. Faced with a determined cannonade from republican troops under General Charles-François du Périer Dumouriez, the duke of Brunswick ordered his army to retreat.

The victory gave new heart to the Revolution. Its forces had faced the worst that the old order of Europe could throw against them, and they had held their ground. In fact, the great bulk of the French army was composed of former royalist regulars, but its composition did not diminish its moral triumph. The German poet Johann Wolfgang von Goethe, who had watched the fighting from the Austrian side, was in no doubt as to the battle's importance. "From this day and this place dates a new era in the history of the world," he told his companions. "Some day you will be able to say—I was there."

Fortified by the good news, the newly assembled convention set to work. Within days of the battle at Valmy, the suspect monarchy was formally abolished, and the foundations of republican France thereby laid. But it was not enough to change the institutions of government: Even the old calendar was scrapped. September 22, 1792, the date of the monarchy's abolition, became the first day of Year I of Liberty; and after a year of committee work, the reform went even further. Twelve new months, each divided into three *décades* of ten days, were created and given new and highly poetic names. For example, the rainy period between mid-January and mid-February became Pluviôse, the month of showers, while Thermidor and Fructidor were respectively the warmth-giving and fruit-bearing periods between mid-July and mid-September. The royal weights and measures went the same way as the Ancien

Régime's months. The foundations of a new metric system were laid, based on the gram and the meter—one ten-millionth of the inaccurately measured distance between Paris and the equator.

With the monarchy out of the way as an institution, there remained the problem of Citizen Capet—the name given to the deposed Louis XVI, whose ancestor, Hugh Capet, had become France's first king back in AD 987. Louis and his wife provided the solution. With the same lack of political sense they had displayed since the Revolution began, Louis and Marie Antoinette had been covertly canvassing military support from fellow monarchs and from French aristocrats who had fled the country. In November 1792, a secret iron closet containing Louis's correspondence was discovered in a wall of the Tuileries; the letters found inside the safe were innocuous enough, but the very fact of their concealment gave Louis's enemies the opportunity they had been waiting for. In December, he was put on trial before the Convention. The charge against him was treason.

The legal and constitutional issues involved were complex, and Louis's guilt, in the judicial sense, was far from clear. But guilt and innocence were of small importance: The trial was an act of republican politics, not of law. France was surrounded by enemy armies, and there were rumblings of internal dissent. The new republican government had to show foreigners and Frenchmen alike that the Revolution would be defended. By an almost unanimous vote, the ex-king was found guilty.

Even so, many deputies shrank from regicide, the next logical step. The Girondist group of deputies argued passionately for clemency, but after an all-night meeting on January 20, 1793, a small Convention majority condemned Louis to die the next day beneath the blade of the guillotine—the killing machine the Revolution's early reformers had adopted as a humane means of execution.

The machine was set up in the Place de la Révolution, formerly named after Louis's grandfather, Louis XV. On the gray, drizzling morning of January 21, Citizen Capet was driven slowly through silent crowds to the drumbeat of his National Guard escort. From the scaffold he addressed his people for the last time. "I die innocent and I forgive," he said. "I pardon my enemies and pray that my blood will be of service to France, that it will appease God's anger." He tried to say more, but a hastily ordered drumroll hid his words, and a few moments later the blade fell.

The executioner held the king's severed head for all to see. "Long live the Republic," thundered the crowd. "Long live freedom! Long live equality!" There would be no turning back.

The king's execution provoked a wave of outraged protest from the governments of Europe; if one crowned head could so easily be removed from its shoulders, the others could hardly rest easy. And the Convention's leaders were in no mood for conciliation. In January, Danton pronounced that the people should fight to expand France's territories to their natural frontiers: the Alps, the Pyrenees, the Rhine, and the Mediterranean. In rapid succession, the Convention declared war on Britain, Holland, and Spain. Revolutionary armies flooded outward from France's borders, determined not only to seize those natural frontiers but also to fulfill their government's promise to give "fraternal help to all peoples who want to recover their liberty." For a few brief weeks they seemed unstoppable.

But France's enemies had begun to regain some of their nerve, and the poorly

A contemporary engraving shows choirs of Parisians hymning the Supreme Being from an artificial mountain, at a festival in the Champs de Mars on June 8, 1794.

A radical's inkwell comprises a red bonnet, symbol of the Revolution, crushing a cleric, symbol of reactionary thought.

The anticlerical thrust of the Revolution created deep divisions throughout France. In July 1790, the National Assembly passed a law requiring all clergymen to be elected by secular assemblies instead of being appointed by the Church. Those clerics who refused to recognize this law were stripped of their posts. Three years later, the Parisian authorities closed all churches and the Assembly abolished religious holidays.

However, these measures caused offense to believers and provided a focus for opposition to the Revolution. For this reason, the radical leader Maximilien Robespierre compromised in 1794 by creating the cult of the Supreme Being, a republican deity that embodied civic virtue and opposition to tyranny.

THE CHURCH USURPED

trained Revolutionary levies began to suffer defeat after defeat. In frustration, Dumouriez, the victor at Valmy, deserted to the Austrians and their British allies. Worse still, civil war broke out at home. The staunchly Roman Catholic peasants of the western region of the Vendée had always resented the Civil Constitution of the Clergy, which had outlawed the priests they most trusted; now they were spurred to revolt by attempts to conscript their sons to defend the revolution they disliked. In Bordeaux, Nantes, Lyons, Marseilles, and other provincial cities, discontent boiled over into insurrection. The crisis marked the start of what was to be known as the Reign of Terror. It put the nation on a war footing. A fearful government now saw political opposition as treason.

Then in March, as the fighting in the Vendée began, the Revolutionary Tribunal was set up to sniff out traitors. In April, the powers of government began to pass into the hands of the newly created Committee of Public Safety. Led at first by Danton, the Committee rapidly developed into a kind of collective dictatorship, ruthlessly determined to wage war against all enemies of the Revolution inside and outside of France.

Even as the Revolution was being defended, though, the Convention's factions were locked in a struggle for its control. The Girondists, blamed for military defeat and economic failure alike, soon fell: Backed by rioting and near-rebellion from the Parisian sans-culottes, the Jacobins were able to force the arrest of Brissot and his supporters early in the month of June. The Jacobin purge continued, and by July, Danton and his supporters, once considered to the left of the Jacobin mainstream, had lost their places on the Committee of Public Safety, which was now dominated by the extremist wing of the Assembly under the general leadership of Robespierre.

As a machine capable of winning wars, the Committee proved to be extremely effective. Conscription was increased, at least outside the disaffected areas; a levy of heretofore-unheard-of dimensions during August gave France a force of 650,000 men. As before, many came from the Revolution's own National Guard and brought their radical fervor with them; and these new soldiers, although at first disorganized and badly

A contemporary illustration of republican playing cards demonstrates the penetration of Revolutionary ideals into French society. The traditional four jacks in the pack have been replaced by equalities *(right column)* of duty, rights, rank, and race. In the adjoining column, the queens have become freedoms of the arts, marriage, the press, and the professions; and in the column second from left, the kings are spirits of war, peace, the arts, and commerce. The aces have become laws. Citizen Bonhomme, an aristocrat turned Revolutionary, designed these cards after the execution of King Louis, at a time when eradication of references to all things royal had become a preoccupation among republicans.

The serenity of Queen Marie Antoinette, surrounded by her children in a painting by Élisabeth Vigée-Lebrun, contrasts shockingly with her haggard appearance during the last weeks of her life, as recorded *(inset)* by the portraitist Sophie Prieur just seven years later. Popular hostility during the Revolution had focused more on the Austrian-born queen than on her husband Louis, providing fertile ground for rumors of her alleged extravagance, treason, and even incest. When she followed Louis to the guillotine at the age of thirty-seven, her elder son Louis Joseph *(standing by crib)* had died of tuberculosis, and she had been forcibly separated from both her daughter Marie Thérèse *(standing)* and her younger son Louis Charles *(on her lap)*.

supplied, greatly outnumbered the small professional armies that were invading France.

One by one, the foreigners and their émigré aristocrat supporters were pushed back across the borders. Marseilles and Lyons fell to Revolutionary troops. And although royalists handed the port of Toulon to the encroaching British, it was recaptured in December 1793: Readers of official dispatches noted that republican success was attributable in large measure to an unknown Corsican artillery officer, a strong Jacobin supporter named Napoleon Buonaparte.

In the meantime, the Revolutionary Tribunal worked overtime. The Law of Suspects, passed in September, packed the nation's jails with counterrevolutionaries. And as what was called the Great Terror ran its course, the definition of counterrevolutionary grew steadily less discriminating. Aristocrats and returned émigrés were obvious targets, as were republican generals who had suffered defeat. Of those who went to the guillotine, some died as tragic figures: Marie Antoinette endured a

151

EXPORTING THE RADICAL MESSAGE

Fired by Revolutionary zeal, France's ruling Assembly dispatched troops in 1792 to free its neighbors from autocratic monarchy. But the people of the Austrian Netherlands and the Rhineland perceived the would-be liberators as atheist invaders and joined their Austrian and Prussian rulers in resisting. The French offensive rallied opposition to the Revolution both abroad, among those who sought to repel its forces, and at home, among those who wanted to restore the power of the king and the Church. Gradually, the war became a matter not just of aggression but also of defense, as the Revolutionaries fought to stave off a counterattack from the monarchies they themselves were assailing. To meet the growing threat, the Assembly stepped up recruitment by declaring a national emergency and later introducing mass conscription. By 1794, more than one million men were fighting in the armies of the republic.

A royalist soldier's badge links a cross, symbolizing Christianity, with a heart, symbolizing the monarchy. Support for the king and Church centered in western France, in the Vendée, but was crushed by a republican army in 1793.

An illustrated song sheet bears the words of the "Marseillaise," a stirring marching song brought to Paris in July 1792 by volunteers from Marseilles, responding to the Revolutionary government's appeal for troops.

slanderous trial with great dignity before being led to execution in October of 1793. Some of the accused were simply pathetic: Madame du Barry, middle-aged former mistress of Louis XVI's grandfather, had to be dragged, screaming, to the scaffold. Aristocrats, however, were only a minority of the Terror's victims. Records were not always well kept, but around 85 percent of the 35,000 people who were executed were probably commoners.

The Revolution found its most conspicuous victims among those who had themselves created it. The Girondist deputies went to the scaffold shortly after Marie Antoinette. Those who had helped put Robespierre in power found to their surprise that they, too, were dangerous counterrevolutionaries: The guillotine claimed them in March 1794. Danton and his group followed within a week: "Show my head to the people," he told the executioner. "They don't see one like it every day."

In the provinces, the Convention sent out its most trusted deputies, some of them traveling with portable guillotines. The defeat of the Vendée rebels in December 1793 brought a terrible republican revenge. There were shootings and beheadings throughout the countryside, and at Nantes, approximately 2,000 people were systematically drowned.

Meanwhile, the man at the center of the Terror, Robespierre, devoted much time to organizing an extraordinary spectacle: the Festival of the Supreme Being. It was an extreme example of the anticlericalism—and anti-Christianity—that had always been a powerful force in the Revolution. With the painter Jacques-Louis David in charge of props and stage management, the Tuileries palace was transformed into a classical amphitheater. The high point of the ceremony came in June 1794, when Robespierre himself ritually ignited a huge papier-mâché monument representing the enemies of happiness; from the ashes arose a scantily clad actress as Wisdom, come to invite the participants to give their homage to the Author of Nature.

At the time of the festival, the Supreme Being appeared due for some thanks. Belgium had been recaptured from the Allies, and France had clearly passed through its period of greatest danger. Yet the Terror raged more fiercely than before, especially in Paris itself. At Robespierre's insistence, a new law obliged revolutionary tribunals—where justice was already almost nonexistent—to choose only between death and acquittal; and in June and July of 1794, a total of 1,376 enemies of the people were executed in Paris, more than in the entire previous year.

From this point on, a sort of nausea of the guillotine set in, and Robespierre and his faction were no longer able to count on the support of the street mobs. No one felt safe, least of all the surviving Convention deputies and the other members of the Committee of Public Safety itself.

On July 26—Thermidor 8, according to the Revolutionary calendar—Robespierre finally overreached himself. Speaking before the already guillotine-depleted Convention, he demanded yet another far-reaching purge of its deputies, in a bid to eradicate the enemies of the republic. The next day, the Convention turned against him: Its members, conscious that they were voting for their necks, ordered Robespierre's arrest. There followed a disordered night in the streets of Paris, but the turn of events had taken Robespierre by surprise, and forces loyal to the Convention were able to suppress his disorganized supporters. He himself was shot through the jaw, perhaps in a suicide attempt. In the morning, he was carted, in great pain, to the guillotine to which he had sent so many others. Within days, his entire faction had followed him there, and the Great Terror was at an end.

For the first time since the death of the king, the guillotine was almost idle. A few more extremists were executed, but the Revolutionary Tribunal was steadily divested of its powers and eventually abolished. Among the condemned radicals were some of the tribunal's own servants, including the former public prosecutor and the more bloodthirsty of the deputies who had brought massacre to the provinces. In general, the new regime preferred the so-called dry guillotine—exile to the unhealthy colony of French Guiana. For the most part, France breathed a sigh of collective relief. The Terror had burned itself out.

From that point on, the primary goal of the government was not to further extend the Revolution, but simply to preserve the gains it had already made—that is, its gains as perceived by the property-owning victors of the Thermidor coup. Much of the work had already been completed. The great armies created by the iron-handed Committee of Public Safety were now well established outside France's 1789 borders, and the allies were in disarray; most auspicious of all, military success meant that the cost of French troops was borne by the lands they occupied, not by the strained Revolutionary economy. Inside France, though, there were still plenty of internal enemies. Despite the great swaths cut by the Terror, there were enough surviving aristocrats—and enough royalist sentiment—to make a right-wing coup a real possibility. More dangerous still was the growing discontent of the old sans-culotte movement, especially since the Thermidorians had responded to commercial pressure by putting an end to the Terror's price-control system, which guaranteed cheap bread. Chronic food shortages and the ever-increasing cost of living kept the Paris poor constantly on the verge of riot.

According to the Thermidorians, the Revolution was virtually over. But they were rapidly learning that it could not be turned off like a faucet. That spring, the army had to be called out to put down violent demonstrations by civilians and National Guardsmen alike. Unrest simmered throughout the capital.

The government's search for stability led to the Constitution of the Year III—the third constitution since 1791. Far less democratic than its 1793 predecessor, it withdrew the right of universal suffrage, allowing only the propertied classes the right to vote; a two-tiered assembly, elected annually, was to select five directors who would wield executive power. To the sans-culottes and the former Jacobins—their clubs had been abolished the previous year—it was a betrayal, and the mood of discontent gave the country's conservatives the chance they had been waiting for. Tremendous crowds, drawn primarily from the more prosperous parts of Paris, assembled to protest against the Convention's obvious attempts to ensure itself a clear two-thirds majority in the Assembly.

The government reacted vigorously. Artillery was assembled under the command of the up-and-coming Buonaparte, who was now one of France's youngest generals. With cannon and musket fire, he dispersed the mob, leaving several hundred people dead and wounded. The massacre confirmed the Directory as the supreme authority in France—and it demonstrated the Directory's resolve to maintain its position. From that time on, there was no doubt in anyone's mind that the new government was prepared to turn its guns on its own people.

In fact, the Directory endured only a little more than four years. It was not the most inspiring period in the annals of the Revolution: As an adjective, the name Directoire would be associated with extravagant women's fashions and highly decorative fur-

THE TERROR

"Oh Liberty, what crimes are committed in your name," cried Madame Jeanne-Manon Roland, a celebrated radical intellectual, as she was led to the guillotine on November 8, 1793. Accused of antirevolutionary activities, she became yet another victim of the wave of arrests and executions that had begun that spring and came to be known as the Reign of Terror.

No one was safe; fallen politicians, generals, even nuns were taken. Some of the worst excesses took place in the provinces: At Nantes, 2,000 alleged royalists were drowned in one day.

During the winter of 1793-1794, approximately 35,000 people were executed. June 10, 1794, saw the passing of a law that denied a defense to the accused and effectively made rumor sufficient evidence for conviction. In Paris alone, 1,376 people died during the seven weeks of this, the Great Terror.

Ironically, its end was marked by the guillotining on July 28 of its principal architect, Maximilien Robespierre. His head was stuck on a pole, where it provided a model for a waxwork (above) by the Parisian sculptress Madame Marie Tussaud, who took it with her when she moved to London in 1802.

(right) depicts an anthology of punishments carried out by the Revolutionary authorities. In every French town and in many villages, committees such as the one pictured below carried out their functions of inquiry, vigilance, and supervision, ordering arrests where deemed necessary. Revolutionary tribunals would then decide the fate of those brought to trial; if condemned to death, the instrument of their execution was most likely to be the guillotine (far right), the most humane means of dispatch. The diagonal blade of this device was designed to slice cleanly through the neck of the victim, who was tied face down to the wooden bench below. Death by beheading had previously been a prerogative of the aristocracy alone, until a Parisian politician by the name of Dr. Joseph-Ignace Guillotin pressed successfully for it to become the standard method of execution.

A painting by Antoine-Jean Gros dated November 1796 shows a dashing young Napoleon Bonaparte at the Battle of Arcole, in northern Italy, where he led the French army to victory over the Austrians. The ambitious son of a Corsican notary, Napoleon had risen to the rank of brigadier general by the age of twenty-four, approaching each military assignment with single-mindedness and sometimes ruthlessness. With characteristic disregard for political convention, he followed up his Italian victories by negotiating his own peace treaty with the defeated Austrians.

niture, not the forging of a nation's destiny. It was also the period of the *jeunesse dorée*, the gilded youth who ostentatiously displayed and spent the wealth its fathers had managed to acquire even during the stern days of the Terror. For the poor, it was a time of great hardship, without the redeeming sense of Revolutionary struggle that had helped them endure the even harder years they had just passed through.

The Directory could claim some genuine achievements. At the time it came to power, billions of the certificates backed by the Church-owned lands seized in 1790 were still in circulation, though almost worthless; they were replaced first by another land-based certificate, then, in 1797, by traditional banknotes that were backed by the government's gold holdings.

A great deal of that gold came from success in war, which the Revolutionary armies were learning to turn into a profitable enterprise. Captured or extorted bullion flowed into France's treasuries from the Netherlands, from the Rhineland, and especially from the Austrian territories of northern Italy, where, in 1796, General Bonaparte—he had dropped the Corsican, un-French "u" from his name—had begun a brilliant campaign.

In fact, the Directory's military efforts were almost everywhere crowned with success, in part at least because of the most efficient system of conscription in Europe. A plan to guarantee French security by creating a ring of satellite republics around the nation's borders—in Switzerland as well as in Italy and the Netherlands—was well under way; an English attempt to land émigré troops in Brittany was crushed, and with it a final royalist rising in the Vendée.

The military, however, would be the new rulers' undoing. The Directory was never truly popular, and throughout its tenure, it had to resist attempts from both left and right to seize power. The army's help became indispensable, but it came at a price. For the Directory introduced the generals to politics, and thenceforth the military coup d'état became a part of French political life.

The first plot against the new regime came in 1796. The so-called Conspiracy of the Equals was organized by a pamphleteer with the improbable name of Gracchus Babeuf. But he was no real threat. The Directory's police force was able to penetrate Babeuf's plot at an early stage, and he was arrested; almost as an afterthought, he was guillotined a year later.

Much more serious were the events that occurred during 1797 and 1798. Elections had increased the number of conservatives in the five-man Directory to two, and the three republicans asked for Bonaparte's aid to rectify the situation. The Corsican by now was clearly France's leading general, not only winning victories but even putting into action his own foreign policy: His 1797 treaty with Austria had set a diplomatic seal on his Italian victories. But Bonaparte possessed caution to match his ambition. Keeping himself distant—for the moment—from Parisian turmoils, he sent an able subordinate, Pierre-François-Charles Augereau, who used locally based troops to supervise purges of both the Directory and the Assembly—where a similar shift to the right had taken place—until a satisfactory republican majority was all that remained.

It was a bad precedent. When the following year's elections produced an assembly that this time was too republican for the directors' tastes, they used their military support to annul the results in more than 100 constituencies. Predictably, the 1799 elections brought a similar crisis; once more, the directors in power used arrest and forced dismissal to maintain the existing order. But the status quo was becoming steadily less comfortable: Great Britain, France's only surviving enemy the previous year, had organized another major coalition. Many doubted the Directory's ability to wage successful war against it.

At this point, Bonaparte seized his long-awaited opportunity. Since the 1798 coup, he had been campaigning in Egypt, in the first stage of an ambitious attempt to seize India. But although he was victorious on land, the British navy destroyed his fleet, leaving his army sick and stranded among the pyramids. The troubled political situation back home gave him a chance to cut his Egyptian losses. He reached southern France in October 1799 and was given a conqueror's welcome as well as an invitation to join the Directory's latest internal conspiracy.

This time he accepted. The five-man Directory would be replaced by three consuls, including, as a reward for services rendered, General Bonaparte. And when, in November, the Jacobins in the lower assembly refused to accept the abrogation of the constitution, they were driven from their chamber by Bonaparte's troops. A few hours later, a handful of less recalcitrant deputies was persuaded to give some sort of assent, and therefore at least a semblance of legality, to the changes. But the bayonets remained, and their message was unmistakable: Not just the unlamented Directory but the Revolution itself was finally at an end.

There was remarkably little opposition. After a decade of upheaval, the yearning for order and authority was almost tangible. Within a few weeks, Bonaparte had established himself as the master of his nation—buttressed by a new and highly authoritarian constitution that a plebiscite of his weary fellow citizens backed almost unanimously. Within four years, as Napoleon I, Bonaparte was wearing an imperial crown. Throats that had yelled themselves hoarse crying the words of the old Revolutionary slogan *Liberté! égalité! fraternité!* were now shouting "Long live the Emperor!" with just as much enthusiasm. It was as if the Bastille had never fallen, the guillotine had never existed.

Had it been worth it? Certainly the Revolution had failed to transform its early idealism into the political paradise on earth of which so many of its supporters had dreamed. But the changes it had brought, despite the betrayals and the massacres, were far-reaching and permanent. First, French men and women were for the most part better off materially, and freed forever from the arbitrary moils of the Ancien Régime. Social and political relationships were not immutable: A determined people could change them whenever it had the will. The relationship between rulers and the ruled would never be the same again, and neither party would ever forget it. For the Revolution had happened, and could happen again.

Outside France, the example of even a flawed revolution was a reminder to the rest of Europe, an encouragement to the oppressed, and a warning to the oppressors. It had been an enormous test-bed for social and political ideas from which future revolutionaries—and counterrevolutionaries, too—could draw practical lessons. Time and again over the next two centuries, some or all of these ideas would be put into practice. Sometimes they would succeed and sometimes fail; but the world had clearly entered a new age.

THE INDUSTRIAL DAWN

The Age of Enlightenment saw men probing into practical matters with as much energy as they employed questioning political and spiritual assumptions. All over Europe, thinkers sought new ways around old problems, but it was in Britain that this creativity was first put to commercial use on a large scale. There, before the century was out, manufacturers found a way to smelt iron ore using cheap coal instead of costly charcoal; others harnessed the power of steam to drive machines previously dependent either on the limited muscle power of man or beast or on the unpredictable forces of wind or water. As the innovations were put to use, Britain's small handicraft workshops gave way to mass-production factories.

This technological revolution came about not only through the inventiveness of individuals but also through the favorable economic and political climate that Britain enjoyed. The new industrialists were enterprising private businessmen with a vested interest in developing new technology that would increase output and cut costs. Unlike their European rivals, they went about their business unhindered by domestic war or revolution and unfettered by government restraints. In France, by contrast, the state not only ran its own subsidized factories but also kept tight control over privately owned ventures, and was supported in its restrictive role by powerful but uni-maginative trade guilds. And whereas rigid class divisions—and even serfdom—still existed in some European countries, Britain boasted a large middle class with both the money and the taste for new products.

At the beginning, the new inventions wrought only small-scale changes on the face of Britain: A 1777 painting *(above)* shows Abraham Darby's pioneering ironworks in an otherwise untouched Shropshire countryside. Few people realized at the time that these piecemeal advances were the beginning of a vast mechanization process that would sweep across western Europe and eventually become known as the Industrial Revolution.

In an 1814 illustration from a book entitled *The Costume of Yorkshire,* a young woman uses a traditional, single-spindle wheel to spin yarn, while an older woman winds the finished product into skeins. By the time this illustration appeared, the wheel had been largely superseded by smaller versions of the spinning jenny pictured on the right. However, the wheel was still used for producing the strong, hard, twisted thread that was needed for the warp of wool fabric.

The industrial pioneer Richard Arkwright exudes prosperity in a 1790 portrait. A former traveling barber, Arkwright sits by a model of his water frame, a machine that not only produced a strong yarn but also achieved fine quality by first stretching the raw cotton through a series of rollers.

A portent of change in rural Derbyshire, Richard Arkwright's Cromford cotton mill stands beside the watercourse that powers its machines. The mill, which opened in 1771, operated continuously, keeping hundreds of workers at their machines in a succession of shifts. Such a concentration of labor and large-scale machinery, unusual for the time, illustrates Arkwright's quick grasp of the economic potential of mass production.

In the last three decades of the century, a series of inventions brought radical changes to the process of producing cloth. Up until the 1770s, it had required as many as ten spinners, each using a single-spindle wheel, to keep one weaver supplied with thread. James Hargreaves's spinning jenny, with between 8 and 120 spindles, greatly increased one machine's output, as did Samuel Crompton's mule, which produced a fine but strong yarn.

The first effect of the new technology was that the home-based spinners who took in work from clothiers and merchants began replacing their wheels with jennies. Next, local entrepreneurs started to install mules in small-scale workshops. Finally, Richard Arkwright's water frame—a machine that produced a sturdier yarn than did the jenny—turned spinning once and for all into an industrial rather than a domestic process. Arkwright not only adapted the water frame so that it could be powered automatically, first by water and later by steam, but he also took out a patent, which allowed it to be used only as a large-scale factory machine. By the late 1790s, the mule and the water frame—and the factory system—dominated cotton spinning.

The established wool industry in Yorkshire adapted slowly to the new methods, partly because of its own conservatism and partly because woolen fiber was less suited to machine working than cotton fiber. Rival and hitherto less successful manufacturers in Lancashire now seized the opportunity to take advantage of the new technology and to diversify into cotton.

Crowds of black-hatted merchants and clothiers compare quality and prices in an 1814 illustration of a Yorkshire cloth-trading hall. Production of all textiles flourished in the eighteenth century, but cotton experienced an unmatched rate of growth.

During the first sixty years, the average yearly increase in output was just 1.3 percent, but in the following decades that figure surged upward, peaking at 12.7 percent between 1780 and 1790.

Cheapside

HARNESSING THE EARTH'S RESOURCES

The finding of new ways to use nature's resources made a crucial contribution to the early Industrial Revolution. In 1700, Britain possessed vast reserves of coal, which until that time had been used only as a domestic fuel; if used in a smelting furnace, coal's impurities—particularly sulfur—made the finished iron too brittle. In 1709, Abraham Darby devised a means of extracting the impurities by heating the coal in airtight conditions; the resulting coke provided a cheap alternative to charcoal. The break with charcoal became complete in 1784 when Henry Cort perfected a coal-fired furnace that could remove the impurities from crude pig iron to create wrought iron, a purer and more malleable form of the metal.

Earlier in the century, Thomas Newcomen had achieved another remarkable breakthrough with the invention of his atmospheric engine, later improved upon by James Watt, who successfully harnessed steam. Both engines were used to pump water, but Watt's also provided a direct power source for rotating machinery.

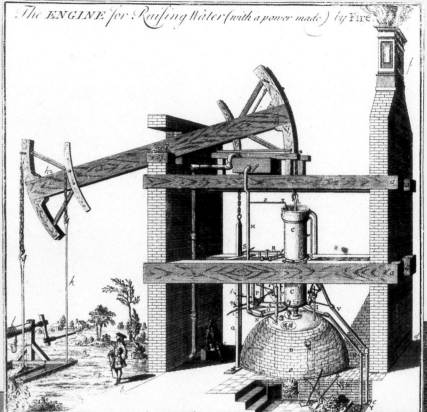

The ENGINE for Raising Water (with a power made) by Fire

In an engraving *(top)*, flames heat water in a Newcomen pump's hemispherical boiler. The steam would rise into a cylinder (C) and condense when cold water was poured in, creating a vacuum, which pulled down a piston at the right-hand end of a wooden beam. The reintroduction of steam released it, sending the left-hand piston down into the water-filled mine shaft. A 1788 aquatint *(above)* shows a pumping machine in action at a Welsh mine.

In a painting executed soon after its completion in 1780, a horse and coach hurry across the iron bridge at Coalbrookdale, in Shropshire. This was the world's first iron bridge, its construction made economical by the availability of iron made cheaply in coke-fired furnaces. Built under the aegis of noted ironmasters John Wilkinson and Abraham Darby III, the five-rib, single-span bridge was cast at Darby's nearby ironworks. Measuring 100 feet in length and 45 feet in height, the bridge took three years to assemble.

A mid-eighteenth-century painting of Backbarrow Furnace in Yorkshire shows ironworkers filling molds with molten metal *(center)*, carried from a glowing furnace, which is still fired by charcoal. Although coke had fueled furnaces at Coalbrookdale for more than thirty years when this picture was painted, charcoal was the most commonly used industrial fuel until the second half of the century.

A 1758 panorama of Abraham Darby's Coalbrookdale ironworks presents a picture of thriving industry: In the foreground, a team of horses departs to deliver a new cast-iron steam-engine cylinder. Plumes of smoke rise from heaps of coal that are being converted into coke.

In a contemporary engraving *(right)*, the duke of Bridgewater points proudly to the Barton Aqueduct *(depicted below in a colored engraving)*, which carries a section of his Worsley-to-Manchester canal over the Irwell River. Most canal enterprises were financed by industrialists who would benefit from faster, more efficient transportation. The pottery magnate Josiah Wedgwood helped to finance a canal linking the Trent and Mersey rivers and opened a new factory, which he named Etruria, on a site near the proposed canal. To mark the factory's opening day (June 13, 1769), Wedgwood molded with his own hands six vases, one of which *(inset)* is shown here.

JUNE XIII .M.DCC.LXIX.
One of the first Days Productions
at
Etruria in Staffordshire
by
Wedgwood and Bentley.

BUILDING A NETWORK OF WATERWAYS

Finding the roads too bad and the rivers not always conveniently located, the new entrepreneurs created an extensive network of canals in order to transport raw materials and finished products to the areas where they were needed. A Roman introduction to Britain, man-made waterways had aroused scant interest until they were championed by Francis Egerton, duke of Bridgewater. In 1759, he commissioned a twelve-mile-long canal, which went straight from his Worsley coal mines to the city of Manchester; the consequent savings on transportation costs halved the price of coal in northern England and initiated a flurry of waterway construction. By 1800, approximately 3,000 miles of canals had been built in Britain.

Two nineteenth-century engravings depict the pioneering engineer Thomas Telford *(right)* and his masterpiece, the Pontcysyllte Aqueduct in North Wales. Soaring more than 120 feet above the Dee River and anchored on pillars of masonry, the majestic structure carried the Shropshire Union Canal across the valley in a 1,007-foot-long trough of iron. Construction work took ten years: The aqueduct opened on November 26, 1805.

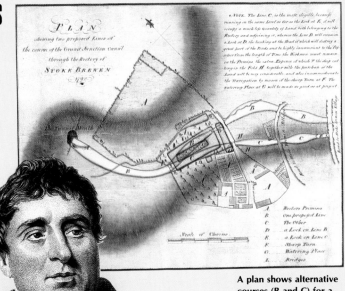

A plan shows alternative courses (B and C) for a Midlands canal. Locks (E) allow for grade changes.

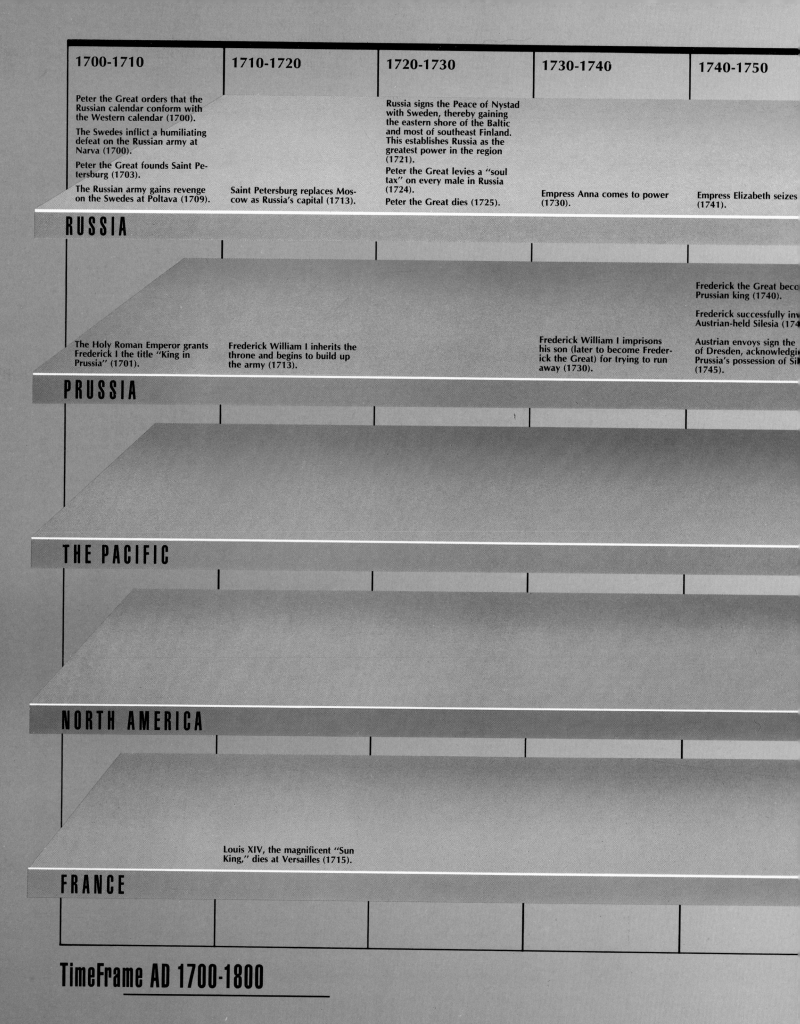

1700-1710	1710-1720	1720-1730	1730-1740	1740-1750
Peter the Great orders that the Russian calendar conform with the Western calendar (1700). The Swedes inflict a humiliating defeat on the Russian army at Narva (1700). Peter the Great founds Saint Petersburg (1703). The Russian army gains revenge on the Swedes at Poltava (1709).	Saint Petersburg replaces Moscow as Russia's capital (1713).	Russia signs the Peace of Nystad with Sweden, thereby gaining the eastern shore of the Baltic and most of southeast Finland. This establishes Russia as the greatest power in the region (1721). Peter the Great levies a "soul tax" on every male in Russia (1724). Peter the Great dies (1725).	Empress Anna comes to power (1730).	Empress Elizabeth seizes (1741).

RUSSIA

The Holy Roman Emperor grants Frederick I the title "King in Prussia" (1701).	Frederick William I inherits the throne and begins to build up the army (1713).		Frederick William I imprisons his son (later to become Frederick the Great) for trying to run away (1730).	Frederick the Great beco Prussian king (1740). Frederick successfully inv Austrian-held Silesia (174 Austrian envoys sign the of Dresden, acknowledgi Prussia's possession of Si (1745).

PRUSSIA

THE PACIFIC

NORTH AMERICA

	Louis XIV, the magnificent "Sun King," dies at Versailles (1715).			

FRANCE

TimeFrame AD 1700-1800

-1760	1760-1770	1770-1780	1780-1790	1790-1800
...ven Years' War begins, ...Russia, Austria, and ...against Prussia and Great ...(1756).	Peter III becomes czar (1762). Catherine, later known as Catherine the Great, becomes empress after overthrowing her husband Peter III (1762). Catherine the Great launches an expansionist war against the Turks (1768).	Catherine's forces put down the peasant rebellion led by Emelyan Pugachev (1774).	Catherine's Statute for National Education sets up a network of high schools and primary schools in provincial capitals (1786).	Russia, Prussia, and Austria divide Poland among themselves (1795). Catherine the Great dies (1796).
...ench philosopher Voltaire ...p residence in Prussia at ...ck's invitation (1750). ...ick marches his army into ..., thereby beginning the ...Years' War (1756). ...ussians incur heavy losses ...battles of Zorndorf (1758) ...nersdorf (1759).	Frederick is victorious at the battles of Liegnitz and Torgau (1760). The combatants in the Seven Years' War sign a peace treaty. Prussia is allowed to keep Silesia (1763).	Frederick gains West Prussia in the first partition of Poland (1772).	Frederick persuades fourteen German states to form the League of Princes, with himself at the head (1785). Frederick dies (1786).	Prussia and Russia divide more of Poland in a second partition (1793). Prussia, Russia, and Austria carry out a third and final partition of Poland (1795).
...s *History of Navigation* ...*Southern Lands,* Charles ...sses alerts the govern- ...of western Europe to ...ategic importance of the ...Pacific (1756).	The explorer Louis-Antoine de Bougainville claims the Falkland Islands for France (1764). The British sea captain Samuel Wallis discovers Tahiti (1767). Bougainville arrives in Tahiti (1768). Lieutenant James Cook starts his first expedition, to Tahiti, New Zealand, and Australia (1768).	Cook departs on his second expedition, which takes him to the southernmost navigable point of the Pacific (1772). Cook, now a captain, leaves Britain on his last voyage, traveling as far north as the Arctic Circle and as far south as New Zealand (1776). Cook is killed in Hawaii (1779).	The first British convicts to be transported to Australia arrive in Botany Bay (1788).	The second British convict ship arrives in Australia (1790).
...pulation of Britain's ...an colonies reaches 1.5 ..., more than six times its ...1688 (1750). ...can colonists join with ...troops to fight the French ...th America (1754). ...itish capture Quebec ...he French (1759).	Britain passes the Sugar Act, imposing an import tax on foreign goods imported into its American colonies (1764). After American protests, Britain repeals the Stamp Act, which had been intended to levy a tax on all documents (1766).	British tea is thrown overboard at the Boston Tea Party (1773). The War of Independence begins at Concord (1775). The Declaration of Independence is signed (1776). The Americans force General Burgoyne's surrender at Saratoga, ending the northern phase of the war (1777).	The British surrender to joint American and French forces at Yorktown, thus ending the war (1781). The Americans and British sign a peace treaty in Paris (1783). Captain Daniel Shays leads a farmers' rebellion (1786). The United States Constitution is ratified (1788).	George Washington dies (1799).
...st volume of Didérot's ...*opédie* is published, en- ...ating the spirit of the Age ...ghtenment (1751). ...e sides with Austria and ...against Britain and Prus- ...he start of the Seven ...War (1756).		Upon the death of Louis XV, Louis XVI becomes king of France (1774). France enters the American War of Independence against the British (1778).	The French government goes bankrupt largely as a result of debts from the American war. A bad harvest leads to hunger and food riots (1788). Louis XVI convenes the Estates General, a meeting of the three estates—nobles, clergy, and commons (1789). Revolutionaries storm the Bastille (1789).	A radical government institutes the Terror, a purge that claims 35,000 lives in one year (1793). King Louis XVI and Queen Marie Antoinette are guillotined (1793). The moderate Directory replaces the radical government (1795). Napoleon Bonaparte overthrows the Directory (1799).

PICTURE CREDITS

BIBLIOGRAPHY

GENERAL

Anderson, Patrick, *Over the Alps.* London: Rupert Hart-Davis, 1969.

Archenholz, Baron J. W. von de, *A Picture of Italy.* 2 vols. Transl. by Joseph Trapp. 1791.

Beckford, Peter, *Familiar Letters from Italy to a Friend in England.* 1787.

Berg, Maxine, *The Age of Manufactures.* Oxford: Basil Blackwell in association with Fontana, 1985.

Bourrit, Marc Théodore, *A Relation of a Journey to the Glaciers in the Dutchy of Savoy.* Transl. by C. and F. Davy. 1775.

Bracegirdle, Brian, and Patricia H. Miles:
Great Engineers and Their Works: The Darbys and the Ironbridge Gorge. Newton Abbot: David & Charles, 1974.
Great Engineers and Their Works: Thomas Telford. Newton Abbot: David & Charles, 1973.

Briggs, Asa, *The Age of Improvement.* London: Longmans, Green and Co., 1959.

Burgess, Anthony, and Francis Haskell, *The Age of the Grand Tour.* London: Paul Elek, 1967.

Cable, Mary, and the Editors of Tree Communications, *Treasures of the World: The African Kings.* New York: Select Books, 1984.

Case, S. L., and D. J. Hall, *A Social and Economic History of Britain.* London: Edward Arnold, 1974.

Cranston, Maurice, *Philosophers and Pamphleteers.* Oxford: Oxford University Press, 1986.

Darnton, Robert, *The Literary Underground of the Old Regime.* Cambridge, Mass.: Harvard University Press, 1982.

Davidson, Basil, *Black Mother: Africa, The Years of Trial.* London: Victor Gollancz, 1961.

Dunn, Richard S., *Sugar and Slaves.* London: Jonathan Cape, 1973.

Edwardes, Michael, *Clive, the Heaven-Born General.* London: Hart-Davis, MacGibbon, 1977.

Edwards, Paul, ed., *Equiano's Travels.* London: Heinemann, 1967.

Equiano, Olaudah, *The Interesting Narrative of the Life of Olaudah Equiano, or Gustavus Vassa, the African.* Vol. 1. London: Union-Street, Marylebone, 1789.

Fage, J. D., *An Introduction to the History of West Africa.* Cambridge: Cambridge University Press, 1955.

Gay, Peter, *Voltaire's Politics.* New Haven: Yale University Press, 1988.

Gay, Peter, and the Editors of Time-Life Books, *Age of Enlightenment* (Great Ages of Man series). New York: Time-Life Books, 1966.

Hadfield, Charles, *British Canals.* Newton Abbot: David & Charles, 1969.

Hampson, Norman, *The Enlightenment.* London: Pelican, 1968.

Hibbert, Christopher, *The Grand Tour.* London: Weidenfeld and Nicolson, 1969.

Hogg, Peter, *Slavery: The Afro-American Experience.* London: The British Library, 1979.

Honour, Hugh, *The Image of the Black in Western Art.* Vol. 4, Part 1. Cambridge, Mass.: Harvard University Press, 1989.

Hopkins, A. G., *An Economic History of West Africa.* London: Longman, 1973.

Klein, Herbert S.:
African Slavery in Latin America and *the Caribbean.* Oxford: Oxford University Press, 1986.
The Middle Passage. Princeton, N.J.: Princeton University Press, 1978.

Lovejoy, Paul E., *Transformations in Slavery.* Cambridge: Cambridge University Press, 1983.

Mackenzie-Grieve, Averil, *The Last Years of the English Slave Trade.* London: Putnam, 1941.

Martin, Bernard, and Mark Spurrell, eds., *The Journal of a Slave Trader.* London: Epworth Press, 1962.

Nicolson, Benedict, *Joseph Wright of Derby: Painter of Light.* Vols. 1 and 2. London: The Paul Mellon Foundation for British Art, in association with Routledge & Kegan Paul, 1968.

Pannell, J. P. M., *An Illustrated History of Civil Engineering.* London: Thames and Hudson, 1964.

Pike, Edgar Royston, *Human Documents of the Industrial Revolution in Britain.* London: George Allen & Unwin, 1966.

Plimmer, Charlotte, and Denis Plimmer, *Slavery.* Newton Abbot: David & Charles, 1973.

Pope-Hennessy, James, *Sins of the Fathers.* London: Weidenfeld and Nicolson, 1967.

Porter, Roy S., and Mikuláš Teich, eds., *The Enlightenment in National Context.* Cambridge: Cambridge University Press, 1981.

Pottle, Frederick A., ed., with Frank Brady, *Boswell on the Grand Tour.* London: Heinemann, 1955.

Ransford, Oliver, *The Slave Trade.* London: John Murray, 1971.

Rawley, James A., *The Transatlantic Slave Trade.* London: W. W. Norton, 1981.

Smollett, Tobias, *Travels in France and Italy.* 1766.

Sutton, Ian, ed., *The Eighteenth Century: Europe in the Age of Enlightenment.* London: Thames and Hudson, 1968.

Trease, Geoffrey, *The Grand Tour.* London: Heinemann, 1967.

Venturi, Franco, *Italy and the Enlightenment.* Transl. by Susan Corsi, ed. by Stuart Woolf. London: Longman, 1972.

Walvin, James, *Slavery and the Slave Trade.* London: Macmillan, 1983.

Williams, Eric, *From Columbus to Castro.* London: Andre Deutsch, 1970.

RUSSIA

Alexander, John T., *Catherine the Great: Life and Legend.* Oxford: Oxford University Press, 1989.

Anderson, M. S., *Peter the Great.* London: Thames and Hudson, 1978.

Cronin, Vincent, *Catherine: Empress of All the Russias.* London: Collins, 1978.

Cross, A. G., *By the Banks of the Thames: Russians in Eighteenth Century Britain.* Newtonville, Mass.: Oriental Research Partners, 1980.

Cross, Anthony, ed., *Russia under Western Eyes: 1517-1825.* London: Elek Books, 1971.

Curtiss, Mina, "The Empress Anna's Ice Palace." *History Today,* February 1973.

Donnert, Erich, *Russia in the Age of Enlightenment.* Transl. by Alison and Alistair Wightman. Edition Leipzig, 1986.

Duffy, Christopher, *Russia's Military Way to the West: Origins and Nature of Russian Military Power, 1700-1800.* London: Routledge & Kegan Paul, 1981.

La France et la Russie au Siècle des Lumières. Paris: Ministère des Affaires Étrangères, Association Française d'Action Artistique, 1986.

Kahan, A., *The Plow, the Hammer, and the Knout: An Economic History of Eighteenth-Century Russia.* Chicago: University of Chicago Press, 1985.

Kochan, Miriam, *Catherine the Great.* Hove, East Sussex: Wayland Publishers, 1976.

Madariaga, Isabel de, *Russia in the Age of Catherine the Great.* London: Weidenfeld and Nicolson, 1981.

Massie, Robert K., *Peter the Great: His Life and World.* London: Victor Gollancz, 1981.

Raeff, Marc:
Imperial Russia, 1682-1825: The Coming of Age of Modern Russia. New York: Alfred A. Knopf, 1971.
Origins of the Russian Intelligentsia. New York: Harcourt Brace Jovanovich, 1966.

Shonbinsky, S. N., "Court Jesters and Their Weddings" in *Historical Narratives from The Russian,* ed. by H. C. Romanoff. London: Rivingtons, 1871.

Troyat, Henri, *Peter the Great.* London: Hamish Hamilton, 1988.

PRUSSIA

Asprey, Robert B., *Frederick the Great: The Magnificent Enigma.* New York: Ticknor & Fields, 1986.

Carsten, F. L.:
Essays in German History. London:

Hambledon Press, 1985.
A History of the Prussian Junkers.
Aldershot: Scolar Press, 1989.
Dorn, W. L., "The Prussian Bureaucracy in the Eighteenth Century" in *Frederick the Great, A Profile,* ed. by P. Paret. London: Macmillan, 1972.
Duffy, Christopher:
The Army of Frederick the Great.
Newton Abbot: David & Charles, 1974.
Frederick the Great: *A Military Life.* London: Routledge & Kegan Paul, 1985.
Feuchtwanger, E. J., *Prussia, Myth and Reality.* London: Oswald Wolff, 1970.
Hinrichs, C., "The Conflict between Frederick and His Father" in *Frederick the Great, A Profile,* ed. by P. Paret. London: Macmillan, 1972.
Hubatsch, Walther, *Frederick the Great of Prussia: Absolutism and Administration.* London: Thames and Hudson, 1975.
Koch, H. W., *A History of Prussia.* London: Longman, 1978.
Mckay, D., and H. M. Scott, *The Rise of the Great Powers: 1648-1815.* London: Longman, 1983.
McNaught, Kenneth, *The Pelican History of Canada.* Harmondsworth, Middlesex: Penguin, 1985.
Mander, John, *Berlin: The Eagle and the Bear.* London: Barrie and Rockliff, 1959.
Mitford, Nancy, *Frederick the Great.* London: Hamish Hamilton, 1970.
Parker, Geoffrey, *The Military Revolution: Military Innovation and the Rise of the West, 1500-1800.* Cambridge: Cambridge University Press, 1988.
Reiners, L., *Frederick the Great.* London: Oswald Wolff, 1960.
Ritter, Gerhard, *Frederick the Great:* London: Eyre & Spottiswoode, 1969.

THE PACIFIC
Allen, Oliver E., and the Editors of Time-Life Books, *The Pacific Navigators* (The Seafarers series). Alexandria, Va.: Time-Life Books, 1980.
Australia, by the Editors of Time-Life Books (Library of Nations series). Alexandria, Va.: Time-Life Books, 1986.
Beaglehole, J. C.:
Exploration of the Pacific. London: A. & C. Black, 1934.
The Life of Captain James Cook. London: A. & C. Black, 1974.
The British Museum Yearbook 3, *Captain Cook and the South Pacific.* London: British Museum Publications, 1979.
Brosse, Jacques, *Great Voyages of Discovery: Circumnavigators and Scientists, 1764-1843.* New York: Facts on File Publications, 1983.
Cameron, Ian, *Lost Paradise: The Explo-*

ration of the Pacific. London: Century Hutchinson, 1987.
Carr, D. J., ed., *Sydney Parkinson: Artist of Cook's "Endeavour" Voyage.* London: British Museum Publications (Natural History), in association with Croom Helm, 1983.
Cobbe, Hugh, ed., *Cook's Voyages and Peoples of the Pacific.* London: British Museum Publications, 1979.
Dodd, Edward, *Polynesian Seafaring.* Lymington, Hampshire: Nautical Publishing Company, 1972.
Gilbert, John, *Charting the Vast Pacific.* London: Aldus Books, 1971.
Hughes, Robert, *The Fatal Shore.* London: Pan, 1988.
Lewis, David, *The Voyaging Stars.* Sydney: Collins, 1978.
Maclean, Alistair, *Captain Cook.* London: Collins, 1972.
Moorhead, Alan, *The Fatal Impact.* London: Hamish Hamilton, 1966.
Ortzen, Len, *Stories of Great Exploration.* London: Arthur Barker, 1975.
Parry, John H., *Trade and Dominion: The European Oversea Empire in the Eighteenth Century.* London: Weidenfeld and Nicolson, 1971.
Porter, Peter, and the Editors of Time-Life Books, *Sydney* (The Great Cities series). Amsterdam: Time-Life Books, 1980.
Rienits, Rex, and Thea Rienits, *The Voyages of Captain Cook.* London: Hamlyn, 1968.
Smith, Bernard, *European Vision and the South Pacific.* New Haven: Yale University Press, 1988.
Syme, Ronald, *The Travels of Captain Cook.* London: Michael Joseph, 1972.
Withey, Lynne, *Voyages of Discovery: Captain Cook and the Exploration of the Pacific.* London: Hutchinson, 1987.

NORTH AMERICA
The American War of Independence, *1775-1783: A Commemorative Exhibition Organized by the Map Library and the Department of Manuscripts of the British Library Reference Division.* London: British Museum Publications, 1975.
Bernstein, Richard B., with Kym S. Rice, *Are We to Be a Nation? The Making of the Constitution.* Cambridge, Mass.: Harvard University Press, 1987.
Boatner, Mark Mayo, III:
Cassell's Biographical Dictionary of the American War of Independence. London: Cassell, 1973.
Encyclopedia of the American Revolution. New York: David McKay Company, 1966.
Bowen, Catherine Drinker, *Miracle at Philadelphia.* London: Hamish Hamilton, 1967.
Brogan, Hugh:
Longman History of the United States of America. London: Longman, 1985.
The Pelican History of the United States of America. London: Penguin, 1968.

Countryman, Edward, *The American Revolution.* London: Penguin, 1987.
Cresswell, Donald H., comp., *American Revolution in Drawings and Prints: A Checklist of 1765-1790 Graphics in the Library of Congress.* Washington, D.C.: Library of Congress, 1975.
Dull, Jonathan R., *A Diplomatic History of the American Revolution.* New Haven: Yale University Press, 1985.
Freeman, Douglas Southall, *George Washington.* 7 vols. London: Eyre & Spottiswoode, 1948-1957.
Hofstadter, Richard, William Miller, and Daniel Aaron, *The American Republic to 1865.* Englewood Cliffs, N.J.: Prentice-Hall, 1959.
Jensen, Merrill, *The New Nation.* New York: Alfred A. Knopf, 1967.
Mackesy, Piers, *The War for America.* Cambridge, Mass.: Harvard University Press, 1965.
Maier, Pauline, *From Resistance to Revolution.* London: Routledge & Kegan Paul, 1973.
Middlekauff, Robert, *The Glorious Cause.* Oxford: Oxford University Press, 1982.
Miller, John C., *Origins of the American Revolution.* London: Faber & Faber, 1945.
Morgan, Edmund S., and Helen M. Morgan, *The Stamp Act Crisis: Prologue to Revolution.* Rev. ed. Chapel Hill: University of North Carolina Press, 1963.
Morris, Richard B., and the Editors of LIFE, *The Making of a Nation: 1775-1789.* Vol. 2 of the LIFE History of the United States series. New York: Time Inc., 1963.
1776: *The British Story of the American Revolution.* London: National Maritime Museum, 1976.
Ward, Christopher, *The War of the Revolution.* Vol. 2. New York: The Macmillan Company, 1952.

FRANCE
Behrens, C. B. A., *The Ancien Régime.* London: Thames and Hudson, 1967.
Bindman, David, *The Shadow of the Guillotine: Britain and the French Revolution.* London: British Museum Publications, 1989.
Chronicle of the French Revolution. Essex: Longman, 1989.
Cobb, Richard, ed., *The French Revolution: Voices from a Momentous Epoch, 1789-1795.* London: Simon & Schuster, 1988.
Cobban, Alfred, *Old Régime and Revolution: 1715-1799.* Vol. 1 of *A History of Modern France.* 3d ed. London: Penguin, 1963.
"The French Revolution: 1789-1989." *History Today,* May 1989.
Furet, François, and Denis Richet, *La*

Révolution. Paris: Réalités Hachette, 1965.
Gaxotte, Pierre, *La Révolution Française.* Paris: Flammarion, 1963.
Gombrich, Sir Ernst H., "The Dream of Reason: Symbolism of the French Revolution." *FMR,* No. 32, 1989.
Hampson, Norman:
Danton. London: Gerald Duckworth, 1978.
The First European Revolution: *1776-1815.* London: Thames and Hudson, 1979.
The French Revolution: *A Concise History.* London: Thames and Hudson, 1975.
A Social History of the French Revolution. London: Routledge & Kegan Paul, 1963.
Hibbert, Christopher, *The Days of the French Revolution.* London: Penguin, 1989.
Hobsbawm, E. J., *The Age of Revolution.* London: Weidenfeld and Nicolson, 1962.
Jean-Richard, Pierrette, and Gilbert Mondin, *Un collectionneur pendant la Révolution: Jean Louis Soulavie (1752-1813).* Paris: Éditions de la Réunion des Musées Nationaux, 1989.
Kafker, Frank A., and James M. Laux, eds., *The French Revolution: Conflicting Interpretations.* 2d ed. New York: Random House, 1976.
Knapton, Ernest John, *France: An Interpretative History.* New York: Scribner's, 1971.
Lefebvre, Georges, *The French Revolution from Its Origins to 1793.* Transl. by Elizabeth Moss Evanson. London: Routledge & Kegan Paul, 1962.
Matrat, Jean, *Robespierre: Or the Tyranny of the Majority.* Transl. by Alan Kendall with Felix Brenner. London: Angus & Robertson, 1975.
Padover, Saul K., *The Life and Death of Louis XVI.* London: D. Appleton-Century Company, 1939.
Schama, Simon, *Citizens: A Chronicle of the French Revolution.* London: Viking, 1989.
Soboul, A.:
The French Revolution, *1787-89.* London: New Left Books, 1974.
A Tale of Two Cities. London: Manorial Research, 1989.
Tocqueville, Alexis de, *The Old Régime and the French Revolution.* New York: Doubleday, 1955.
Tulard, Jean, *La Révolution Française á Paris: Á Travers les Collections du Musée Carnavalet.* Paris: Musées, 1989.
Wendel, Hermann, *Danton.* London: Constable, 1936.

ACKNOWLEDGMENTS

The following materials have been reprinted with the kind permission of the publishers: Page 55: "My youth, the fire of passion . . ." and page 69: "No face which did not show relief and hope . . .," quoted from *Frederick the Great,* by L. Reiners, London: Oswald Wolff Books, 1960. Page 65: "I tell you, I lead a dog's life . . .," quoted from *The Army of Frederick the Great,* by Christopher Duffy, Newton Abbot, Devon, England: David & Charles, 1974.

The editors also wish to thank the following individuals and institutions for their valuable assistance in the preparation of this volume:
England: Coventry—Maxine Berg, Senior Lecturer in Economic History, University of Warwick. Hull—Elizabeth Frostick and Penny Wilkinson, Wilberforce House, Hull City Museums and Art Galleries. London—Robert Baldwin, Head of Navigational Sciences, National Maritime Museum; Kenneth Bale, The Council for World Mission; Trevor Chriss, A. C. Cooper Ltd.; Michael Kerrigan; Tim Lott; Caroline Manyon; Jackie Matthews; Rosemary Seaton, School of Oriental and African Studies; Deborah Thompson; Juliet Thorp, Yale University Press. York—James Walvin, Provost, Alcuin College, University of York.
France: Paris—François Avril, Curateur, Département des Manuscrits, Bibliothèque Nationale; Antoinette Decaudin, Documentaliste, Département des Antiquités Orientales, Musée du Louvre; Marie Montembault, Documentaliste, Antiquités Grecques et Romaines, Musée du Louvre.
West Germany: Bonn—Angie Lemmer. Nuremberg—Hermann Maué, Germanisches Nationalmuseum. West Berlin—Heidi Klein, Bildarchiv Preussischer Kulturbesitz.
Italy: Rome—Ann Wise.
Scotland: Saint Andrews—H. M. Scott, Lecturer in Modern History, University of Saint Andrews.

INDEX